A popular phrenological pamphlet which was quickly reprinted to capitalize on Guiteau's notoriety. This vulgarized psychological explanation was widely current in the United States of the 1880's. *Courtesy of the Library of Congress.*

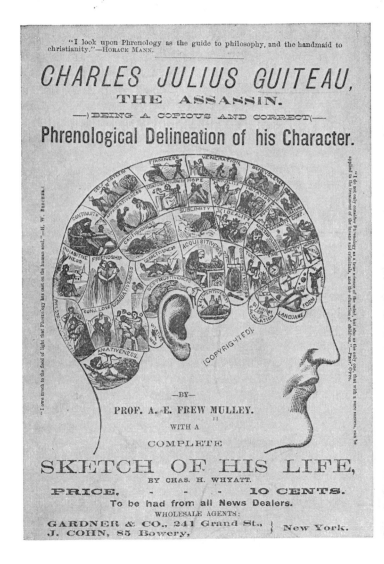

THE TRIAL
OF THE ASSASSIN
GUITEAU

THE TRIAL
OF THE ASSASSIN
GUITEAU

Psychiatry and Law in the Gilded Age

Charles E. Rosenberg

The University of Chicago Press
Chicago and London

Library of Congress Catalog Card Number: 68:16713
The University of Chicago Press, Chicago 60637
The University of Chicago Press, Ltd., London W.C. 1
© 1968 by The University of Chicago. All rights reserved
Published 1968. Printed in the United States of America

For Leah and her mother

Acknowledgments

I have accumulated many debts in the writing of this book. It began in 1960–61 at the Institute for the History of Medicine of the Johns Hopkins University. Professor Owsei Temkin, Director of the Institute, provided both guidance and initial encouragement. For a number of reasons, I then put the project aside, and I owe its completion to the constant and thoughtful encouragement of Richard Hofstadter and Erwin H. Ackerknecht.

In a study of this kind, the historian must inevitably find himself dependent upon the specialized knowledge and good offices of others expert in medicine and the law. I should particularly like to thank psychiatrists Otto Marx, Martin Kesselman, and Jacques Quen for their careful reading of the manuscript, and pathologist and historian of pathology Esmond Long for his thoughtful evaluation of the Guiteau autopsy report. A novice in the law, I was saved from more than a few legal blunders by the kindness of Professor Louis B. Schwartz of the Law School of the University of Pennsylvania and Professor Lawrence Friedman of the University of Wisconsin Law School; both read carefully and criticized an earlier version of this manuscript. Of course, none of these scholarly samaritans are in any way responsible for remaining errors and indiscretions.

I have also incurred a debt of gratitude to Mr. Justin G. Turner of Los Angeles and to Dr. Robert Ravel of Strafford, Pennsylvania, both of whom were kind enough to have allowed me to consult manuscript materials in their possession relating to the trial. Richard Wolfe, Librarian of the Rare Books Department of the Countway Library of Medicine, was also helpful in calling my attention to relevant materials in that library and in facilitating their use. I should like, finally, to thank my wife Carroll for her unfailing encouragement and acute editorial judgment.

Introduction

James Abram Garfield has a secure, if small, place in the history of the American presidency. Yet it is the manner of his death, rather than any accomplishment of his administration, that distinguishes Garfield in the minds of most Americans: after less than a year in office he was assassinated. There would seem otherwise to be little remarkable in his career, nothing to set him apart from the other stout, imposing, and reassuringly bearded postbellum presidents. Graduates of college and university courses in American history may also recall that the unfortunate Garfield was the victim of a disappointed office seeker, that he died a martyr to the cause of civil service reform. Only the most knowledgeable and retentive of memory are aware of the assassin's name, Charles Julius Guiteau.

Like many traditionally accepted pictures from the American past, this is neither complete nor strictly accurate. Garfield's role as martyr was somewhat inadvertent. And the most interesting aspect of the assasination, it may well be argued, was not the passage of a moderate civil service reform—in 1883, two years after Garfield's death—but the presidential assassin's trial. For Charles J. Guiteau was not really a disappointed office seeker. He was in fact no office seeker at all, but rather a victim of mental illness whose delusional system prescribed this role for him. Guiteau's trial lacked the suspense of many other great trials—for it seems clear that Americans would have tolerated nothing but the death sentence—but it held an overwhelming interest for contemporaries. It was the most celebrated American "insanity trial" of the nineteenth century, and perhaps only the Harry K. Thaw and Leopold-

Loeb cases in the twentieth century rival it in prominence. (In world psychiatric literature as well, the Guiteau case occupied an extraordinarily prominent place.) The following pages are an account of this trial and, through it, something of the reactions of Americans in the Gilded Age to mental illness, to psychiatry, and to individual character and personality.

In the days and weeks immediately following the assassination and at the President's death (he lingered in pain from July 2, 1881, until September 19), Americans sketched unendingly repetitious pictures of Garfield and his assailant. In the creation of these highly stylized images they could not but express much that was central in American social thought, as well as something of the inconsistency and ambivalence with which these values were formulated. Contemporary biographies of the virtuous Garfield and the correspondingly iniquitous Guiteau functioned as mirrors of American social values, the actual facts of their lives shadowed and foreshortened by the need of Americans to teach, to warn, and to reassure.

Garfield's career illustrated the potential for achievement in American life; he had, in the much-quoted phrase of Horatio Alger, followed the road "from towpath to President." (Garfield had been briefly a canal boy during his poverty-stricken Ohio boyhood.) He had been a tattered and hungry youth, fatherless at an early age and self-educated; he had risen to a college presidency, to a Civil War commission as brigadier general, to congressional prominence, and finally to the presidency.

During Garfield's last illness and especially at his death, Americans created an immense body of eulogistic sermons, addresses, and editorials; only the death of Lincoln had precipitated so concentrated an outpouring of grief.* The

* The following remarks are based on a reading of more than three hundred sermons, editorials, and addresses

need of civil service reformers, moreover, to represent Garfield as a martyr to honesty in government intensified and consciously directed the emphasis of many such productions. (Henry Adams found the process thoroughly distasteful; "The cynical impudence," he wrote, "with which the reformers have tried to manufacture an ideal statesman out of the late shady politician beats anything in novel-writing. They are making popular capital. They lie and maneuver just like candidates for office.")

The countless retellings of the late President's life affirmed in each biographical detail the continued pertinence of the self-made man as ideal social type. Garfield had worked his way through Williams College, graduating with honors. Returning to Ohio, he was appointed professor at little Hiram College; soon he became its acting president. In Congress he was a notorious and habitual reader of books (with Charles Sumner, the two legislators most likely to be found in the congressional library). Clerical and journalistic eulogists emphasized Garfield's reliance in debate upon cool and deeply learned analysis, not upon emotion or party prejudice. Despite Garfield's methodical scholarship—he kept voluminous subject files of notes and clippings on matters of public concern—he was no sickly and effeminate introvert. On the contrary, he was immensely strong and tenacious, a punishing fighter when insulted, though no bully. In politics, eulogists agreed, Garfield's career had never been sullied by the compromising stratagems of the "mere politician." He never sought office; it sought him, a fitting reward for his scholarship and probity. (This was a particular striking emphasis; roughly two-thirds of the memorial addresses I have read emphasized Garfield's never having sought the nomination of the Re-

---

occasioned by Garfield's death. Such writings, of course, represent the overt—indeed, pedagogical—intent of men self-consciously restating society's agreed-upon values; as such they must be approached with due caution.

publican party's deadlocked convention.) Having worked his way from poverty to national eminence, moreover, Garfield had a profound respect for the dignity of labor and the human potential in even the most uncompromising circumstances. In piety and domestic virtue the murdered President had set a standard for other Americans to emulate; he had been a stern yet doting father, a devoted husband, a loving son, a conscientious churchgoer.

The formal structure of Garfield's public biography was an improbable mosaic of these and other laudable yet often inconsistent traits. He was ceaselessly ambitious, yet humble and modest; scholarly and methodical, yet courageous and astonishingly vigorous; pious and uxorious, yet competent in the harsh arts of the soldier. Conventional wisdom could not, quite obviously, accept the configuration of personality traits which ordinarily made the self-made man.*

Guiteau's life, as we shall see in much greater detail, represented a starkly didactic contrast. The assassin's biography illustrated the consequences of vice, of crime, and of irresponsibility. The trial of Guiteau, as one contemporary put it, taught a great lesson: "the striking contrast between Guiteau and Garfield . . . the value of right principles, honesty and industry, in contrast with indolence, vanity, and deceit as the main-springs of action." If Garfield, in the qualities assigned him, seemed to demonstrate

---

* The public image of Garfield represents a marked contrast with that assigned Andrew Jackson by his contemporaries, especially the "tamed" strength of Garfield as contrasted to the primal forcefulness and intuitive wisdom with which popular myth endowed Old Hickory. The construction of such public myths is hardly a random process, and the contrast between the popular images of Jackson and Garfield may well reflect the need of an increasingly stable and institutionalized society to articulate new and more appropriate ideals of behavior.

the potential of American life, Guiteau, in his eccentric peregrinations and compulsive rhetoric, provided a wry comment on America as it was. Religion, business, law, politics—the consuming interests of American life—all found a place in Guiteau's baroque delusional system. And viewed in the skewed perspective of his madness, each appeared with expressionistic intensity, distortion—and clarity.

There is no doubt that Guiteau suffered from mental illness; this much is unquestionable. The precise diagnosis is another matter. This has not been my task, nor am I trained to make such judgments. Those twentieth-century clinicians, however, who have studied the case of Guiteau tend to agree in their evaluation of the assassin's mental status: he was, in the facetious words of one such author, "a common garden variety of paranoid schizophrenia."

The bulk of this book concerns itself with Guiteau's trial and the medical and legal ideas it dramatized. The problems of evaluating criminal responsibility are in some ways no more settled today than they were during the presidency of Chester Arthur. We discuss with equal vigor the conduct of witnesses, the ground rules of judicial procedure, the admission of evidence, and the basic rules of law governing criminal responsibility. Then as now, debate on the limits of criminal responsibility reflects the status of psychiatry and the psychiatrist in the lay mind. As these images have changed, the grounds of debate have changed as well—but not sufficiently to bridge completely the distance between medical thought and legal practice. I have tried, however, to avoid didactically explicit references to the present, except where such references seemed useful in helping to explain particular historical assumptions and practices.

I have, on the other hand, hoped in the reconstruction of this incident to create a microcosm of American psychiatry in the 1880's. Both defense and prosecution were prodigal in their expenditure of expert testimony—and equally unrelenting in their demands upon the jurors' patience. This testimony—and the lay and medical comment it evoked—provides an organic cross section of psychiatric thought in this immediately pre-Freudian generation. The expert testimony reflects with equal clarity personal and social antagonisms that split the institutional structure of the profession during these decades.

In the Guiteau trial, for example, as in many other prominent "insanity" trials held in the years between 1880 and 1900, medical witnesses for the prosecution and defense endorsed contradictory views of the symptomatology and etiology of insanity so as to bolster their legal positions (a practice, of course, not completely historical). Psychiatrists for the prosecution argued that the defendant understood the nature and consequences of his act, appeared to reason coherently, and hence, following the generally accepted rule of law, was guilty. Psychiatrists for the defense, on the other hand, argued that he might seem rational, even intelligent, and still not be responsible for his actions. The cause of an individual's criminality, they were convinced, often lay in heredity, in a congenital disposition toward lack of moral perceptivity and control. Indeed, the argument frequently continued, such men could often be identified through physical stigmata that seemed to accompany hereditary mental illness and criminality.

Mid-twentieth-century sympathies are most frequently with such physicians and lawyers who are fighting—as we see it—to save a mentally ill individual from capital punishment. We applaud their ability to cite German authorities, we approve their invocation of science, and we sympathize with their opposition to the vengeful moralism of the prosecution's expert witnesses. Yet if we examine the content of their ideas, it becomes clear that we are faced with a seemingly anomalous circumstance; in a schematic sense at least, the ideas of the witnesses for the prosecution appear in some ways closer to modern views than do those of the defense experts. We tend to think of personality in dynamic terms and to reject the idea that heredity alone can cause insanity, or that insanity is often the behavioral expression of congenital malformations. Defenders of traditional morality at the end of the nineteenth century refused to accept such seemingly materialistic arguments. They viewed the criminal act as the consequence not of a diseased or deformed brain, but as the result of traits originating in the habitual actions of earliest childhood. Conservatives in matters of legal medicine were particularly alarmed by the concept of "moral insanity"—the idea, that is, that insanity might be marked by antisocial behavior and emotional symptomatology without overt delusion or apparent irrationality. The human personality was a whole, they argued, and one part of it, such as the moral sense, could not be diseased while another, such as the reasoning faculty, remained healthy.

In a sense, of course, this analysis is merely ironic; the prosecution witnesses were not really forerunners of modern personality theory, and defense witnesses seem to us liberal, not because their ideas are correct in detail, but because their *esprit* and values seem right to us. It seems more important that they quote German sources as transcendent authorities—even if these authorities are wrong—than that they quote the Bible or the rules of criminal jurisprudence. The heart of the matter lies in one's attitude toward the criminal offender. Then as now, "forensic liberals" assume a deterministic stance, conservatives a less deterministic one. That the scientific ideas with which the determinism is justified have changed in this century seems less important than that they serve the same social function. The seeming "quaintness" of many of the formal ideas expressed during the Guiteau trial should not blind one to the internal logic of the social and institutional needs they expressed.

My interest in the assassination of President Garfield and the trial of his assassin began quite by chance. A half dozen years ago, I was at work on a study of hereditarian ideas in the second half of the nineteenth century. While reading the works of European and English criminologists of the fin de siècle, I came upon surprisingly frequent references to the case of Guiteau; almost every important European criminologist and many psychiatrists of that generation had at least referred to Garfield's assassin, some as evidence for the hereditary origin of criminality, others because of the medicolegal issues raised by his trial, others because of a vague animus against the United States and its institutions. As a student of American history, I naturally found my interest in the case growing. I turned, still largely impelled by curiosity, to the records of the trial itself. The proceedings, I discovered, had been printed in three stout, closely printed octavo volumes, amounting to almost three thousand pages. Despite my initial dismay at this abundance of material, reading the testimony only increased my interest. It was hard to believe that such a trial had ever taken place; certainly it could only have taken place in the America of Jay Gould and Colonel Sellers. Guiteau, a sometime lawyer, participated in his own defense and his comments and asides turned a somewhat grim procedure into a surrealistic one. Fascinated, I then turned to newspapers, to magazines, to sermons, and to medical and legal journals in an effort to learn more about American reactions to this strange proceeding. The results fill the following pages. The manuscript was half written when the events of November 22, 1963, lent its subject a dismaying and unexpected contemporaneity.

CONTENTS

ILLUSTRATIONS

JULY THE SECOND

Far into the nineteenth century, Washington remained a small, rather provincial city. Life was seasonal. Oppressed by heat and malaria during the summer, the capital did not awake to its foreshortened and unnaturally frenetic life until fall and the convening of Congress.

No period in the city's life cycle was more feverish than the scrambling, office-seeking months following the election of a new president. The spring of 1881 had been hectic, even more than was usual in these postinaugural months. The Republican party was seriously split. The Stalwarts, the faction of the party's old guard, and the seemingly more flexible Half-breeds, led by James G. Blaine, had fought bitterly since the nominating convention the previous year. The president, James A. Garfield—sometime Ohio congressman, a man of bearing and for the time at least average probity—had been the choice of a deadlocked convention, a compromise after the Stalwarts and their leader Roscoe Conkling had failed to secure the nomination of Ulysses S. Grant for a third term. Unable to overcome Half-breed opposition, they had succeeded at least in blocking the nomination of Blaine, the Half-breed standard-bearer. Perhaps Garfield's well-known indecisiveness had made him palatable to both wings of the party. Soon after his inauguration, however, it became apparent that the Ohioan intended to cast his lot with Blaine and the Half-breeds. Blaine himself was made Secretary of State and Garfield began methodically to oppose Conkling and his fellow senator from New York, Tom Platt, on matters of patronage within their own state. Conkling and Platt then resigned melodramatically from the Senate, precipitating an unusual special election, one in which they hoped to be overwhelmingly reelected by New York's complaisant legislature; with this vote of confidence they would be able to return to Washington with added prestige. But as spring turned into summer, New York's senate remained deadlocked, unable either to reaffirm their selection of Platt and Conkling or to choose successors.

Never, observers agreed, had such ill will divided the party of Lincoln. The more partisan did not limit themselves to observation; charges of corruption—usually true—and conspiracy filled news and editorial columns. Unless the rift were healed, prospects for the Republican party did not seem bright in the next presidential year.

June was ordinarily quiet in postbellum Washington. In 1881, however, the city was still busy, but beginning to exhibit symptoms of its accustomed summer lethargy. The pressure for office could not, even in the first months of a new term, continue indefinitely. The President, it was announced, would be making an excursion early in July. Accompanied by his family and several cabinet members, Garfield planned to attend the commencement of his alma mater, Williams College, and then take a much-needed vacation. He was to leave Washington on the 9:30 A.M. limited express, Saturday, July 2.

The President left himself little time. His carriage did not arrive at the station until 9:25, and he then sat for several minutes talking with his close friend, the Secretary of State. Blaine lightheartedly toyed with his cane, throwing it again and again into the air before stepping down from the carriage with the President and entering the almost-deserted Baltimore and Potomac Station. A servant followed carrying the President's bags.

A slight, dark-bearded, and shabbily dressed man suddenly whirled toward the two heavyset, imposing figures as they passed. He drew a stubby revolver, leveled it at the President's back, and fired. He fired again after running a few steps toward his victim. As Garfield sank to the floor, the man turned and walked hurriedly toward the exit. He had not spoken a word.

Patrick Kearney of the District of Columbia police stood outside the Sixth Street entrance to the station. He still felt a glow of well-being; the President had stopped and asked him the time as he entered the station. Suddenly Kearney heard two shots; he turned immediately and ran toward the entrance. As the officer pulled open the heavy door he bumped into a slight, dark man, obviously agitated. "I have a letter to send to General Sherman," he gasped. Kearney did not let him pass, however, coming as he did from the scene of a shooting. Almost immediately, the ticket-taker and depot watchman ran up and seized the man. He had shot the President.

Garfield lay on the floor, his crushed top hat beside him, his gray traveling suit stained with blood. A circle of on-lookers had already formed around the husky man. He was soon placed on a coarse mattress that several railroad men had carried from one of the worker's rooms. The first phy-sician arrived within a few minutes. This was Dr. Smith Townsend, the District Health Officer, who assumed im-mediately that the President was dying. He administered brandy and aromatic spirits of ammonia, then inserted his finger into a wound low on the right side of Garfield's back. Some hemorrhage followed. The assassin's other shot had inflicted a flesh wound on the President's arm. The wound in his back, Dr. Townsend assured the Presi-dent, was not a serious one. "I thank you, doctor," the Civil War veteran replied, "but I am a dead man."

A few minutes later, bystanders carried the President, still on the mattress, to a police ambulance (through crowds which had somehow gathered almost immediately around the station). At running speed, the horses returned Garfield to the White House. Servants quickly prepared a second-floor bedroom and made the President as comfortable as possible; in the room and in the corridor outside it there was chaos. Throughout the long day, an average of five or six physicians, three or four attendants, and a half-dozen others of Garfield's official family occupied the sickroom. Reporters milled aggressively at the door, waiting to interrogate anyone coming from the bedside. Doctors summoned hurriedly from government posts and private practice agreed unanimously that the President's condition was too grave to permit probing for the bullet. Most contented themselves with introducing their fingers into the wound.

There seemed little hope of his survival. Garfield was pale, his extremities cold—and with no massive external bleeding it seemed likely that the President was dying of internal hemorrhaging. The physicians began to issue half-hourly bulletins on the condition of their morphine-deadened patient. Four cabinet members—Attorney General Wayne MacVeagh, Postmaster General Edward James, Secretary of the Treasury William Windom, and Secretary of War Robert Todd Lincoln—spent most of the night in the sickroom. "How many hours of sorrow," Lincoln observed to a reporter, "I have passed in this town."

Officer Kearney, as soon as he saw the President lying on the waiting room floor, had hurried his prisoner out of the depot. As they left the Sixth Street exit, the assassin turned and said mildly: "I did it. I will go to jail for it; Arthur is President, and I am a Stalwart."

Kearney's excitement seemed out of place as he brought his prisoner into the morning quiet of the station house; and detectives assumed he was joking when the patrolman reported in his rich brogue that the insignificant man with him had shot President Garfield. Kearney himself was so agitated that it was not until reaching the station that he thought to ask for the assassin's revolver. He thought as well for the first time to ask his prisoner's name. The slight, shabbily-dressed man produced a thick pile of cards from his pocket and eagerly handed one to the officer. It read:

CHARLES GUITEAU, CHICAGO, ILL. He was a lawyer, Guiteau volunteered, and born in the United States. The assassin had brown hair, the police books noted as well, weighed about 130 pounds, had a sallow complexion and thin whiskers; he was dressed in a dark suit and a black slouch hat. Guiteau's pockets produced a number of items in addition to his pistol and visiting cards. Most interesting was a letter addressed "to the White House." It was dated that morning, July 2, and seemed clearly to support the idea that the assassin had been politically motivated. "I am a Stalwart of the Stalwarts," it confessed. A similar letter was found outside the station, sealed and addressed: "Please deliver at once to General Sherman, or his first assistant in charge of the War Department":

To GENERAL SHERMAN:
   I have just shot the President. I shot him several times, as
I wished him to go as easily as possible. His death was a
political necessity. I am a lawyer, theologian and politician.
I am a Stalwart of the Stalwarts. I was with General Grant and
the rest of our men, in New York during the canvass.
I am going to the jail. Please order out your troops, and
take possession of the jail at once.
                              Very respectfully,
                                 CHARLES GUITEAU

   Guiteau was not allowed to linger in police headquarters. The captain, determined, as the Washington *Post* put it, "to abide by the forms of the law," swore out a warrant against the prisoner and dispatched Guiteau to the district jail to await a hearing. A mob had already gathered outside headquarters and Guiteau seemed anxious to leave for the relative security of the prison. Two detectives accompanied him in the hack, and as they moved away toward the jail, Guiteau became suddenly quite garrulous. His only motive in killing the President, he told Detective George McElfresh, was to unite the Republican party. Suddenly Guiteau leaned forward and asked McElfresh whether he were himself a Stalwart. "Yes," the detective admitted. Pleased, Guiteau smiled and promised to have him made chief of police.

Could this commonplace little man have undertaken so desperate an act without help or encouragement? Americans wondered; rumors of accomplices and plots filled newspaper columns. Helpful and seemingly omnipresent informants reported that Guiteau had been seen conspiring with single men or groups of men, that he was a Chicago Socialist and well known at their meetings, that he had been seen drinking with a number of respectable men in a Washington hotel. Late Saturday, the Attorney General summoned James Brooks, chief of the Secret Service to his office. There must not be allowed to remain the slightest possibility that Guiteau had conspired with anyone, McVeagh explained; every lead, even the most fragmentary, would have to be investigated. At midnight, Brooks was still at work, talking to the assassin in his cell. The Secret Service chief, a man of proven ability, immediately called his most reliable investigators to Washington and put them to work. (They were to spend a good deal of time sequestering the lunatic and eccentric who drifted into the city, attracted there by the morbid stimulus of the assassination.)

Despite rumors of massive lynching parties—and despite equally persistent rumors that the assassin had been transferred to a heavily armored monitor anchored in the Potomac—Guiteau was lodged quietly in the district prison. Regulars with cannon guarded the isolated building.

The cannon might, it seemed, prove necessary. Americans were deeply shocked by the assassination. Within half an hour of the shooting, crowds gathered outside newspaper offices in the larger cities, waiting for telegraphic bulletins to be posted. Along Philadelphia's Chestnut Street and in New York's printing house square, crowds filled sidewalks and despite a hot sun spilled over into roadways. At first it was assumed that the President had died, and in New York flags were lowered; at eleven, however, with the arrival of more accurate news, they were raised and public interest—if it were possible—increased. Six policemen were stationed at each of New York's newspaper offices, clearing a path for pedestrians through the dense crowd. The *Tribune* reported that streetcar drivers on Park Row had to bring their horses to a walk and then shout themselves hoarse in an effort to move through the tightly packed street. By noon, extras had been set in type, printed, and sold out. By noon, as well, the President, a somewhat colorless figure a few hours before, had become a leader of towering stature.

Americans found the assassination bewildering. Most simply assumed that it had been the work of a lunatic. To others it implied developments more alarming than the random act of an unbalanced mind. Some, for example, learning of the assassin's foreign-sounding name, were convinced that the assault on President Garfield was a consequence of uncurbed immigration; the nihilism which had so recently done away with the czar had apparently found an American home. "If this is the outgrowth of Nihilism," General Grant told reporters, "I am in favor of crushing it out immediately by the prompt execution of the would-be assassins and their followers."

The stock market dipped suddenly; despite hectic flurries of trading, averages were lower by four or five points at the day's end. Fortunately for the market's stability, however, July 3 was a Sunday and Monday was the Fourth of July—both days on which no trading could take place.

Clergymen of every denomination found a Sabbath text in the assassination. Some even read medical bulletins from their pulpits; most sought a meaning in so unnatural and unexpected an act. The reformist in politics were quick to emphasize a connection between the spoils system and the assassination; such attacks, these ministers argued, were the logical consequence of a political system predicated on self-aggrandizement, not principle. Other clergymen saw God's hand in the assassination, chastising the nation for impiety, or intemperance, or perhaps for tolerating the blasphemies of Mormonism. Some of the less zealous, however, suspected the presence of more mundane influences in the assassination: Guiteau might well have been the tool of a factional plot. Despite the persistence of such suspicions, most clergymen, like responsible Americans generally, felt certain that it was the act of an individual—not even office-seeking politicians would stoop to assassination. There was some consolation, as Henry Ward Beecher assured his congregation that Sunday, in at least one aspect of the tragedy: it had been the act of an isolated lunatic, not the culmination of a plot, as such an incident would almost inevitably have been in Europe. While clergymen sought to define the ultimate moral significance of the assassination, many of their listeners that Sunday must have been far more concerned with prospects for the President's recovery.

His chances did not seem good. Still under sedation, he was very weak, and Washington physicians, though naturally unwilling to forgo the prestige of treating so eminent a patient, were grateful when two of the country's leading surgeons, D. Hayes Agnew of Philadelphia and Frank Hamilton of New York, arrived as consultants. But this was only one incident in a nationwide medical furor aroused by the President's condition; north and south, from all walks of life, Americans sent advice and good wishes. A South Carolina physician offered a vial of his "Elixir of Life"— and the blessings of South Carolinians. From Paris, J. Marion Sims, the great gynecological surgeon and an American with a truly international reputation, cabled his advice; from a small town in Ohio, Garfield's old regimental surgeon was summoned. A merchant sent three bottles of extra choice old Jamaica rum, a Baltimorean a cow (which, for a time, passersby could see tethered behind the White House). Advice was most abundant. "Eat raw onions—raw onions—raw onions to strengthen stomach," a New Yorker telegraphed. At a meeting of New York's Chamber of

Commerce, merchants and bankers contributed $40,000 toward a trust fund for Mrs. Garfield and the children.

Despite this concern for his survivors, the President soon rallied, sat up, and began to take some light food. On July 16, two weeks after the shooting, Dr. Frank Hamilton, questioned by a *Tribune* reporter, felt able to report decisively that "ultimate recovery is beyond all reasonable doubt." Even earlier, the more militant among religious leaders felt able to congratulate themselves on the "supernatural element in this miracle of healing"; the prayers of Americans seemed to have been answered. (By the end of the month, an enterprising Cincinnati publisher had produced an extended *History of the Attempted Assassination of James A. Garfield.*)

Not everything, of course, was left in divine hands. No effort was spared in helping the President in his fight for life. Even the heat of Washington's summer was mitigated by American ingenuity; on July 10, Navy engineers began to implement an imaginative plan for cooling the air in the President's sickroom. That day the first shipment of an ultimate half-million pounds of ice was delivered to the White House.

On the twenty-third, however, the President's condition suddenly worsened. He vomited, complained of chills, and his temperature soon rose to 104°. Again, Hamilton and Agnew rushed to Washington, and on the morning of the twenty-fourth, Agnew made a drainage incision below the wound—a procedure repeated on August 12. Since early in July, moreover, Garfield had been running an intermittent, low-grade fever (a result, physicians felt, of Washington's ever-present malaria; they treated it routinely with quinine). As August progressed, the President seemed to hold his own, but a severe cough and a parotid abscess left him weakened and in pain. By the end of August, the broad-chested Garfield had shrunk from his normal 200 pounds to about 120. The prognosis was not promising.

And the first week of September brought record high temperatures, a heat wave extraordinary even for Washington. On the sixth, the President was moved—in an effort to escape the oppressive heat—from Washington to his oceanside cottage at Elberon, New Jersey. He traveled on a special train and for the last few miles on track laid especially for his trip—leading almost to the door of his summer home.

But despite the cooling breezes of the Jersey shore, the President's condition continued to deteriorate. On the seventeenth it became critical, and at 10:35 on the evening of the nineteenth, he died. (As an autopsy showed, the immediate cause was the rupturing of an aneurysm in the splenic artery, the artery having originally been injured by the bullet or probes.) On September 22, the President lay in state at the Capitol, his face terribly emaciated, his hands shrunken and twisted.

The crowds were immense. And the atmosphere, in one reporter's words, resembled that of a country fair; sellers of magazines, engravings, and photographs of the late President, venders of lemonade and ice water pounced upon the noisy and sun-baked crowd, determined to improve so rare an opportunity. Two days later Garfield was buried in his native Ohio. Chester Arthur, the Vice-President become President, proclaimed Monday, September 26, as a day of prayer and mourning.

But this formal observance was merely a concluding episode in a week of energetic and international lamentation. Parnell and Queen Victoria telegraphed their condolences almost simultaneously to Mrs. Garfield; Moses Montefiore, it was reported, telegraphed to Palestine and had prayers said in the holy cities. In Buenos Aires, flags were lowered to half-mast, the national and provincial legislatures adjourned, and all official business canceled. There was no end to the number of strange bedfellows united in their mourning of America's chief executive. In Dublin, the City Corporation interrupted its sessions in

honor of the late President, and in Liverpool the Conservative Club draped its balconies in black. And throughout the United States, of course, in schoolrooms, in G.A.R.
halls, in city councils and from pulpits, the life and virtues
of James A. Garfield, his stoic conduct during his last
illness, and his heroic death were extolled and embellished.
No grief in the world's history, one Presbyterian clergyman
decided, had ever compared to this. "Israel's grief for
Samuel," he observed, "was only a small thing, compared
with America's grief for Garfield. The land of Canaan
was not as large as the State of New Jersey." Probably no
greater concentration of sermons and oratory had ever
been produced by Americans, a people given traditionally
to excess in such matters. Local committees directed mass
memorial meetings; businesses, institutions, and private
homes covered their façades with lavish displays of black
crepe. In New York, even ferryboats and locomotives were
draped in black, while many New Yorkers wore mourning
bands around ther hats. No community was too small or too
remote to raise its prayers heavenward. In Deadwood,
Dakota Territory, a full-scale memorial service began with
"Asleep in Jesus" and closed with "Nearer, My God, to
Thee." Even before Garfield's death, engravers, printers,
and lithographers, creators of "beautiful Oil Chromos,"
and "splendidly illustrated" biographies had begun their
labors. Garfield's name and imposing bearded head were
soon to be found embossed on trays and enamels, etched in
glass, and engraved on steel.

But commercialism could not blur the question the
President's death seemed to raise: If God had removed so
admirable a Christian gentleman, surely this removal must
at least illustrate some moral truth—though the ultimate
meaning of his death might remain hidden to man. The
clearest lesson of the assassination lay, it seemed, in the contrasting character of the protagonists. The lives of Garfield
and Guiteau seemed to illustrate far more than a need for
civil service reform—or the need for adequately protecting

the chief executive's life. The contrasting biographies of Garfield and Guiteau dramatized the moral potential of American life. If Garfield embodied the possible achievement of the self-made man, the difficult yet accessible road from towpath to president, the career of Charles J. Guiteau, another midwestern boy, demonstrated to Americans another side of the American dream: the extent to which vice and depravity could hypertrophy in the same fluid environment that had so inspired James A. Garfield.

2

CHARLES J. GUITEAU

September 8, 1841–July 2, 1881

On May 8, 1833, at Denmark, Lewis County, New York, Jane Howe married Luther Guiteau, the youngest of eleven children of a hard-working local physician. As his name suggested, the young man was of Huguenot background, of a family consistently pious and respectable, if not distinguished. The fourth of Luther and Jane's six children, Charles Julius, was the only Guiteau to attain fame.

In 1839, the young couple moved to Freeport, Illinois. There the last three of their children were born, the first of these, Charles Julius on September 8, 1841. After the delivery, Jane Howe Guiteau—as family legend recalled it—remained in her room for several months and had her head shaved. She suffered, it seemed, from a "brain-fever" though her illness might possibly be diagnosed today as a postpartum psychosis. Neither of Mrs. Guiteau's last two children lived to his second birthday. She herself died on September 25, 1848, and, as the family Bible recorded, was "buried in the burying ground at Freeport, Ill. by the side of her children Charles H., Luther T., & Julia Catherine." Charles, seven at his mother's death, was the youngest of the three surviving Guiteau children.

Luther Wilson Guiteau was, in many ways, a difficult man. A hard-working and competent businessman, elected county clerk, and for many years cashier of Freeport's Second National Bank, Guiteau was a harsh and sometimes neglectful father. In religion, moreover, he was, to say the least, opinionated; in many of his neighbor's views, fanatical. By any standards, his religious opinions were extreme —even in an age still harboring an abundance of evangelical enthusiasm. The world was a very dramatic place to Luther Guiteau, one which he viewed in essence as a stage for the confrontation of God and the Evil One; each soul, and indeed every happening in the world, was an objective to be gained in this continuing struggle. Selfish or sinful actions, he always explained, were a consequence of submission to the pervasive forces of Evil; benevolence came only through faith and submission to God. No action, however small, could be ignored, and young Charles Julius Guiteau received a saving beating whenever his behavior indicated symptoms of the Evil One's hegemony. Luther Guiteau's views were, thus far, not terribly uncommon in antebellum America.

Even in this comparatively strenuous theological climate, however, his convictions attracted attention, for the respectable Freeport man of business had become a convert to the doctrines of John Humphrey Noyes, founder of New York State's Oneida Community. Established by Noyes and a handful of his perfectionist followers in the 1840's, the Oneida Community was, as Noyes termed it, a "Bible Communism." The communism extended, moreover, to sexual relations and child rearing as well as to property and work. Noyes, influenced by the millennial perfectionism endemic in the 1830's, had become convinced that he was without sin, that indeed all men could perfect themselves and live without sin. The second coming of Christ had, Noyes believed, already taken place during the destruction of the Temple in A.D. 70. A kingdom of saints already existed in Heaven and groups of human beings could perfect themselves in faith and, if successful, come into spiritual contact with the perfect realm of heavenly grace. Hence the Oneida Community.

Luther Guiteau had always cherished a desire to join the community, though prevented by circumstances and family responsibilities from ever actually doing so. His faith in

Noyes never wavered, however; it was a faith equal to his belief in revelation itself. Luther Guiteau believed as well that to the truly faithful all things were possible. Men now alive might never die, were their belief sufficiently pure; disease was not of God and could be banished by a faith vigorous and untainted. Like a handful of other disciples scattered throughout the country, Luther W. Guiteau read and reread Noyes's theological works and eagerly awaited copies of the community's circular.

Charles Julius was actually raised by his sister Frances, almost six years older than her younger brother. "Franky" was always closest to the boy, even after her marriage to George Scoville, a Chicago lawyer. But Frances was not always with Charles; in her early teens she left each fall to attend a nearby academy for young ladies. In the one letter of Guiteau's childhood that has been preserved, we can visualize the eleven-year-old writer, casually educated, obviously still disturbed by his mother's death four years before. "Dear Sister" he began:

you ou me a letter I want you to Wright to me how do you do
... well how do you like going to School at Rockbord [that
is, of course, Rockford] ... I go to Union School I like to go
the Union School thay have five teachers in the Union School
... I and Wilson [his older brother] ... ar verry well I
cant think of any thing.

JULIUS

Young Julius—children a hundred years ago were often called by their middle names—was not a happy child; even his name was unfortunate. Julius, with its grand Roman echoes, was, in antebellum America, a "nigger name," and the boy was always sensitive about it. Guiteau was extraordinarily slow in learning to speak and had as well great difficulty in pronouncing certain words. Yet he was at the same time extremely "nervous," his body always in motion. Years later, his brother recalled their father having offered Charles ten cents if he could keep his hands and feet still for five minutes—and the boy being incapable of earning the reward.

In 1853, when Charles was twelve, his father married a local woman—a good housekeeper, levelheaded, and more than a little skeptical of Oneida and Noyes—but also something of the stepmother. Five years after his father's second marriage, spelling improved, Charles Julius wrote his sister that "we live more pleasantly together now than we have since Father's marriage. I feel more at home than I have heretofore."

Perhaps this was because he was no longer at home all the time. Charles worked long hours, helping his father at the office; he split wood and cared for the family's horse. Like any ambitious son of respectable, churchgoing Americans, he was a moral and enterprising young man. Young Guiteau was an avid reader of Greeley's New York *Tribune,* that avatar of right-thinking Republicanism, and he found in its pages the models for his dreams of success. But he knew that such success could come only through hard work, that it had to be conceived of in moral as well as material terms. He would, he wrote his sister in 1859, try to perfect and educate himself, "physically, intellectually, and morally."

I think I should live according to the laws of health and physiology to arrive at the first part (physically). Secondly, to improve my mind by reading, writing, studying, and thinking as much as possible without over taxing the brain (intellectually). Thirdly, to keep my moral character pure and spotless.

The slight, fairly short young man had taken up gymnastics and weight lifting; in the three months he had had his dumbbells, Charles reported exuberantly that his chest had increased in girth from twenty-nine to thirty-three inches. Guiteau had become a convert not only to Greeley's Republicanism, and to something of his father's piety, but to the utopian health enthusiasms of the day as well. He was an avid reader of W. W. Hall's popular *Journal of Health* and a devotee of the phrenological and hydropathic publications of Fowlers and Wells in New York; a new dawn of health, Charles believed, was now possible, for the "race" as well as the individual. In pursuing his intellectual development, the young man had not only learned to write clearly and spell properly; he had even, he informed his sister, taken up German. ("A person who undertakes to master the German language has gotten himself into a scrape," Guiteau reported. Even at his most appealing, conscious humor was never one of his attributes.)

Most important, he could not wait to leave Freeport and the domination of his zealous father. Charles's heart was set on continuing his education, a necessary stepping-stone to achievement and independence. "I want," he wrote his sister, "to go to School two or three years steady if I can & I can if my will is large enough. (Where there is a will there is a way.) I think mine is sufficient." Guiteau would be a self-made man.

The problem was Luther Guiteau. He had no intention of subsidizing his son's college education; if Charles were to go anywhere it would be to the Oneida Community. In 1859, however, a new opportunity presented itself.

Charles's maternal grandfather, a retired steamboat captain, died in Wisconsin and left Charles—his favorite among the Guiteau children—a legacy of $1,000. His heir immediately began writing for college catalogues. "I want," he decided, "to obtain the most practical knowledge in the shortest time and at the least expense possible." Michigan appeared to be the most promising among the many possibilities. An aunt lived in Ann Arbor and, fortuitously, a law clerk in Freeport recommended Michigan warmly—the best university in the West, he declared. After much pleading and cajoling, his father finally gave permission for young Julius to attend college, though on his own responsibility and at his own expense. The cost, Charles calculated, would not be too great, certainly no more than $200 a year.

Registering for a degree might prove wasteful, but two or three years of disciplined study would, he felt, be an excellent preparation for the law career that he ultimately planned.

Ann Arbor proved a disappointment. Guiteau had rarely been away from home and family; he was always lonely. He discovered, moreover, that he had not prepared sufficiently for university work and would have to spend some time at Michigan's preparatory school. He felt, Charles wrote his brother-in-law, more miserable and destitute than he ever had before.

Not surprisingly, the lonely young man found increasing consolation in religion. He began, with a seriousness he had never been able to manage at home, to read the *Oneida Circular* and the *Berean,* Noyes's collected theological writings. Soon he began to correspond with several young men at the Oneida Community. By March of 1860, he could confide to one of these Oneida correspondents that "I feel that Christ is the only friend I have in the world, except those that are united to him in the truth." "I confess," he concluded joyously, "my union with Christ and the church of God at Oneida." With the coming of spring, he waited only for June and the semester's end so that he might—as his father had never done—take up residence in the community. In April, 1860, he wrote to his "dear beloved friends at Oneida" that

My confidence in you is continuously increasing and especially in Mr. Noyes. I have perfect, entire and absolute confidence in him in all things. I believe him to be a man directly inspired of God.

The writings of Noyes, Charles's letter continued, were as much the legitimate product of divine inspiration as those of the Apostles. The whole community, indeed, offered a promise of achievement and acceptance, an emotional warmth which to the lonesome young man must have seemed a very real and moving religious experience. "I feel united to you *all* by the body of Christ. I desire to be a true medium by which the truths that have been revealed to me by God, through Mr. Noyes, may be made known to the world." In June of 1860, he left Ann Arbor for New York State.

He was not to be happy at Oneida either. Charles was neither a steady nor diligent worker and never became popular with the Community's other young people. They soon christened him "Gitout" and regarded warily his alterations between brooding silence and garrulous enthusiasm. Guiteau was never shy in expressing belief in his mission, in his calling to a vocation higher than that of kitchen worker or shipping clerk in the Community's steel trap factory. Years later a neighboring farm boy employed by the Community recalled that Charles had usually done satisfactory work in the trap factory. At times, however, he would become confused and make ludicrous mistakes; he was always nervous and quick-tempered. If anything was said to anger him, Charles would gesticulate wildly and talk in a mysterious "understanding" manner. "At other times he would sit for hours in a corner talking to no one." He would spend hours writing, then tear up what he had written and throw it into the stove.

Most unhappily, the sallow young man was never popular with the girls of the Community. Anathematized as a haven for free love, sexual relationships at Oneida were—in their way—quite decorous (though members were not to indulge in the impiety of allowing an exclusive affection for one partner to interfere with their love of God). Guiteau was able neither to charm young ladies nor to prevail upon any of the older men to intercede for him.

The Community had, moreover, relied almost since its inception upon the institution of "criticism" to regulate social behavior. The individual to be criticized sat in a room surrounded by a circle of those community members who knew him best; the erring one would then have to endure their sharp and experienced observations. In Oneida one did see oneself as others did and it was not always a pleasant experience. During these sessions, Guiteau was forced to listen again and again to the charge of "egotism and conceit"; the other community members seemed unable to understand the significance of the mission to which he had been called.

For at least four years, however, Guiteau's faith in Noyes continued undimmed. As late as 1864, for example, when visiting the Community's branch near Wallingford, Connecticut, he took the opportunity of hearing Henry Ward Beecher. Though Beecher had previously been a hero to Guiteau, he now seemed boring and superficial compared to Noyes. "He failed entirely," Charles wrote, "to comprehend the great spiritual object of Christ's mission, which was to destroy the works of the devil and to save his people from their sins." Guiteau was impressed, too, with the pious and moral life led by Community members, and the earnest attempts all made to improve their education. (Guiteau always credited his lifelong abstention from tobacco, alcohol, and profanity to his years at the Community.) Gradually, however, a demanding restlessness overcame the young man. The Oneida fellowship seemed confining; his mission had yet to be fulfilled.

As early as 1863, Charles Julius had begun to suspect the character of his vocation. He was to be a great newspaper editor, greater even than his childhood idol, Horace Greeley; for his paper would be dedicated to spreading the millennial communism of the Community. "This is the only way," he wrote in 1863, "to pierce the atheistic materialism of the day."

On April 3, 1865, he left the Community. Its leaders had been generous; Charles departed with $50 worth of books, $100 worth of new clothes, $100 in cash, and a note for $800. (When he entered the Community, Guiteau had contributed the $900 remaining from his inheritance.) The decision to leave, Charles felt, was not his, but God's. The Deity, as Charles explained formally to the elders, acted directly upon nations, upon communities, and upon men, "just as a musician plays upon the keys of a piano." "But," he continued;

God makes no *blunders*. The millions inhabiting the earth are before Him, and he selects the right man every time for the right place; and in this He always successfully check-mates the devil's moves.

He had been chosen, Guiteau explained, to found the first of what would be a chain of daily newspapers. There were thousands of clergymen in America, Charles pointed out to the Community, but no theocratic newspapers. Here was a "splendid chance for some one to do a big thing for God, for humanity, and for himself." Instead of Americans spending an hour or two in religious contemplation once a week, Guiteau would

present them with a theocratic daily each morning at the breakfast table. . . . It would entirely discard all muddy theology, brain philosophy and religious cant, and seek to turn the *heart* of men toward the living God. . . . It would flood the land with communistic matter, just as phrenologists, physiologists and their cliques have with their peculiar specifics. Do you say that the establishment of a great daily paper is a stupendous work and only to be accomplished by extraordinary talents and energy. . . . However presumptuous it may seem, I am nevertheless constrained to confess the truth about myself. Therefore, I say boldly, that I claim *inspiration*. I claim that I am in the employ of Jesus Christ & Co.; the very ablest and strongest firm in the universe. . . . I *know in my heart* that I am ONE with Christ, Paul and Mr. Noyes, forever and ever. . . .

His plans, he concluded, were to stay in New York, to live frugally on the income from his $900 (a diet of lemon-ade, dried beef, and soda crackers would suffice), and to prepare for his editorial duties by reading and writing. He had been celibate at the Community and would remain so in New York; he had no particular friends to distract him at the Community and would have none in New York. But now his time would be his own; success was an ever-present possibility. Look at Horace Greeley, Guiteau argued, who had arrived in New York City thirty years before, homeless, friendless, and destitute; what American was now more influential? Charles concluded on a defensive note:

If a man have big ideas he is usually deemed *insane;* but I trust the community will not thrust the charge of insanity at me; but will allow me quietly to follow my own inspiration.

Guiteau settled in Hoboken and quickly set to work. Within a few weeks he had written and issued a prospectus for the *Daily Theocrat,* describing its mission and soliciting subscribers and advertising. But the lonely young man was unable to continue. Three months after leaving the Oneida Community he reapplied for admission, humbly even obsequiously. He prayed, he wrote the Oneida elders on July 20, 1865, "for a true spirit of humility and repentance, and that I may become a *little child,* and loyally yield myself to the Community spirit, and be a partaker of its life and love." God, he hoped, would reward them for their forbearance. As a gesture of good faith, the penitent, would-be editor donated his inheritance to the Community's printing department.

His second stay was a short one. On November 1, 1866, Charles again fled the Community. At his first leave-taking he had consulted with the elders and had subjected himself to the criticism of his peers; he had no intention of undergoing the experience again. Writing to the Community from New York, he asked for the return of the money he had donated to the printing department. His father, disturbed by Charles's defection, advised Noyes to send the money, though he was certain the young man would simply waste it.

By August of 1867 the money was spent. Guiteau returned to Freeport, spent some trying days with his father, then left for Chicago. His brother-in-law, George Scoville, had offered him a place as a clerk in his law office and as a boarder in his home.

Charles was again and again to turn for sympathy to his sister and her husband; they alone offered understanding in the face of his father's moral onslaughts. John Wilson Guiteau, Charles's older brother, sided consistently with his father and resented not only Charles but Scoville as well.

After a few months in Chicago, however, restlessness again overcame the would-be attorney. He had decided, he announced to his father and to the Scovilles, to return to journalism. And Chicago did not offer sufficient opportunities; Charles planned, it appeared, to return to New York and obtain a position as assistant editor on Henry Ward Beecher's *Independent,* one of the country's more influential weeklies. Through his contacts at the Y.M.C.A., Charles explained, and his acquaintanceship with Beecher, he felt assured of finding editorial work. Both father and brother-in-law tried to discourage the young man; it seemed clear that his chances for success were minimal. Charles would not be dissuaded, however, and asked his father for the loan of $100 to establish himself in New York. Despite his well-founded misgivings, Luther Guiteau finally gave his son fifty dollars. The editor-to-be arrived in New York with thirty-five dollars and soon found a satisfactory boardinghouse in Brooklyn Heights, near Beecher's Church of the Pilgrims. By December 11, he had only five dollars left and found himself writing to his sister for money—a procedure to which Charles was soon to accustom himself. The assistant editorship had been scaled down; Charles hoped now only to sell subscriptions and advertising on commission.

But a connection with the *Independent* had, it soon became clear to his family, been merely a cloak for Guiteau's true motive in returning to New York. His late worship of Noyes turned to the bitterness of rejection, Charles had become obsessed with the idea of taking revenge on the Oneida Community—and, at the same time, making a small fortune. At his brother-in-law's office, he had learned of the possibility of bringing suit to receive compensation for work performed, even where there had been no specific agreement to this effect. He decided that the threat of such a suit would be sufficient to force a settlement on the Community. As soon as Guiteau arrived in New York, he prevailed upon one John H. Dean, a young lawyer he had met through the Y.M.C.A., to undertake an action against Noyes and the Community. Charles demanded $9000, a figure arrived at by estimating wages of $1500 a year for the six years he resided at Oneida. At first Guiteau was confident; there seemed to him little likelihood that the Community would chance a public suit in which their sexual practices might become known. Charles had even made plans for investing the settlement he confidently awaited. ("When I get the money," he wrote his sister, "I am going to buy half a dozen Chicago lots, and let them grow.")

But the Community, of course, had no intention of paying. His client, Noyes wrote to Dean, had no valid claim, either in law or equity. Like all Community members, Guiteau had agreed to accept board, room, and education in lieu of wages; indeed, he had signed an agreement to this effect as soon as he had come of age. Perhaps more to the point, Noyes continued, was the fact that Guiteau had been neither a competent nor reliable worker in his years at the Community. He had been "moody, self-conceited, unmanageable, and a great part of the time was not reckoned in the ranks of reliable labor." It was hardly surprising, Noyes continued, for Guiteau had confessed while at the Community to having stolen money from previous employers; he had admitted as well to having frequented brothels, thus contracting a venereal disease; and to having become addicted to masturbation. One could hardly expect much in the way of productive work from a young man such as this, undermined in both moral and physical health.

Rebuffed, Guiteau grew increasingly bitter—a bitterness

proportionate to his earlier worship of Noyes. Though his attorney soon dropped a cause for which no fee seemed likely to be forthcoming, Guiteau continued to write letter after letter to the Community. Their tone became progressively abusive and threatening. If he had never entered the Community, he wrote in March, "I should have had a good law practice, and a nice family, and other things to match; but now I have neither." If the claim was not paid, he blustered, the Community's leaders would soon find themselves in prison. Ten years in Sing Sing would be an unpleasant experience for the autocratic Mr. Noyes.

I shall request Gov. Fenton [of New York] to order the Community to disband, and to confiscate their property to the State. A similar order will be obtained from Gov. English of Conn. . . . [The community, it will be recalled, had a branch at Wallingford.] It means *war to the teeth,* not a newspaper war, not a moral war; but a criminal war for them, and a war of dispersion for their community.

It made no difference that he had signed a waiver of compensation, Charles wrote his brother, John Wilson. The Oneida Community was a despotism and all contracts made within it were therefore void. "Whether I can get my money out of them or not, I want to see the Community 'wiped out.'" Charles had even arranged for the printing of an "Appeal" describing the sexual idiosyncrasies of the Community and calling for the extirpation of this moral cancer; he sent it to the Attorney General in Washington, to New York State officials, and to prominent ministers and editors in New York.

The essential and peculiarly insidious flaw in the Community, Guiteau later explained to a reporter, lay in Noyes's power to make members accept him as a prophet, convincing them that belief in him would bring salvation, while resistance would mean eternal damnation. "The idea," Guiteau continued, "produced a terrible spiritual suction." But it was all hypocrisy, Charles concluded. The Community had been founded not to establish the Kingdom of God on earth, but to satisfy Noyes's abnormal sexual instincts. ("All the girls that were born in the Community," Guiteau recalled indignantly, "were forced to cohabit with Noyes at such an early period that it dwarfed them. The result was that most of the Oneida women were small and thin and homely.") Finally, the Community's leaders instructed their attorney in New York to threaten Guiteau with prosecution for attempted extortion. His own threatening letters, Guiteau was told, would be evidence sufficient to have him imprisoned as a blackmailer.

Luther Guiteau was probably the most alarmed and humiliated participant in the sordid affair. His unworthy son, as he had feared, had attacked the godly Noyes and his Community. At Noyes's suggestion—though after some hesitation—the elder Guiteau wrote to New York's newspapers defending the Community. His son's original motivation, Luther explained, in joining the Community had been lechery, not piety; frustration and jealousy, not outraged morality, inspired his attack on the Oneida brotherhood. Noyes was quick to reassure his midwestern disciple that he harbored no resentment against his son. "I am sure," he wrote, "I have no ill will toward him. I regard him as insane, and I prayed for him last night as sincerely as I ever prayed for my own son, that is now in a Lunatic Asylum."

Whether because of the Community's threat of prosecution or because he lacked funds, Guiteau abruptly left New York early in 1868. He beat a hasty retreat to Illinois, to his family and the only security he knew. After a stop in Freeport, Charles moved to Chicago and a place in the law offices of Reynolds and Phelps. He copied documents and performed other routine office tasks while using his spare time to study for the bar. General J. S. Reynolds must have been a tolerant sort, for Charles Julius' fellow clerks recalled that Guiteau had been moody and unreliable, never able to finish a piece of work he had begun.

At first Charles seemed contented enough, despite an occasional exacerbation of the chronic bitterness he felt toward his father. Not only had Luther Guiteau supported the now hated Noyes in opposition to his own son, but he had repeatedly asked his son-in-law not to provide Charles with further loans. "How affectionate 'Father' must feel," he wrote sarcastically to his sister, "to advise Mr. Scoville not to let me have any more money. Great magnanimous man! How happy he must be!"

After a few months of desultory studying—and after an even more casual examination—Charles was admitted to the Illinois bar. The young man now had a trade.

And soon a wife as well. Like many evangelical and unmarried young men, Guiteau spent much of his time at the Y.M.C.A., where he became acquainted with their librarian, Miss Annie Bunn. Annie was a young Philadelphia girl who had come to Chicago at eighteen and soon found employment at the Christian Association. (She was, apparently, the mother of an illegitimate child.) She was enthusiastic about Guiteau, whom she described to her family as a "lawyer and a Christian." In 1869 they were married. Their union, however, proved not all that she might have wished.

Her husband was, first of all, a rather poor provider. His practice, even at its most expansive moments, consisted almost exclusively of bill-collecting, a field in which Guiteau's persistence and surface plausibility were indeed useful. (His one venture as courtroom advocate did not encourage further attempts; Charles's plea was so incoherent, even farcical, that it was remembered many years later by onlookers. The next trial at which he appeared as counsel was his own.) Often there was no money in the house and even when there was, Guiteau still met board bills by the simple expedient of flight. Almost immediately after their marriage, moreover, he began to treat Annie with uncommon brutality. Though he would sometimes be affectionate, at other times and almost without provocation, she recalled, he would strike her, pull her around the room by the hair, and kick her. Often he would beat her and sometimes lock his unfortunate wife in a closet for hours—and on a few occasions all night.

Mrs. Guiteau, like others who knew him, was shaken by her husband's inability to tolerate contradiction. Disagreement, even in small matters, provoked Guiteau into a fury. "I am your master," he would shout at his wife, "you are to submit yourself to me." Yet Charles was generally quiet and sedate, never making jokes, never given to frivolous amusements, never addicted to minor vices. He read avariciously; after an absence of ten years he was remembered by both the librarian and the director of New York's Y.M.C.A. Both recalled his frequent visits to their reading room and his erratic behavior.

After the Chicago fire, Guiteau and his bride moved to New York. Neither his personal nor his business habits changed, however. A fellow lodger in a New York boarding house in the summer of 1872 recalled him with some distaste. The Chicago lawyer beat and abused his wife, and the other boarders were relieved when he was ejected for failing to pay his bills.

In the summer and fall of 1872 he was particularly difficult. Guiteau spent much of his time in buttonholing New Yorkers who knew Horace Greeley—the Democratic candidate for President—and asking for their endorsement should Greeley win and be in a position to dispose of offices. Throughout the summer before the election, Annie recalled, he wrote campaign speeches and attended public meetings. Charles was convinced that he would be appointed minister to Chile if Greeley should be elected. "He talked about it day and night at home," continually making plans for his tenure of office. As the election approached he became so agitated that he could not sleep, but would pace to and fro reading and rereading his speeches, interrupting only to ask his wife's opinion of particularly dramatic effects.

Annie was forced, moreover, to participate in Charles's

imaginative financial arrangements. She too had to face the cold eyes of landladies and the harassment of bill collectors. Mrs. Guiteau was useful, as well, in establishing trust and credit. For example, soon after the Guiteaus returned to New York, they joined the Reverend Dr. Robert S. McArthur's Calvary Baptist Church; shortly thereafter, Mrs. Guiteau appeared in the reverend doctor's study and asked for the loan of $100. The fire, she explained, had left them temporarily short of funds. The minister provided the money and, needless to say, never saw it again.

He was not greatly surprised to learn some years later of the Guiteaus' divorce and the circumstances that had made it possible: Charles had, in 1874, purposely slept with a prostitute so that his wife might have the requisite legal grounds for a New York divorce.

Charles's New York legal affairs were as tangled as his personal life. He had, as his office boy recalled, "plenty of quiet cheek," borrowing law books and office equipment as needed. Stationery was ordered in immense quantities, though rarely paid for. (Cards and letterheads were always a weakness.) Guiteau spent most of the day at his desk, writing and correcting, then throwing the crossed-out sheets into the wastebasket. His manner of walking quietly, of avoiding the eyes of anyone he spoke with—yet all the while speaking in an urgent and confidential manner— made him seem the very picture of a seedy, unsuccessful shyster. His practice bore a similar stamp. Though he haunted the city prison for clients, Guiteau remained—as he had begun in Chicago—essentially a bill collector. (Charles occasionally sold some insurance on commission; this was never a major interest, however, though, as in his collection work, Guiteau's persistence had a certain value.) Guiteau was, moreover, a somewhat casual recipient for delinquent accounts; he charged a commission of 50 per cent and, as often as not, failed to pay the client his portion.

James Gordon Bennett's *Herald* finally warned its readers of this local attorney and his individualistic practice. The

Herald pointed to a particular case in which Guiteau had taken a bill of $350 for collection. When the debtor settled for $175, Guiteau refused to remit any of this sum to his client. His answer to the unfortunate creditor's demands was a simple one: All lawyers charged 50 per cent to collect past-due bills; he had collected his half and nothing, therefore, was due the client. Guiteau was furious with the *Herald*. He had always been an admirer of James Gordon Bennett for his journalistic success—if not always for his politics.

Guiteau decided now to humble Bennett as he had previously sought to humble the Oneida Community. He would, he informed friends, sue Bennett and the *Herald* for $100,000 for libel. Guiteau indeed went so far as to approach one of New York City's most prominent lawyers as possible counsel. The would-be plaintiff brought with him an opening speech of thirty-two closely written, foolscap pages. The case never came to trial; another of his victims brought suit against the erratic bill collector and Guiteau returned abruptly to Chicago. (Charles spent short periods of time in jail both in Chicago and New York for his financial idiosyncracies.)

Charles skittered from city to city, from project to project, from charlatanry to petty fraud; his youngest child was obviously a severe trial to Luther Guiteau's patience. Early in May of 1875, Luther wrote to John Wilson, his older son now respectably settled as an insurance agent in Boston, that he thought his younger brother, "capable of any folly, stupidity, or rascality. The only possible excuse I can render for him is that he is absolutely insane and is hardly responsible for his acts." Charles lacked faith— had allowed himself to become possessed by some satanic force; even when Charles appealed for bail so that he could leave Chicago's municipal prison, his father felt it incumbent upon himself to refuse. Perhaps a few weeks in prison might have an educative effect. "I do not desire your deliverance from jail," he explained to his son, "so much as I do that you may be brought to repentance and obedience to Christ."

But Charles was just then elaborating his most ambitious scheme; rather than found a new daily he would buy one. The Chicago *Inter-Ocean,* he had become convinced, could be converted from an ordinary daily into the most influential paper in the West. "I proposed," he recalled with enthusiasm, "to put Horace Greeley's Republicanism into it and James Gordon Bennett's snap & enterprise." The central element in Guiteau's plan was to transmit the New York *Tribune's* news columns telegraphically to Chicago each day and print them in the *Inter-Ocean.* Guiteau inspected possible buildings for his paper, selected several steam presses, even discussed rates with the telegraph company. Early in the fall of 1875, the prospective publisher sought backing for his project. He first approached Charles B. Farwell, prominent Chicago businessman and philanthropist. As Farwell recalled the incident, Guiteau asked to borrow $200,000; with this, he promised, he would make Farwell President of the United States. Guiteau made a similar proposal to Potter Palmer; he even turned to his father for help and in the middle of October visited Freeport. He hoped that the older man would intercede with a local banker and arrange a $25,000 loan to help buy the *Inter-Ocean.* Not surprisingly, he was disappointed. His father refused even to discount his note for $200. This new scheme of Charles's, Luther Guiteau wrote to his daughter Frances, could hardly be the product of a sound mind:

To my mind he is a fit subject for a lunatic asylum, and If I had the means to keep him would send him to one for a while at least. His condition in my judgment has been caused by an *unsubdued will,* the very spirit of disobedience to authority . . . disobedience to God and the spirit of truth, which culminated with a quarrel with Mr. Noyes and the O.C.

His son, it was clear, had been motivated by Satan, by his yielding to the blandishments of the satanic forces which filled the world. (Luther, as well as his sons John Wilson and Charles, believed that insanity was the result of a species of satanic possession.)

Had Luther Guiteau known of his son's behavior while visiting sister Frances at her Wisconsin summer home late that spring, he would have been even more alarmed. Charles, more or less destitute, had visited the Scovilles, and one particularly hot day Frances asked him to cut some wood for the stove. He left the house and set to work. A short time later, Frances walked past, and, as she did, he turned and lifted his axe as if to strike her. She dodged and ran into the house. When inside she sent the hired man to watch her brother and then called the family physician. When Dr. Rice arrived he spoke with Charles for some time; he experienced, the doctor recalled, little difficulty in concluding that he was insane and recommended that Frances place her brother in an asylum. Before anything could be done, however, Charles disappeared as abruptly as he had come.

After the failure of his *Inter-Ocean* enterprise, Charles was again at loose ends. But he began almost immediately to fit himself for a new vocation. Guiteau had always enjoyed attending religious meetings; indeed, he had become something of a connoisseur of evangelical preaching. In 1876, he started to attend Dwight Moody's revival meetings—and soon grew so enthusiastic that he began to serve each evening as an usher. During the day, Guiteau was accustomed to spend much of his time in libraries and reading rooms; almost all his reading now was in theology. God, salvation, and the Evil One had never been far from his mind—as all the Guiteaus believed, they constituted the world's essential and immanent fabric. Guiteau again felt himself called to some great task.

Though his customary collecting of late accounts had come to provide a more-or-less reliable living, Charles began to lose interest in law. "My mind was running on Theology," he recalled. "I was like a woman in childbirth.

I had something in me and I had to get it out." Inspired by Moody's eloquence and success, Guiteau laid aside the business of law and "went into theology." He would be a great lecturer, a popular oracle like Beecher or Moody, but—Charles believed—with a more novel and significant message. A great truth, Guiteau was convinced, had been divulged to him; like Paul, he had been chosen to preach a new gospel.

Guiteau began a new life. He moved from town to town, lecturing in rented and begged auditoriums, leaving a trail of unpaid boarding-house keepers, printers, and tailors. Eastern railroads, too, helped spread this new dispensation: Guiteau's normal mode of travel consisted of boarding trains and then staying on until put off at the first stop, boarding another train and repeating the process. (A slow but not unreliable means of travel—though one trainman did throw Guiteau off a moving express. That he was not injured always seemed to Charles a sign of his divine calling.) Guiteau would arrive at a town, arrange for the use of an auditorium and the printing of handbills advertising his appearance. Newspaper advertisements soon appeared, announcing a lecture by Charles J. Guiteau of Chicago, "lawyer and theologian" (in at least one handbill he described himself as "The Little Giant from the West"). In March of 1878, for example, Guiteau spoke at the Newark Opera House; his subject, "Is there a Hell?" Tickets were ten and fifteen cents. The *Newark Daily Journal* reported the next day under the headline, "Is there a Hell?" that

FIFTY DECEIVED PEOPLE ARE OF THE OPINION THAT THERE
OUGHT TO BE

The man Charles J. Guiteau, if such really is his name, who calls himself an eminent Chicago lawyer, has fraud and imbecility plainly stamped upon his countenance, and it is not surprising that his "lecture" in the Opera House last evening did not leave a pleasant impression on the minds of the fifty people who assembled to hear him. . . .

His lecture was a wonderful production of genius. It

consisted of the averment that the second coming of Christ occurred in the year 70 when Jerusalem was destroyed; interesting readings from the book of Genesis, and the prediction that the world would soon come to an end.

Although the impudent scoundrel had talked only fifteen minutes, he suddenly perorated brilliantly by thanking the audience for their attention and bidding them goodnight. Before the astounded fifty recovered from their amazement, or the half dozen bill collectors who were waiting for an interview with the lecturer had comprehended the situation, the latter had fled from the building and escaped.

This was the pattern in all Guiteau's lectures. He shuffled papers, spoke incoherently for a few minutes, then abruptly left the podium and the room. Insofar as a theme could be found in his talks, it was the thesis of John H. Noyes: Christ had appeared for a second time at the destruction of the Temple in A.D. 70. Thus, in the intervening years, perfect sinlessness had always been a possibility for those of sufficient faith. Though Guiteau became indignant at the allegation, his theological writings were essentially disorganized excerpts from Noyes's *Berean*. It is likely, however, that Guiteau did not himself realize this; his mode of composition had a romantically spontaneous quality.

I weave the discourse out of my brain as cotton is woven into a fabric. When I compose my brain is in a white heat, and my mind works like lightning. This accounts for the short epigrammatic style of my sentences. I write so rapidly I can hardly read it . . . I divest myself of all unnecessary clothing. I eat and sleep mechanically.

This description would hardly have surprised the few readers of Guiteau's *The Truth: A Companion to the Bible,* a work in which he took immense pride. *The Truth* was— essentially—an exhortation to do good in the manner of a rural evangelist, interspersed with somewhat more apocalyptic admonitions. It had been published by an unwary and unpaid Boston printer and imprinted with the name of a commercial publisher, though the publisher had never heard of the work. Guiteau was certainly motivated by a genuine detestation for drinking, smoking, chewing, dancing, and the theater—vices to which he never succumbed and which he associated with the self-indulgent, the depraved, and members of the lower orders. Charles was, as he himself put it, a "high-toned gentleman" at all times.

Guiteau spent the three years between 1877 and 1880 writing, speaking, selling his theological tracts. In 1880, however, a new purpose again filled his life: Charles became a politician. (The year 1880 also saw the death of Charles's father.) His theological peregrinations seemed to have reaped neither temporal nor eternal profits. The "lawyer and theologian" became a "lawyer, theologian, and politician."

Guiteau had been interested in politics since his boyhood in Freeport; only in 1872, however, when he could identify with his childhood idol Greeley, had he become intensely involved in a specific political campaign. In 1880, Guiteau associated himself emotionally with the Stalwart faction of the Republican Party and their attempt to nominate Grant for a third term. When Garfield was chosen, however, Guiteau adopted the Ohioan's cause and transferred his operations from Boston to New York. The small, shabby man with the catlike walk and confidential manner became a familiar figure among the hangers-on at the Republican campaign headquarters in New York's Fifth Avenue Hotel. He cornered prominent politicians and asked to be provided with speaking engagements, pressing upon them copies of a campaign speech he had composed.

The speech, entitled "Garfield vs. Hancock," is an almost incoherent mélange of bloody-shirt clichés; in it, however, Guiteau felt that he had originated a major Republican issue. This was, in Guiteau's terminology, the "Rebel War claim idea." The government, Guiteau argued, could not be given over to the traitorous Democrats; it would mean an emptying of the treasury, economic crisis and—very likely—civil war. Guiteau, of course, was only one among an assortment of marginal souls who hovered about the campaign headquarters.

He never impressed party functionaries with any quality other than persistence, and the Republicans managed to wage the campaign without his services. (Except for one speech that Guiteau delivered in his usual disjointed manner to a group of about a dozen Negroes; this was not a high-priority assignment in the plans of New York City's Republican managers.) Garfield's election was, nevertheless, a joyous event. "We have cleaned them out," he wrote immediately to the President-elect, after the victory, "just as I expected. Thank God." Guiteau had never met Garfield.

Greeley's election had conjured up visions of Latin American indolence for Guiteau, and Garfield's election too meant plans. Vienna, however, not Chile, was Guiteau's new destination. As early as November 11, Guiteau wrote politely to Secretary of State William Evarts asking whether all of Hayes' appointees would resign and new appointments be made by Garfield. In October and then in January, Guiteau had written to Garfield, mentioning his impending marriage to a woman of wealth and his consequent fitness for the ministry in Vienna. (The heiress, Charles explained later, was a lady he had seen at church in New York; though he had never been introduced or spoken with her, Guiteau was convinced that she would marry him.) With the new year, the sometime lawyer and theologian moved to Washington so that he might, like thousands of other would-be appointees, better prosecute his cause. Soon after the new President's inauguration he became a familiar face in the corridors of the State Department and the anterooms of the White House. Guiteau submitted applications—duly filed—for the ministry to Austria, for the consul-generalship to Paris, and even for the consulship in Liverpool. Despite such wavering, however, the Paris position sooned replaced the Austrian one in

Guiteau's affections. He preferred, he explained to Secretary Blaine, life in Paris to that in Vienna. Guiteau's letter to Blaine on March 11 was marked "private" and enclosed a copy of his campaign speech, "Garfield vs. Hancock." It explained his claims:

I think I have a right to claim your help on the strength of this speech. It was sent to our leading editors and orators in August. It was about the first shot in the rebel war claim idea, and it was *this* idea that elected General Garfield. . . . I will talk with you about this as soon as I can get a chance. There is nothing against me. I claim to be a gentleman and a Christian.

On the twenty-fifth he wrote again to Blaine, explaining something of his credentials:

I vote in Chicago, although I have been in New York for nearly a year. I was running the canvass with the National and State committees last fall. I asked Gen. Logan to sign my applications and he said he had already signed so many applications for consuls that he did not think it would do any good; but, he added: "I have no objection to your having the Paris consulship."
This is the only office I ask for myself or friends, and I think I am entitled to it.
I ask it as a personal tribute. . . .
I am very glad that the President selected you for his Premier. It might have been some one else.

While awaiting his commission and bombarding Blaine and Garfield with insinuating letters, Guiteau made do in his usual style.

When he arrived in Washington, he sought a place in a most respectable boarding house, Mrs. Lockwood's at 810 Twelfth Street (possibly because Senator Logan also boarded there). Though his appearance was not too reassuring, Charles was given a room in an isolated part of the house. Guiteau received his mail, however, at the more elegant Riggs House, one of Washington's best hotels. The Riggs supplied stationery as well, stationery with a dignified letterhead suitable for a prospective minister or consul. At Mrs. Lockwood's he was a difficult guest, constantly bothering General Logan with his importunities, appearing with his unnaturally quiet steps suddenly at the side of fellow boarders. At dinner, he attacked the food with the single-minded intensity of one who had missed many meals. Ladies expecting him to pass the plates were quickly disappointed. In the middle of the month, when Mrs. Lockwood presented her first bill, Guiteau decamped with practiced efficiency and left a note in which he promised payment as soon as he received the $6,000-a-year position that was to be his. General "Blackjack" Logan, a shrewd and, in his fashion, worldly politician, took one glance at Guiteau's parting note and assured his landlady that its author was a lunatic.

From Mrs. Lockwood's, Guiteau moved to a less imposing, though still respectable boarding house on Fourteenth Street. Most of his time was spent on the benches in Lafayette Square. When not in the park, he visited the White House or State Department, sending in his card each day and badgering the secretaries with demands for attention. He was a bit odd, but officials in the executive departments were accustomed to eccentrics; indeed they found them a source of some amusement. Guiteau became, in the words of one Washingtonian, "a kind of butt, sent around from place to place, his own egotism sustaining him."

But Charles was coming to the end of his path, his life increasingly unrelated to others. He had no source of income, no lecturing, no books to sell, no bills to collect; he had no family; he had never had any friends. His clothes, shabby enough when he reached Washington, were deteriorating. Even in March, with snow on the ground, he went about without boots or an overcoat. By June, his worn sleeves were pulled down over his hands and his coat buttoned up to his neck, for he had no collar and possibly lacked a shirt as well. His communications to the President became, despite the rebuffs of secretaries, increasingly familiar. On April 29 and May 7, he wrote urging Garfield to compromise with Senator Conkling and change his decision to remove the Stalwart Collector of Customs in New York. On the tenth he wrote an intimate and encouraging letter to the President, advising him to run again in 1884. "I will see you about the Paris consulship to-morrow," a postscript concluded, "unless you happen to send in my name today."

Yet the exhilarating enthusiasm that had inspired him since the election was beginning to fade. Blaine and Garfield, the gracious patrons of his imaginings, had deserted him. Blaine, in fact, meeting him at the State Department on May 14, had snapped at him, "Never bother me again about the Paris consulship so long as you live." At the same time, Stalwart editorialists were confirming Guiteau's fears about the character of Garfield and Blaine and the future of the Republican party. They seemed clearly bent on proscribing the Stalwarts—Conkling, Grant, and Logan among them, men whose careers Charles had admired and whose integrity and ability he did not question.

Guiteau's letters became increasingly intense. On May 23, he wrote the President warning of Blaine's duplicity. The Secretary of State "is a wicked man," he cautioned, "and you ought to demand his *immediate* resignation. Otherwise, you and the republican party will come to grief." Guiteau had already been forbidden the White House anterooms by secretaries who had ceased to find him amusing.

At some time in the middle of May, lying exhausted one night in his bed, it occurred to Guiteau that the President should be "removed" and that he, Charles Julius Guiteau, was the man for the job. The idea, he recalled, revolted him at first but would not be banished. Like all the other acts and plans of his life, it had to be considered in its essential character: Was it truly a divine inspiration or was it a prompting of Satan? After a few weeks of prayer for heavenly guidance—about the beginning of June—Charles concluded that his inspiration was indeed a "divine pressure," not a devilish temptation. On June 8, he borrowed fifteen dollars from a distant relative, ostensibly to settle his board bill.

His next stop was a gunshop. Unlike most Illinoisians, Guiteau knew nothing of firearms; he did know that he needed a revolver of the largest caliber. He wanted no mistakes. A helpful fellow customer showed Charles how to load the snub-nosed, forty-five caliber English revolver he had chosen. Guiteau selected one with an inlaid grip, thinking it would be far more elegant when displayed later in the patent office. The next three weeks he followed the President, noted his daily routine, even attended church with the Chief Executive—then inspected a side window to see whether it might be possible to shoot Garfield as he sat in his pew. When not thus occupied, Guiteau made several excursions to the Potomac's muddy bank to practice with his new revolver.

There was no question now in Charles's mind of the necessity for Garfield's removal. In his room on June 16, he wrote an "Address to the American People," explaining the need for the act he planned:

I conceived of the idea of removing the President four weeks ago. Not a soul knew of my purpose. I conceived the idea myself. I read the newspapers carefully, for and against the administration, and gradually the conviction settled on me that the President's removal was a political necessity, because he proved a traitor to the men who made him, and thereby imperiled the life of the Republic. At the late Presidential election, the Republican party carried every Northern State. Today, owing to the misconduct of the President and his Secretary of State, they could hardly carry ten Northern States. They certainly could not carry New York, and that is the pivotal State.

Ingratitude is the basest of crimes. That the President, under the manipulation of his Secretary of State, has been guilty of the basest ingratitude to the Stalwarts admits of no denial.

. . . In the President's madness he has wrecked the once
grand old Republican party; and for this he dies. . . .
    I had no ill-will to the President.
    This is not murder. It is a political necessity. It will make my
friend Arthur President, and save the Republic. I have
sacrificed only one. I shot the President as I would a rebel, if
I saw him pulling down the American flag. I leave my
justification to God and the American people.

Still, Guiteau could not quite bring himself to shoot the
President. Once he came upon Garfield walking at night
with Secretary Blaine; somehow he was not able to pull
the trigger. A few days later, on June 18, when Charles had
definitely decided to remove the President as he met Mrs.
Garfield at the railroad station, Guiteau again held his fire.
He could not bear to shoot the President then, Guiteau
wrote that night: Mrs. Garfield looked so frail and clung
so pathetically to her husband's arm. (A sufferer from
malaria, the First Lady spent much of her time at the
Jersey Shore.)

Thursday, June 30, Guiteau disappeared from his boarding house and registered at the Riggs House. He had
learned from newspaper reports that the President would
be leaving at 9:30 Saturday morning from the Baltimore
and Potomac depot. Friday night, the would-be assassin
composed another explanation for his intended act. "The
President's tragic death," he began

was a sad necessity, but it will unite the Republican party and
save the Republic. Life is a fleeting dream, and it matters
little when one goes. A human life is of small value. During
the war thousands of brave boys went down without a tear. I
presume the President was a Christian, and that he will be
happier in Paradise than here.
    It will be no worse for Mrs. Garfield, dear soul, to part with
her husband this way than by natural death. He is liable to
go at any time anyway.
    I had no ill-will towards the President. His death was a
political necessity. I am a lawyer, a theologian, a politician. I
am a Stalwart of the Stalwarts. I was with General Grant and

the rest of our men in New York during the canvass. I have some papers for the press, which I shall leave with Byron Andrews and his co-journalists at 1440 N.Y. Ave., where all the reporters can see them.

I am going to the jail.

CHARLES GUITEAU

Early Saturday morning, Guiteau ate a full breakfast at the Riggs, charging it to his bill. He then walked to the river at the foot of Seventeenth Street. Charles placed a stick in the mud of the river bank and practiced with his revolver for a few minutes. The now confident marksman walked to the station, arriving at eight-thirty; he had an hour to wait. Part of this time he consumed in necessary errands: he had his shoes shined, negotiated with a hack-man to drive him to the congressional cemetery near the District prison at nine-thirty, and left a package of papers at the newsstand addressed to a New York *Herald* reporter together with a letter for Byron Andrews, Washington correspondent for the Chicago *Inter-Ocean*. This accomplished, he went into the deserted men's washroom and checked his revolver. He emerged at about nine. He had still a half-hour to wait.

3

THE PRISONER, PSYCHIATRY, AND THE LAW

The District of Columbia jail was a sturdy building, squatting on a bluff overlooking the Anacostia River. It stood alone; Washington was a small city, and almost a mile lay between the prison and the eastern terminus of the city's two horsecar lines.

President Garfield had been shot on a Saturday morning. The next day the sun had scarcely risen before a stream of visitors—on foot and in carriages—began to arrive at the prison. By midafternoon, reporters had to push their way through a knot of curiosity seekers in front of the gate. A smaller group stood in the shade of a tree to the east of the building, looking toward the barred windows in hopes of catching a glimpse of the assassin.

There was none to be had. Even the impatient swarm of newspapermen filling the jail's rotunda were unable to see or question Guiteau. The warden, General Crocker, who had rushed back to Washington from his vacation, spent a hectic day fending off reporters. Repeatedly and defensively the warden recited his instructions: the prisoner could not be seen without the consent of Attorney General Wayne MacVeagh or District Attorney George Corkhill. In the prison's high domed rotunda, outside the door to the warden's office, a detachment of troops stood ready to defend the assassin.

In the afternoon the prisoner did appear briefly in the rotunda; he was to have his picture taken. Clark Bell, a prominent Washington photographer, had been summoned to record the would-be assassin's features. ("Think," a

43

popular writer mused, "of Science squatting down and using a pencil of sunshine to paint the face of Charles Julius Guiteau! Michael Angelo molding the head of a toad with a paste of diamonds.") The pictures were quickly taken and Bell was pounced upon by the still hopeful reporters. Guiteau, the photographer confided, had been positively garrulous, deeply concerned that his pictures be flattering.

Monday was the Fourth of July and again crowds of ordinary Washingtonians made the long trip to the district jail in hopes of seeing the prisoner. But again the slight assassin did not appear. Only Secret Service men and the District Attorney were privileged to speak with the new celebrity. The government's primary responsibility was to allay suspicions that Guiteau had been motivated neither by insanity nor individual depravity, but by conspiratorial design. The bitterness accompanying the Republican party split had been too deep and too public. Guiteau, however, remained adamant in his denials. He had acted alone, he insisted; his inspiration had been divine, not political.

Though he was behind bars, guarded by police and regular troops, unseen even by the ubiquitous newspapermen, the assassin's name was immediately known throughout the country. Within a few days, the outlines of his career began to appear piecemeal in newspapers and weeklies. Those who had, to their regret at the time, brushed against Guiteau during his legal or evangelical peregrinations found themselves local celebrities. Hotel clerks, boardinghouse keepers, YMCA secretaries, printers, clergymen, and lawyers reported their encounters with the elusive Guiteau. Gradually, the elements of a biography emerged. The assassin represented a familiar species: the deadbeat, the semicriminal petty swindler. Mixed with these were characteristics of the religious and political fanatic, both familiar American types.

Meanwhile the prisoner seemed in high spirits. After years of irregular eating and consistent obscurity, he now dined regularly and enjoyed the knowledge that he was a figure of national importance. (Guiteau ate a surprising quantity of food for a slight man, gaining over ten pounds during the summer. Sensationalist accounts of the assassination imaginatively pictured Guiteau's supposedly Lucullan prison fare—details that would hardly endear the prisoner to less affluent Americans, the presumable audience for such pamphlets.) Guiteau maintained with consistent optimism that his imprisonment was in itself quite important, indeed necessary, to the fulfillment of his mission. The sudden notoriety would certainly provide readers for his theological works and for an autobiography he planned to complete in prison. Early in June, for example, he wrote to the "Chicago Press":

I expect to issue shortly through a first-rate New York
publishing house a book entitled
     The Life and Theology of Charles Guiteau
     Prepared by Himself
     It will be a good-sized volume of 500 pages.
Part 1. My life, I dictated to a short-hand writer. The story of
     my life is pointed and graphic, and reads like a
     romance, and tells of my acquaintance with public
     men, and of my attempted removal of the President.
Part 2. My Theology, is my contribution to the civilization of
     the race. It is a reprint of my book *The Truth*
     issued in Boston nearly two years ago.

At the top of the sheet, the prospective autobiographer had scrawled: "Put quick headlines on to this matter. C.G."

It seemed clear to Guiteau that the government's case must be a frail one indeed. How could he, the sometime lawyer submitted, be guilty of an act in which he displayed no volition, in which he acted simply as an instrument of the Deity? The President's survival, Guiteau argued throughout the summer, was merely a consequence of

the disadvantage under which I executed the Divine Will: to
wit: I shot him as he was rapidly receding from me and
the bullet did not strike him in a vital part, but notwithstanding

this, it would have proved speedily fatal had it not been for
the prayers and supplications of the people who were
justly horrified by the President's distressed condition . . . the
prayers and entreaties of the American People changed
the Deity's original intention. . . .

The most annoying aspect of his imprisonment was the
necessity of remaining incarcerated until his trial and inevitable acquittal. Certainly, Guiteau thought, he would be
free on bail by fall.

It was not simply a matter of convenience that he be
temporarily free; it was a financial necessity. The subtle
questions of law, theology, and politics, which would inevitably be discussed during his trial, demanded the best of
legal talent. And such lawyers were expensive. But in a
few months on bail, Charles was convinced, he could make
at least $30,000 lecturing. Henry Ward Beecher, he re-
flected, and even that contemptible atheist Robert Inger-
soll, commanded such fees. Some of Guiteau's needs were
more immediate, and he used every opportunity to appeal
for small sums of money. He asked, for example, that
Clark Bell send him a twenty-five dollar royalty payment
for the use of his photograph.

Guiteau's moods, however, did seem to vary somewhat
with the President's condition. (Though he was not supposed to be informed of Garfield's progress, Charles was
apparently able to gather something of his victim's status
from the conversation of warders and official visitors.)
During his more optimistic moments Guiteau argued that
even the President's death could not change the basic legal
situation: it would simply prove the authenticity of his
assassin's inspiration. Temporal punishments would necessarily seem trivial in this eternal perspective.

Guiteau felt a more prosaic assurance as well. Should
the President die, the Stalwarts, always his friends and now
the beneficiaries of his inspiration, would hardly allow him
to come to harm. Colonel George Corkhill, Washington's
district attorney, reported with some indignation that at

one of their interviews Guiteau had slapped him on the knee, leaning forward and remarking: "Colonel, you are a Stalwart?" Guiteau straightened, smiling blandly, when Corkhill admitted that he was.

Nevertheless, as July turned into August the prisoner became increasingly anxious. The President seemed on the road to recovery, while he, the nation's almost savior, remained in virtual isolation. Guiteau was allowed no newspapers and was kept in a wing carefully isolated from other prisoners. The guards were forbidden to communicate with the assassin and he was allowed neither letters nor visitors without the District Attorney's approval. This had been the case since July 19. Two days before, on July 17, the President's several physicians had informed the District Attorney that Garfield seemed well on the road to recovery. The next day Corkhill dismissed the grand jury that he had kept in session since the Fourth; they were to reconvene in September, when, it was assumed, the President's condition would be clarified.

Corkhill's harsh orders did not seem to disturb the assassin greatly. Guiteau was accustomed to spending much of his time alone. He did, however, miss the newspapers. They had been his chief companions for many years and now they would be all the more engrossing. On August 28 he wrote to the District Attorney asking to see at least the New York *Herald* and the Chicago *Tribune,* papers that he was certain were friendly. Guiteau assured Corkhill that there was very little sentiment against him outside of Washington. Even in the District of Columbia, he explained, such hostility was artificially stimulated by the place-holding beneficiaries of Garfield's appointing power, by politicians who feared that they would forfeit lucrative positions if Arthur and the Stalwarts were to assume the reins of government.

As the President's health deteriorated and the summer came to an end, Guiteau seemed to become increasingly agitated. This tension showed itself, for example, in a growing concern for his personal safety. At four-thirty in the morning of August 17th, he either foiled a guard who entered his cell with the intention of shooting him as he slept, or, as the guard reported the incident, suddenly attacked the warder as he routinely entered the cell with gun drawn. With this incident as catalyst, the sometime lawyer and theologian, an experienced correspondent in either capacity, wrote letter after letter demanding that his cell be adequately protected from the prison guards as well as from the hostile outside world. He was, Guiteau warned Warden Crocker, not without influence; the Stalwarts would certainly exact a just revenge if anything should happen to their friend and benefactor. Guiteau demanded blinds and special bars on his cell to discourage the marksmanship of ill-intentioned guards. Finally, as Guiteau put it, he became "tired and sick of this whole business." On September 13, he wrote to one of the judges on the District's supreme bench offering a compromise:

If I should decide [he suggested] to enter a plea of assault with attempt to kill, would the government meet me by giving two years—the lowest time the law allows? I hardly know whether I would do it as I expect to be acquitted, whatever the charge.

The news of the President's death seemed at first to shock the assassin. A guard's chance remark told him of Garfield's demise, and Guiteau immediately sank to his knees in prayer, apparently quite agitated. Despite this immediate confusion Guiteau soon took consolation in the thought that Garfield's death proved irrefutably the genuineness of his inspiration. The Lord had chosen to ignore the prayers of millions of Americans, Guiteau argued, in making his removal of the President final. The assassin was careful to point out as well that his unavailing prayers had been among those of so many other Americans and that he too now prayed for the salvation of the late President's soul—as he would for that of any other Christian. There was no malice in his act, Guiteau stated again and again;

it was not murder but necessary removal. There could be no question of its necessity; Americans, Guiteau wrote late in September, were coming to realize that he had saved the Republican party and averted an almost certain civil war. He would, he felt, "probably not be tried for a year. Not until the excitement all dies out."

And then, of course, the influence of the new president would be at his disposal. Indeed, as soon as he learned of Garfield's death Guiteau threw himself into the affairs of the party. "My inspiration," he wrote to Chester Arthur the day after his predecessor's death,

is a God send to you & I presume you appreciate it. It raises you from $8,000 to $50,000 a year. It raises you from a political cypher to President of the United States with all its powers and honors. . . . For the cabinet I would suggest as follows: State: Mr. Conkling Treasury: Mr. Morton War: Gen. Logan P.M.G. Mr. James Atty. Gen. Mr. E. A. Storrs of Chicago. There is no objection to two or more cabinet officers from the same state. The men & not the state should govern. . . . Let all honor be paid to Gen. Garfield's remains. He was a good man but a weak politician.

Perhaps most important to Guiteau was the appearance in the October 6 edition of the New York *Herald* of the autobiography he had dictated in prison. "I am looking for a wife," he confessed in concluding his life's story. "I want an elegant Christian lady of wealth, under thirty, belonging to a first class family . . . I am fond of female society, and I judge the ladies are of me, and I should be delighted to find my mate."

Despite Guiteau's unflagging confidence in the mood of the American people, September and October brought with them increased hostility. His side of the story had not changed men's minds.

Early in September, General Sherman himself visited the prison and personally rearranged the sentry posts guarding its approaches. A company of troops remained stationed in the rotunda, while an extra detail of District police officers had been stationed at the workhouse a few hundred yards from the prison.

The crowds of onlookers had dwindled during the heat of July and August and as the novelty of the situation declined, but with the President's death they increased once more. All day and into the dusk visitors gathered in small groups, hoping not only for a glimpse of the prisoner but also, perhaps, to be present at the lynching so many would have applauded. Guiteau was moved to a new cell, one closer to the troops in the rotunda and reconstructed especially for his safety. It was of brick, with a massive, iron cored and bulletproof oaken door. A small grille at the top admitted light and air. Presumably Guiteau installed above the door the sign that had graced his previous cell. It bore the legend: "Be faithful unto the end."

These precautions seemed necessary. Each post brought rumors and threats to the District Attorney's office; throughout the eastern seaboard, stories circulated of grim faced men meeting by moonlight and swearing blood oaths to exterminate the assassin. Abuse and threats arrived at the prison from the pens of the ill-balanced and ill-tempered throughout the country. One suggested that the assassin be forced to eat two ounces of his own flesh each day, another that he be given 39 lashes a day until death. An Indiana correspondent enclosed a dozen bedbugs in his letter to the prison, suggesting that they be allowed to multiply in Guiteau's cell. Many warned, even when it appeared that the President would live, that a jail term would simply postpone their revenge. "When your term expires," a Union veteran promised,

and you remain in this country twenty-four hours after, I or some of my pards will get the drop on you, and don't you forget it. You dirty, lousy, lying rebel traitor; hanging is too good for you, you stinking cuss. We will keep you spotted, you stinking pup. You damn old mildewed assassin. You ought to be burned alive and let rot. You savage cannibal dog.

Newspaper stories related incidents in which men expressing sympathy for Guiteau were beaten by mobs—and one
in which such a blasphemer was killed. Many Americans,
even among the educated and legally enlightened, could
not accept the possibility of his escaping with a relatively
light jail term (in the period, that is, before the President's
death). A number of respectable lawyers and editors proposed that Guiteau be tried twice, once for each of the
bullets he had fired; others suggested that attempts on the
President's life be considered, like treason, capital crimes.
And, inevitably, the mentally disturbed throughout the
country found places in their worlds for Guiteau and his
emotion-laden act; they wrote and visited, creating problems for the District Attorney, the Secret Service, and the
Washington police, experienced though all were with eccentricity and "crankiness."

Several attempts, one almost successful, had already
been made on Guiteau's life. Early in the morning of
September 11, as Guiteau stood at his cell window, Sergeant William Mason—a member of the guard of regulars
surrounding the prison—calmly picked up his rifle and,
sighting carefully, squeezed off a shot at the assassin.
Mason, who had always been considered a bit odd by his
fellow soldiers, explained his action quite willingly to reporters. He was, he said, tired of riding across the city's
cobblestones each day to guard such a dog as Guiteau.
The sergeant was not alone in his sentiments: "There is,"
as one popular editorialist phrased it, "an American judge
whose decisions are almost always just, and whose work is
always well done. His name is Judge Lynch; and if he ever
had a job that he ought to give his whole attention to, he
has it waiting for him in Washington." And though organs
of respectable opinion were shocked—the *Nation, Harper's,* and the *Independent* vied in deploring Mason's act—
most ordinary Americans regarded him with admiration if
not affection. Though their officers were embarrassed, his
fellow enlisted men and noncommissioned officers regretted

only Mason's imperfect aim. Several of Washington's less respectable newspapers immediately sponsored a subscription for Mason's defense and his family's expenses. The sergeant's court-martial in 1882 and sentence of eight years imprisonment created an immediate surge of resentment; at least three state legislatures were reported as having resolved to petition President Arthur to lighten the patriot's sentence.

With Garfield's death, Washingtonians turned grimly to the duty of trying his assassin. Few could disagree with the sentiments of a poem published the day after the President's death in the New York *Tribune:*

> That life so mean should murder life so great!
> What is there left to us who think and feel,
> Who have no remedy and no appeal,
> But damn the wasp and crush him under heel?

There seemed little chance of the wasp's escaping.

Respectable editorialists were already congratulating fellow citizens on their laudable respect for the law in having refrained from lynching the assassin. Journalists appealing to a more popular audience, however, were often impatient with the tedious ritual of due process. "The true plan," one urged soon after Garfield's death, "and by far the safest to society, is to get rid of him the easiest and cheapest way—hand him over to the dogs." But such solutions were hardly in keeping with the dignity of the nation or with the memory of the fair-minded dead President. The trial would, hopefully, be conducted with appropriate decorum.

It promised, in any case, to be little more than a formality. The assassin had but one hope, and that frail indeed. It was the defense of insanity.

Guiteau had shot the President. There was no question of self-defense and his premeditation was as undeniable as the act itself. The defendant denied neither the shooting nor his elaborate preparations for it; he seemed, on the contrary, inordinately proud of having been chosen as the Lord's instrument in so important a matter. Such references to the Deity tended, of course, only to provoke; many knowledgeable Americans immediately characterized Guiteau's claim to inspiration as a cynical attempt to avoid punishment.

The defense of insanity was bitterly controversial in 1881. It was, in popular terminology, the "insanity dodge," a last resort in cases otherwise hopeless. For example, it was used by lawyers and jurors seeking a formal justification for the acquittal of obviously culpable yet sympathetic defendants. In the years before Guiteau's removal of President Garfield, American newspaper readers had been treated to a number of trials in which highly paid advocates superintended the acquittal of overly enthusiastic defenders of the nuptial couch. The outraged mate had been temporarily insane at the moment of avenging his or her honor, but quite sane the moment before and after the actual murder. These somewhat ingenuous verdicts of innocent by reason of insanity had begun to try the patience of many respectable Americans; murder, they felt, should never go unpunished. John Ordronaux, one of the nation's leading experts on criminal responsibility, warned in 1880 that the perfectly equitable plea of not guilty by reason of insanity was being steadily undermined by a growing popular prejudice.

The problem rested largely on the rigidity of popular conceptions of insanity and on the prevailing legal rules governing criminal responsibility, rules that reflected and, in a sense, confirmed these views. Americans in 1881, especially those living in rural areas, seemed able to tolerate a far greater degree of deviant behavior than is ordinarily the case today. If one had pressed ordinary Americans for descriptions of mental illness, their replies would almost certainly have come under three general headings: congenital or traumatic mental deficiency, raving mania or stupor, and, finally, irrational belief or illogical action. "Eccentric" or "cranky" one might be but still not an idiot, maniac, or lunatic, the terms used customarily to label these stereotyped categories of mental illness. One might be a fanatic in religion or politics, even a compulsive thief or murderer—and still appear to be within the range of responsible behavior.

These were formal beliefs. Attitudes in any particular criminal case reflected the specific circumstances involved as well. Where these circumstances seemed to demand a verdict of innocence by reason of insanity, jurors had no difficulty in coming to this decision—even if the defendant were neither incoherent nor a violently raving maniac. If an ordinarily sober parent, for example, took an ax and, at the command of Jehovah, slew his previously beloved children, conventional wisdom found no difficulty in judging this an insane act—although the murderer might on all other subjects speak and act rationally. The quality of such an act implied disorder in the mind of its perpetrator.

Yet these offenders might not have been considered exculpable in the light of a strict construction of the legal rule that governed the determination of criminal responsibility in almost every American jurisdiction in 1881. This was the so-called M'Naghten rule.* It had been formulated by the judges of the Queen's Bench in England in 1843 and, although widely criticized by medical men and some lawyers since at least the 1850's, the M'Naghten rule had been adopted not only in England but in most American jurisdictions as well. The test seemed, in a schematic sense at least, an excellent rule of law, easily understood and applied. It held that a defendant was to be considered

* There are at least four variant spellings of M'Naghten— all with excellent pedigrees and some claim to legitimacy. In using the spelling "M'Naghten" I have followed the convention adopted by the *Journal* of the American Psychiatric Association and by the Royal Commission on Capital Punishment, 1949–53.

responsible if he was aware of the nature and consequences of his act and knew it to be forbidden by law.* Even proof that a defendant had acted under the influence of a delusion need not imply a verdict of not guilty by reason of insanity; only certain delusions—only those that would mean a defendant's acquittal if considered literally true—implied irresponsibility. If an individual, for example, shot a neighbor whom he believed to be spreading tales, the jury would still, according to the M'Naghten rule, have to find him guilty—for the law did not permit the execution of slanderers. If, on the other hand, a man was seized with the delusion that a neighbor was attacking him with an ax, the murder might then be construed as an act of self-defense. This was, however, a purely cognitive test, a test of "understanding" in a period when physicians concerned with psychological medicine were well aware that mental illness might often, if not ordinarily, originate in and manifest itself through an individual's emotional as well as his intellectual faculties.

By the 1860's and 1870's, many leaders in English and American psychiatry had come to regard the M'Naghten test as essentially irrelevant. It was, indeed, felt by the more

---

* The central operational passage in the M'Naghten rule holds "that the jury ought to be told in all cases that every man is to be presumed to be sane, and to possess a sufficient degree of reason to be responsible for his crimes, until the contrary be proved to their satisfaction; and that to establish a defence on the ground of insanity it must be clearly proved that, at the time of committing the act, the accused was labouring under such a defect of reason, from disease of the mind, as not to know the nature and quality of the act he was doing, or, if he did know it, that he did not know he was doing what was wrong." This is clearly not a medical test for sanity, but a legal test of responsibility. This logical distinction is, of course, not always easily made in practice. In the nineteenth century, as today, laymen—and lawyers—often found it difficult to view a mind "alienated" by true madness as fully responsible for any of its acts.

critical that any formal rule of law must ultimately prove inadequate as a measure of true responsibility; the guises of insanity were simply too various and protean. As early as 1854, for example, John C. Bucknill, a prominent English authority on insanity and the law, had phrased the problem clearly. The central aspect of the dilemma, he submitted, was that the law did not provide in theory for degrees of responsibility; one was either sane and responsible or insane and absolutely irresponsible. Yet clinical observation, even common sense experience, attested to the existence of every conceivable gradation of mental power and control.

> In nature we find no such sharply defined classification: even the exact boundary of the animal and vegetable kingdoms is not ascertained; and in the kingdom of mind, mind itself is scarcely able to conceive the gradations of power and knowledge. But nature herself must bend to the laws of man! and a dozen farmers and shopkeepers are compelled to divide the world of mind into two parts; and, on the most awful and momentous occasion, on the question of life or death. of a fellow creature, to discern what the most scientific often fail to do, the exact position therein of a particular instance.

And the M'Naghten test was particularly inadequate; responsibility depended in actuality not upon what one knew to be correct, but upon one's ability to conform to such dictates. Not understanding, Bucknill argued, but control should be the logical keystone in any realistic test of criminal responsibility.

The circumstances surrounding Garfield's assassination seemed particularly confusing. Guiteau's crime—assuming that a desire for notoriety could not rationally account for such an act—was unmotivated and hence irrational. Indeed, many Americans did assume immediately that Guiteau must have been insane; his act itself constituted presumptive evidence of mental abnormality. Henry Adams, for example, compared Garfield's misfortune to that which might have overtaken him had a brick fallen on his head.

Henry Ward Beecher assured Americans that the shots in the Baltimore & Potomac Station had emerged not from the convolutions of a plot but from a madhouse. Abram Hewitt, the prominent industrialist, politician, and philanthropist, explained to newspapermen that the same fate could have been his—or any prominent man's—if an insane mind had fastened upon him some imagined wrong. Garfield himself, when informed of his assassin's identity, slumped back in bed, exclaiming that the man must have been mad, for he had no motive.

Yet these instinctive judgments could not be allowed to affect the assassin's fate. Though Guiteau's crime had perhaps been—from any rational point of view—unmotivated, though he was admittedly a bit "cranky," perhaps even unbalanced, none of these considerations mitigated in the slightest the frustration and anger Americans of every class felt toward him. Few could seriously entertain the possibility that a lack of some metaphysical and debatable measure of reason should keep their president's assassin from a much-deserved noose.

Moreover, by many common-sense, rule-of-thumb standards, Guiteau did not seem to be insane. He could hardly have acted at the urging of some irresistible impulse; the assassin had bided his time, had indeed withheld his fire on several occasions when he might easily have shot the president. In the popular mind, an insane act of violence was ordinarily unpremeditated in any rational sense—the madman reached for a knife, a gun, or a hammer and turned raging upon those he happened to encounter. Guiteau, however, had organized and planned the details of his crime with conspicuous order. There could be no doubt of his premeditation, nor of his knowledge that Garfield's "removal" was condemned by human laws. Nor was he ignorant of the probable reactions of ordinary Americans to his selfless and inspired deed; he had been careful to hire a hack to take him to the District jail and away from the fury of the mob. The New York *Tribune,* for example, felt no qualms in censuring the soft hearted who might consider Guiteau legally irresponsible; Guiteau's lengthy premeditation, the editorialist argued, made it clear that anyone considering him insane was probably a bit unbalanced himself.

It must be recalled, that in the moral climate of late nineteenth century America Guiteau had still to answer for his lifetime of petty crime and immorality. Perhaps (and this was the opinion of most educated Americans) Guiteau was compulsive and erratic; perhaps, indeed, his final crime would never have been committed by a precisely normal person. Nevertheless, his long history of instability and immorality demonstrated how thoroughly and instinctively he had schooled himself in vice. Certainly Guiteau had had a disastrous influence in his fanatical father and an even more unfortunate formative period at the Oneida Community. Nevertheless, moral exegetes insisted, Guiteau's character was ultimately his own responsibility. Originally he had possessed a capacity for moral behavior, but this had never been developed, never strengthened through the habitual exercise of restraint, virtue, and moderation. Each time Guiteau—or any other criminal for that matter—succumbed to temptation, he was making it increasingly difficult to return to a moral course; each decision to steal, to lie, to drink, to fornicate, dulled one's moral capacities.

In a generation perhaps overly fond of mechanistic analogies, the capacity for moral action was often seen in physical as well as spiritual terms. This could be observed most strikingly in the drunkard or drug addict; a series of immoral decisions had ultimately destroyed the physiological capacity of these unfortunates for virtuous behavior. Physicians and moralists echoed one another in endorsing this position. (A favorite analogy compared such repeated patterns of action to the pressure of many feet wearing a path across a lawn; after a time it became well-worn and walkers followed it automatically. The neurological thought of the day hypothesized that such routes were worn by habitual actions along certain nerve paths—ultimately making it almost impossible for impulses to travel along any other path.) When such persons eventually committed a major crime it would be—as it might well have been in Guiteau's case—impossible for them to control themselves. But their real inability to exercise restraint at that moment in time need not imply irresponsibility. For ultimately the criminal was responsible for the series of immoral decisions, beginning often in earliest childhood, which had in the end paralyzed his moral faculties. As one Methodist clergyman put it:

men are to be held responsible not only for their immediate choices, conscious volitions, wilful acts, deliberate intentions, but withal for all choices, volitions, wilful acts, intentions— conscious or otherwise, intentional or unintentional—which may be traced to, or regarded as, the natural and legitimate outcome of self-induced character. . . . Why, indeed, should not a moral agent be held to a strict account for all the remote as well as the immediate results of his free, intelligent choices.

Moreover, an individual must be considered responsible not only for conscious acts but also for the indulgences of his imagination. "Where the line between sanity and insanity runs," as another clergyman explained it,

is a difficult question for the expert. But it is actually crossed by the individual whensoever, by the habit of his mind, or by the indulgence of particular imaginations, he allows himself to drift from the world of objective realities into a region of facts distorted or created by his personal conceptions.

These were, of course, arguments of the pious and so- phisticated. Common folk took a shorter view, fearful that Guiteau might escape the scaffold through some excess of misplaced humanitarianism. If he knew the right direction in which to point the gun, as one editor put it, he must then be considered responsible. Guiteau may have been eccentric, but he was clearly sane enough to hang.

These attitudes toward mental illness and criminal responsibility were hardly novel; physicians and educated laymen had in general shared them since almost the beginning of the century. By the 1880's, however, signs of change were apparent.

A new intellectual climate was coming into being, one that tended to emphasize humanitarianism at the expense of traditional moral categories. It was an intellectual climate that deferred not only to the innate value of human life and individual dignity, but also to the values and findings of science. Second, and more specifically, changing views of mental illness and institutional innovation within the medical profession paralleled and tended to support the arguments of those hoping to liberalize the treatment and adjudication of the possibly insane criminal.

Most significant of the changes in psychological medicine in the years after the Civil War was the beginning of a new discipline, neurology. These new specialists were concentrated in the great eastern seaboard cities, New York, Boston, and Philadelphia. Some had been trained in Europe, though all at least deferred to the new values and procedures of European clinical medicine. Their adherence to the aspirations of world science—like the process of specialization itself—foreshadowed the development of modern medicine in the United States.

But a note of explanation seems necessary here; twentieth century readers may well be confused by an unfamiliar terminology. The term neurologist, as used in the late nineteenth century does not have a real counterpart in mid-twentieth century American usage. The neurologists of the 1880's treated all conditions that their contemporaries subsumed under the rubric "nervous"—that is psychoses and neuroses as well as the organic neurological ailments now ordinarily the province of the neurologist. And in the 1870's and 1880's, of course, the mentally ill were by no means all in hospitals. The neurologists regarded the distinction between their work and that of intra-mural psychiatrists—a distinction often emphasized at the time—as both arbitrary and misleading. One did not need to be resident in an asylum to study mental illness. Insanity, the neurologists argued, was simply a deviant variety of normal psychological function; the same mechanisms that governed ordinary mental life also determined the manifestations of mental illness. Sharpening and in a real sense helping to create this emphasis was the somewhat narrow intellectual and institutional posture of the Association of Medical Superintendents of American Institutions for the Insane, the only established organization of American experts in psychiatric matters.

This organization had been founded in 1844 by a number of active and enlightened superintendents of private and state mental institutions. Beginning in the early years of the century, and increasingly by the 1830's and 1840's, physicians and laymen had cooperated to establish a number of such hospitals. They were, as might have been expected, a characteristic product of the peculiarly Jacksonian mixture of religious benevolence, humanitarianism, and social reform. The intellectual leaders in this pioneer generation of American psychiatry—men like Isaac Ray, Thomas Kirkbride, Samuel Woodward, and Amariah Brigham—had no formal training in psychiatry; there was, of course, none to be had. They were, however, humanitarians and, necessarily, optimists, deeply concerned with ameliorating the lot of the mentally ill and encouraging the hope that insanity might be curable. Not surprisingly, they were receptive to any theoretical innovation that implied a more hopeful view of the nature of mental illness and the possibility of cure. Continuity within the asylum superintendent's association came—after the gradual passing of this founding generation—not through shared bonds of education, intellectual assumption, and disciplinary values, but through the institutional position its members occupied. It was almost inevitable that such a group should prove increasingly conservative in succeeding decades. The membership of the

Association was limited to superintendents at hospitals for the insane; not even assistant physicians were eligible, certainly not neurologists in private practice. Younger men, and especially the neurologists, charged the association with narrowness, with unwillingness to accept either specific criticisms or new ideas generally. Most frequent was the charge that the superintendents were, as a group, unduly sensitive to popular opinion. Their institutional and public role, the argument followed, made them unceasingly conscious of the expressed will of common men and the mundane stratagems of local politicians. In the words of George M. Beard, a prominent New York neurologist, medical publicist, and internationally known popularizer of the concept of neurasthenia, the asylums had at the time of their establishment been truly laudable innovations in charity and medical science. "But now," Beard wrote in 1880, "those very asylums, with the far-extending and intricate political, social and mechanical influences involved with them and about them ... are oftentimes the first and last opponents of all measures for the next advance, which is now to be made in the study and treatment of insanity." They represented, the rhetorical New Yorker concluded, the eighteenth, rather than the nineteenth or twentieth centuries.

In many ways such charges were justified; in some instances, at least, the asylum superintendents were clearly more sensitive to the values of the communities they served and the needs of the political party that appointed them than to those of their scientific colleagues. Many of the superintendents felt no strong emotional commitment to contemporary European peers (despite opposition from dissidents within the association whose views were in some ways more similar to those of their outspoken neurological critics). Indeed, they tended on occasion to stubbornly resist ideas that seemed tainted with the materialism of the continent.

None of the superintendents was more prominent or

socially conservative than John P. Gray of New York State's Utica Asylum. In addition to his influence in the councils of the superintendent's association, Gray was the somewhat autocratic editor of the *American Journal of Insanity,* the oldest and most important American journal of psychopathology. No single problem divided American psychiatrists more sharply than the proper definition of criminal responsibility. Gray, and a good many other like thinking physicians, consistently supported the M'Naghten rule, seeking indeed to interpret it as narrowly as possible —and in so doing, they felt, help stabilize the fabric of social order.

The late nineteenth-century controversy over criminal responsibility was, however, more complex than a simple struggle between conservative and liberal, orthodox believer and agnostic. It is ultimately incomprehensible without some understanding of the assumptions of this generation of physicians with regard to mental illness. The problem of categorizing physicians in terms of their attitudes toward the possibly insane criminal is a difficult one, for on most questions regarding mental illness liberals and conservatives were in agreement. All assumed that insanity was, at least ultimately, a physical disease; all assumed as well that emotional pressures in an individual's environment could cause mental illness. Differences, as we shall see, arose over the problem of symptomatology. More conservative physicians, committed to a relatively rigid interpretation of the M'Naghten rule, found its rejection of the emotional and behaviorial manifestations of mental illness quite satisfactory. Liberals, on the other hand, more hospitable to innovation and deterministic explanations of behavior, placed a far greater emphasis on the importance of emotional symptoms in the diagnosis of mental disease.* They

* This was especially true in the stylized courtroom setting. Where the problem of criminal responsibility was not involved, the evidence indicates that American psychiatrists would have ordinarily agreed on their diagnosis of specific cases.

could not, of course, accept the M'Naghten rule's narrow emphasis on knowledge and cognition.

Insanity, American physicians agreed, was a disease of the brain. And disease, no medical man doubted, was of necessity a physical phenomenon; insanity was essentially a material ailment, no different in essence than mumps or typhoid fever. This had been assumed by physicians concerned with mental illness since at least the beginning of the nineteenth century. If mental disease was not physical, it was not a disease at all, not a problem for the physician, but for the clergyman—perhaps even the exorciser. Yet, at the same time, no physician doubted that environmental and emotional causes, tension, anxiety, grief—"moral" causes in the vocabulary of the time—might exacerbate or even cause mental illness (especially in those with some hereditary weakness or predisposition). Business anxieties, sexual fears and frustrations, the shock of bereavement might, it was assumed, all bring about mental illness. But such emotional causes exerted this effect only by means of their action on the body—through the reflex action of the nervous system, perhaps, or through the blood supply. Reflex action, for example, explained how masturbation or "uterine conditions" might injure the brain and thus ultimately produce insanity; similarly, anxiety, grief, and worry might bring physical exhaustion, impair the blood's nutritive qualities, and thus injure the brain's delicate cells. Such hypothetical mechanisms changed during the course of the century—yet the relationships they explained remained unquestioned (the role, that is, of emotional factors in inducing functional changes severe enough to eventually cause brain disease).

Since insanity was ordinarily regarded as a physical disease with a specific course and etiology, it was always important in a trial involving criminal responsibility to uncover a defendant's previous record. If it were persistently criminal and showed no sharp discontinuity in behavior, the act for which he was being tried could be regarded as consistent with his other antisocial acts. His crime was simply the result of evil impulse, not mental illness. Sin was an emotionally real and on the whole unquestioned concept in the 1880's; crimes of rare brutality implied in themselves nothing more than the depths of man's undoubted depravity. If, however, an individual had always lived a blameless existence, abhorred liquor, and worked steadily, and then, let us say, stopped working, became withdrawn, and suddenly committed a murder, it might be assumed that this was the consequence of a disease process.

The more conservative members of the psychiatric fraternity tended to emphasize the specific and discrete onset of mental illness. They rejected logically the idea that insanity might be present throughout life, manifesting itself in compulsive, discordant, and antisocial behavior from childhood. (Though most would at the same time have accepted the idea, with its contradictory implications, that a hereditary tendency or predisposition was a major cause of insanity. The annual reports of American asylums neatly and casually recorded in their statistical tables proportions of their inmates whose ailments seemed to have a hereditary origin.) No one could doubt that mental deficiency—idiocy in the terminology of the 1880's—was hereditary, or that it manifested itself unmistakably from birth. But in such cases the diagnosis was ordinarily so clear that argument seemed unnecessary.

Certainly definitions of insanity had been broadened considerably since the opening years of the nineteenth century. Even the most clinically wary, even the theologically orthodox, had come to assume that absolute irrationality was not an inevitable characteristic of true madness—that surface rationality might obscure the diagnosis of quite decided cases of mental illness. Yet, although such standards were routinely applied in admissions to asylums, admitting officers often proved unwilling to accord a criminal exhibiting the same symptoms the privilege of legal irresponsibility. Though insane "enough" to justify commitment, they believed, an individual might still be held responsible for his willed acts. One might, and in practice most American physicians did, concede that heredity and environment often conspired to impair free agency. Society, the argument ran, must nevertheless protect itself; the merciless prosecution of the vicious must not be impeded —no matter how lamentable the circumstances conspiring to form their vicious character. For, as most philosophers of the law were able to agree in 1881, the function of institutionalized justice was to protect society; if offenders were to go unpunished no man would be safe, nor would his family and property. Society must always have the benefit of the doubt; only unmistakable cases of mental disease should, most physicians and lawyers agreed, be exempt from punishment.

Both humanity and the law assumed, of course, that no truly insane person should be put to death as punishment for his criminal acts. Though opposition to capital punishment as such was comparatively small, only a few self-consciously ruthless intellectuals even suggested that insane criminals should suffer the maximum penalty. The problem, of course, lay in deciding the merits of any particular case. And, in the minds of some theorists, the decision as to whether persons of mental endowment similar to that of a particular defendant would be discouraged by his fate. Though the M'Naghten rule existed, though precedents regarding the admission of evidence and burden of proof existed as well, each case presented the problem in a new guise. The circumstances of the crime, the character of the jury, the personality of expert witnesses all obviously affected the outcome.

The role of expert witnesses was a problem disturbing to conservatives and innovators alike. All disapproved of the existing advocate system in which experts appeared for both sides, leaving the public with a somewhat cynical view of the integrity of those involved. For some time before 1881, concerned American physicians had been urging the appointment of court-designated commissioners to evaluate the responsibility of criminals, serving not as witnesses for either defense or prosecution, but as servants of the state and the judiciary. European precedents were clear enough.

In 1881, however, even in the accustomed adversary setting, the role of the psychiatric expert was still poorly defined. Within the structure of organized medicine, psychiatry was not yet firmly established; in American courts these protospecialists were granted no peculiar status or competence. In theory, any witness might provide evidence relating to a defendant's mental status; these might be friends, relatives, or clergymen. Often general practitioners testified as experts although, as asylum superintendents and neurologists joined in complaining, the psychological knowledge of such practitioners might be no greater than that of an educated layman. Of course, in important cases, men of status, position, and reputation were employed by both defense and prosecution. Common sense conceded their greater competence and hence influence as witnesses.

But it was not merely a question of general practitioner as opposed to specialist. Most jurors and many judges found it difficult to assume that the evaluation of human behavior demanded special competence. Strongly contested cases tended accordingly to become amorphous sessions in competitive biography; judges too were influenced by contemporary medical thought and allowed its assumptions to shape their policy in admitting evidence. Theories of causation in mental illness that—as we have seen—emphasized both heredity and habitual patterns of behavior, sanctioned the usual willingness of American judges to accept evidence relating not only to the defendant's previous life, but to that of his parents, uncles, and first cousins as well. Though such testimony might have seemed rather marginal if not inadmissible in light of the rule of law established in the M'Naghten decision, judges ordinarily admitted such testimony and then simply referred in their charges to the M'Naghten rule.

One theoretical formulation served most frequently to dramatize controversy within the medical profession and between many medical men and the legal world. This was the concept of "moral insanity." The idea of moral insanity had been formulated, elaborated, and gradually accepted in the first half of the century. It grew out of the clinicians' realization that traditional categories of mental disease were too narrow—that their emphasis upon reason and knowledge failed to reflect the importance of emotional and behavioral aberrations in the symptomatology of mental illness. Moral insanity was an explanation of certain types of compulsive and asocial behavior as well as justification for the position that seeming rationality might obscure grave illness.

In legal contexts the term "moral insanity" implied an inability to conform to the moral dictates of society—as a consequence of disease, not depravity, and despite the absence of traditionally accepted signs of mental disturbance. The morally insane offender might seem to be quite rational in conversation, even intelligent, be able to solve problems and be subject to no delusions or sensory misconceptions—yet still be mentally ill. Since the beginning of the nineteenth century, since the work of Pinel and Esquirol in France, of Prichard and Conolly in England, and of Rush and Ray in the United States, most physicians prominent in the treatment of the mentally ill had tended to accept this concept to at least some extent (though perhaps unwilling in some cases to accord legal irresponsibility to the morally insane).

And indeed, in the period of the 1880's conceptions of mental illness were further broadened to systematically include for the first time, neuroses and character disorders as well as the more distinctly marked psychoses. The earlier formulations of moral insanity were shifting too, being redefined in terms of newly fashionable pathological schemes. Many of the staunchest defenders of the idea, noting that persons often exhibited characteristic antisocial traits from early childhood, argued that the disease could be innate. Thus a number of American theorists, attuned to a growing European emphasis on the hereditary causation of mental illness and criminality, were beginning to assume that what their predecessors had called moral insanity was in reality sometimes an inborn condition, a behavioral consequence of structural or functional deformity. Explanations of antisocial behavior in terms of such mechanisms were increasingly fashionable in European medical circles during the second half of the nineteenth century.

Medical men and pioneer social scientists were, during the 1880's and 1890's, particularly devoted to biological and mechanistic explanations of human behavior. This was the generation of Lombrosianism, of the widespread influence of the Italian criminologist's "criminal anthropology." The born epileptic, or insane, or atavistic criminal was becoming a cliché in the writings of "progressive" sociologists, psychiatrists, and penologists. Yet most American physicians in 1881 were still unwilling to accept so thoroughly deterministic a theory; few, however, dismissed these new ideas out of hand. Certainly, most could accept the idea that such hereditary criminals did occur in some families; none essentially questioned the role of constitutional nervous weakness in the causation of mental illness, alcoholism, and mental retardation. It was simply the common sense of the matter.

Historians of psychiatry have sometimes viewed the concept of moral insanity as a forerunner of the more modern concept of the psychopathic personality, of the behavior disorder. In a broad schematic sense, this is certainly true; in practice, however, in the nineteenth century, many if not most of the criminals physicians were willing to diagnose as morally insane would be diagnosed today as actively psychotic. Those who had demonstrated a pattern of emotional instability combined with persistent antisocial behavior were usually characterized as vicious and peculiarly reprehensible criminals. If one believes very strongly in original depravity, one need not strive for environmental and biological explanations with which to understand crime; vice and criminality are simply an inevitable part of the natural order.

And, not surprisingly, in the 1880's convinced defenders of social order and religious faith found in the new coinages of European alienists a threat to individual responsibility and hence social stability int general. Sin, men like John Gray argued, not the metaphysical sentimentalism of moral insanity, caused crime; lust was the proper appellation for nymphomania, depravity for kleptomania, dissipation and weakness for dipsomania. Could the criminal act itself be allowed to serve as proof of its perpetrator's irresponsibility? A defendant, Gray argued in 1878, "may be cunning, shrewd, active; he may deceive the best of men constantly; he may have no delusion whatever, no disease, only this propensity, this thieving; and out of this shall we originate the word kleptomania, and call him a lunatic?"

The circle of New York neurologists, and with them a minority in the asylum superintendents' association, tended, on the other hand, to be receptive to the mechanistic and hereditarian doctrines so fashionable in the scientific world generally, as well as to these new and often controversial disease categories. They tended, moreover, toward a jaunty and sardonic agnosticism; the piety of the asylum superintendents was simply proof of their provincialism, of their allegiance to the values of the state legislature rather than to those of Vienna, Berlin, and London. To these young physicians, it seemed clear that they were dealing, in many cases of "reasoning mania," not with the lesions of a disease process, but with a teratological problem. The individual displaying the signs of moral insanity had, they argued, been born with a constitutional defect or malformation, one which made it impossible for him to conform to the dictates of morality.

These intellectual conflicts, involving such emotionally

charged issues as religion and professional competence, were sharpened and made increasingly bitter by a personal and institutional conflict that had developed between the neurologists, many of them younger men, and the more entrenched and ordinarily more conservative leadership within the asylum superintendents' association. New York State was the scene of the most bitter controversy. Beginning in the mid-1870's, the neurologists centered their protests in the proceedings and meetings of the New York Neurological Society and Medico-Legal Society, and soon in the pages of the *Journal of Nervous and Mental Disease,* the *Alienist and Neurologist,* and the *Chicago Medical Review.* Though not completely partisan, these journals were willing to publish criticism of the American Association, its official publication the *American Journal of Insanity,* and its editor John Gray—criticism both personal and professional.

Probably the most outspoken among the neurologists was Edward Charles Spitzka, a young German-trained neuroanatomist. Born in New York City in 1852, the son of a Czech immigrant, Spitzka had attended New York's public schools, the Medical Department of the University of the city of New York, and had then studied in Europe for three years, largely in Vienna and Leipzig. He returned to New York with a German wife, a worshipful attitude toward German method, and a somewhat bemused view of orthodoxy in religion. His disputatious and outspoken character he had always had. Though his research interests were in neuroanatomy, Spitzka was concerned as a practitioner with mental illness and especially with problems of legal medicine. This interest and his work in neuroanatomy were closely connected; Spitzka was deeply interested in the question of whether the brains of criminals and the insane showed characteristic structural patterns. In his maturity, Spitzka was to become a leading American neuroanatomist. In the 1870's, while still a young man in his twenties, he spent a good deal of time attacking the powerful leadership of the Association of Superintendents of Asylums for the Insane.

In the articles, editorials, and reviews that he began publishing in abundance in 1878, Spitzka accused the Association's membership, and especially Gray and his institution at Utica, of everything from scientific incompetence, extravagance, and religious bigotry to abuse of patients and the juggling of financial accounts. Gray he characterized in print as "an indifferent, superficial man, owing his position merely to political buffoonery." Spitzka —and he was joined by a handful of other like-thinking but on the whole less outspoken neurologists—accused the superintendents and Gray most conspicuously of being far behind European practice in their continued employment of mechanical restraint. They were equally ignorant of advances in diagnosis and of innovations in pathological anatomy. But the incompetence of the asylum establishment was hardly surprising; on the whole they had taken no specialized training, but had risen instead through the ranks of the asylums' self-contained and self-perpetuating bureaucracy. The asylum superintendents were as a group not scientists at all, but placeholding bureaucrats.

And the superintendents, Spitzka charged, had the effrontery to argue that only persons connected with asylums could properly diagnose or treat the diseased mind. In keeping with this narrowness and self-serving intellectual isolationism was their trade-union practice of limiting membership in their association to asylum superintendents alone. It was hardly surprising, Spitzka argued, that debate and discussion in such an organization should revolve around the comparative virtues of heating and plumbing fixtures or the most efficient way to run an asylum's farm or dairy. That no respectable research publications emanated from these well-endowed hospitals was, the young neurologist emphasized, as inevitable as it was unfortunate. Their narrow and invariably self-righteous posture, he continued, necessarily led to shoddy management and

inefficient practice, even in purely administrative and disciplinary matters. Spitzka pointed, for example, to one
asylum

whose record of accidents during the current year, a record
which is by no means exhaustive, sounds like the list of
casualties of a Bulgarian campaign? . . . Three patients beaten
to death, one of whom has twelve ribs broken! One patient
boiled to death, by having the hot water turned on him in a
bath, while the attendant went out of the asylum building
. . . and several patients drowned, by falling off the asylum
dock, in epileptic convulsions!

Though hardly threatened in his position, Gray could
not well have ignored such accusations. The older man was
editor of an influential journal and a long-standing defender
of orthodoxy in religion, in morals, and in legal medicine.
To Gray a lack of religious training, and an excessive and
morbid sentimentalism toward criminals were connected
with European materialism and sensualism. Men like
Spitzka at once embodied and expressed all these dangerous
tendencies. Gray was, moreover, a strong controversialist
and an enduring hater.

In 1878, largely at the instigation of Spitzka, the New
York Neurological Society formally took up the cudgels
against Gray and New York State's asylum establishment.
In public statements and in a petition to the legislature,
the neurologists asked for an investigation of the asylums
and their management. In the spring of 1879 a committee
hearing was held in Albany; the legislators were, of course,
friendly to the superintendents, only confirming the youthful neurologists in their resentment. Spitzka and another
young New York physician, James G. Kiernan (who had
been recently fired from his assistant's position at the
Ward's Island asylum by superintendent A. E. MacDonald),
were the most outspoken witnesses in support of the Neurological Society's petition. Gray and MacDonald were the
most vocal spokesmen for the superintendents. The committee finally concluded that the criticism expressed in the

petition was unfounded and contentious; there was clearly no need for a formal investigation. But the personal confrontation in the legislative hearing room could only have exacerbated the antagonisms already dividing the superintendents and their neurological critics.

Two and a half years later, the same opponents were to confront each other for a second time. The place was a criminal courtroom in the District of Columbia, the occasion the trial of Charles J. Guiteau. Though the assassin was hardly aware of these men or the issues that divided them, his trial was to become a battleground for the ideas and personalities of Gray and Spitzka, the guiding spirits in the prosecution and defense.

4

BEFORE THE TRIAL

President Garfield died late in the evening of September 19, 1881. He had been wounded on July 2. During these two and a half months of sickness and anxiety the government carefully marshalled its evidence.

While the President was still being made comfortable in his White House sickroom, George Corkhill, Washington's district attorney (a minor Republican politician and sometime managing editor of John Forney's sensationalistic *Sunday Chronicle*) began to gather statements and depositions. It was no difficult matter to reconstruct and document the assassin's preparations and the shooting; the hackman who was to drive him to the cemetery, the dealer who had sold Guiteau his bulldog pistol, the horrified witnesses to the assassination itself—ranging from Secretary of State Blaine to the railroad ticket seller—were all quickly located and their statements recorded. Guiteau himself was most helpful in illuminating unexplained portions of his movements and plans. In some ways the District Attorney's most difficult task in the days immediately following July 2 was to sort through and sometimes avoid the scores of would-be witnesses aggressively presenting themselves. From all over the United States acquaintances and victims of Guiteau—and an even greater number of "cranks"—wrote and reported in person. Aside from accumulating depositions, however, Corkhill was loath to take any concrete steps: the President lay critically wounded and keeping the assassin intact was in itself almost a full-time task. On July 7, Corkhill announced that there would be no formal proceedings until the President either re-covered or died.

Though Guiteau's past was rapidly becoming known, the close security under which he was kept helped maintain the curiosity of newspapermen and their readers. Corkhill, for example, refused to make public the contents of the letters Guiteau had left with the station newsdealer. It was impossible, he explained; a number of individuals were mentioned in the letters and, considering the state of public sentiment, it would be unfair to these innocent by-standers. But the District Attorney's motivation in this in-genuous disclaimer and in his decision to keep Guiteau in virtual isolation may not have been quite so bland. For the assassin's letters and statements were indeed odd and it seemed clear enough that his only defense could be in-sanity.

Many Americans, as we have seen, had assumed immediately that Guiteau must have been mad. The editorial-ists of the New York *Herald*, the *Nation*, and the Washington *Post*, for example, and such prominent men as Collis P. Huntington and Senator Logan, stated unhesitatingly that no normal person could have committed so pointless a crime. It was the instinctive common sense of the matter and at the same time the most comforting possible explanation of the assassination. The crime of a madman was a random happening, an act of God that reflected discredit neither on America nor—more cogently in some minds—on the Republican party. In Russia, the czar had been recently assassinated and talk of nihilism and anarchists filled European and American newspapers. Americans were still proud of what they called their institutions and sensitive to European criticism; responsible voices were naturally quick to dismiss Guiteau's act as a psychopathological rather than a political problem.

This immediate and understandable reaction was soon modified. Vengeance might conceivably be cheated if the assassin were declared legally insane; this was a sentiment clear enough before the President's death, harshly exacerbated afterward. Guiteau might be eccentric, but he was hardly irresponsible. Detectives and police officers in the District had since the day of the assassination stated with consistent and heavy-handed certainty that Guiteau spoke and reasoned rationally, certainly enough to understand the nature and consequences of his act. And to hang.

Guiteau, Corkhill assured reporters on the Fourth of July, was perfectly sane. Next Saturday, July 9, he summarized his observations in an interview for his old paper, the *Sunday Chronicle*. The District Attorney simply dismissed the problem of Guiteau's mental condition: "He's no more insane than I am," he told the reporter, "and he scouts the idea of being insane himself; in fact, he gets indignant at any suggestion of that kind. . . . There's nothing of the madman about Guiteau: he's a cool calculating blackguard, a polished ruffian, who has gradually prepared himself to pose in this way before the world . . . he was a dead-beat—pure and simple. . . . Finally he got tired of the monotony of dead-beating. He wanted excitement of some other kind and notoriety, and he's got it."

But such statements were uninformative, almost formalistic. Clearly there were doubts—or at least curiosity—in Corkhill's mind for he began to make exceptions to his initial policy of holding the prisoner virtually incommunicado. He first introduced a young legal colleague, Edmond Bailey, to Guiteau. (Guiteau later maintained that Corkhill had told him the younger man was a correspondent for the New York *Herald;* Corkhill flatly denied this deception.) Bailey, unlike most lawyers, had some knowledge of shorthand, and he spent several weeks with the prisoner, recording tens of thousands of words concerning Guiteau's life, his political and religious ideas, and, of course, the "removal" for which he was confined. Bailey claimed later to have destroyed these notes after showing them to Corkhill; the only surviving portion did—strangely enough—appear in the *Herald*. (A scoop for which the ingenuous

Mr. Bailey received, as he was forced to admit under oath, $500 from the *Herald*.) Guiteau, of course, was delighted to have the attention of a man whom he at least considered a minion of Bennett's *Herald,* an enterprise whose "snap" and success he had always admired. Hoping, similarly, to learn something of Guiteau's more intimate opinions, the District Attorney allowed General J. S. Reynolds of Chicago, onetime legal preceptor of Guiteau, to visit the prisoner—with the understanding, of course, that he should report the substance of their conversation.

Reynolds visited Guiteau in his cell on July 14 and 15. He was first struck, the Chicagoan reported with surprise and indignation, by the assassin's cheerful lack of shame; he seemed completely unabashed. When all the circumstances surrounding the President's removal came before the people, Guiteau assured Reynolds, there would be a unanimous shift of public opinion in his favor. Certainly such leaders of the Stalwarts as General Grant, Roscoe Conkling, and Senator Logan would at the proper moment make themselves known as his friends. It was not until the second day of their talks that Reynolds asked directly about the assassination. It took him two weeks, Guiteau confided in reply, to conclude that his decision was a proper, an inspired one. The deciding factor, he explained, was the situation at Albany. (Platt and Conkling, it will be recalled, had resigned their Senate seats, melodramatically protesting against Garfield's patronage policies in their state; they would, the senators assumed, be re-elected in a ringing endorsement by the state legislature. The legislature, however, failed to cooperate and for months remained deadlocked over the senatorial choice.) It would be tragic, Guiteau felt, if a man of Conkling's rare talents should fail to return to the national scene; with Arthur as president, however, Guiteau was certain that the New York legislature would elect Conkling on the first ballot. The Blaine element would be eclipsed and Stalwarts like Conkling, Logan and Morton would assume the reins of government. Reynolds interrupted to ask whether he had told anyone else of his plans. "Of course not," Guiteau answered as though surprised at Reynolds' naïveté; if he had, a detective might have arrested him. There was no malice in Garfield's removal, Guiteau insisted; it was an act of simple patriotism.

Reynolds was not the only Chicagoan to visit Guiteau. By a remarkable coincidence, Guiteau's brother-in-law, attorney George Scoville, left Chicago for the District of Columbia on the morning of July 2; he had a business engagement in the nation's capital. When he arrived, Scoville was amazed to find that the President had been shot and that his erratic brother-in-law had done the shooting. Scoville hurried to the District Attorney, who was then still preoccupied with quashing rumors of a conspiracy. Corkhill was only too happy to let Scoville speak with the assassin. He spent an hour and a half with Guiteau in his cell and emerged, he explained to the District Attorney, convinced that it had been the act of an individual, of a demented individual. "I am entirely satisfied," he told Corkhill, "that it was an insane act and that he was alone. If the government wishes to hang an insane man . . . I do not think the government can do that with impunity."

While the President lived, of course, interest centered in the surgical, rather than the legal aspects of the case. With Garfield's death the Attorney General turned immediately to the trial of his assassin; it soon became apparent that the government would spare neither effort nor expense in its preparations.

Knowing that insanity was Guiteau's only possible defense, the prosecution methodically began to seek the materials of Guiteau's biography; each motley segment of the assassin's life produced its quota of witnesses attesting to his erratic and sometime criminal behavior. From as far as Leadville, Colorado, for example, Guiteau's ex-wife—now a Mrs. Dunmire—submitted her recollections. She described Guiteau's interest in the 1872 campaign, his sudden fits of temper and his habit of beating and locking her in closets. (The District Attorney learned something else as well about the former Mrs. Guiteau, something he was able to keep from reporters and the public: the illegitimate child that Miss Bunn had had before her marriage to Guiteau. It was a fact that might well, in the moral climate of the 1880's, have discredited her testimony.) New York lawyer Simon D. Phelps recalled his acquaintance with Guiteau in the 1860's. The young man had come to him after leaving the Oneida Community, hoping to find some grounds for a suit against it. One of his principal complaints, Phelps confided to Corkhill's assistant, Edmond Bailey, was unfair treatment in the selection of mates. "The elders themselves monopolized that part of the business, and did not give the young man a chance." Phelps found Guiteau's legal abilities laughable; he was, for example, completely unable to copy even the simplest document accurately. Most disquieting was Guiteau's nervous, restless look. "For instance," Phelps elaborated, "if you were to address any remark to him he would glance at you, and then either look beyond, or simply crosswise of your face." But, Phelps cautioned, he had never thought him insane, simply consumed with egotism, ambition, and unadulterated selfishness. "I have always looked upon him as a sort of Col. Sellers. Enthusiastic, opinionated, and constantly conceiving new schemes, in each of which there would be millions." Besides which, Phelps concluded in his deposition, he had once served on the state legislative committee entrusted with the supervision of mental institutions. "I saw there many men insane on a single idea—but this is not true of Guiteau. He has too many ideas to be insane on one."

Phelps, of course, was only one among scores of those whose statements had to be recorded. Some had simply known Guiteau's father; in a generation convinced of the hereditary character of mental illness, it seemed clear that the elder Guiteau's somewhat individualistic conceptions of salvation and immortality would become an issue at the trial. And the matter was a delicate one, for all of Luther Guiteau's Freeport associates agreed in characterizing him as a bit odd, though strangely enough all agreed that his oddness seemed limited to matters of religion and that in business and public affairs he was prudent and reliable.

Another class of witnesses appeared in even larger numbers—the cranks. Many such, seeking either notoriety, a witness's per diem, or some obscure goal of their own, presented themselves and unfolded elaborate stories of their intimate acquaintance with Guiteau and of damning confidences he had made. Others reported having seen the assassin plotting with groups of well-dressed or suspicious men. For example, one Humphrey Morris, of Philadelphia, appeared at the District Attorney's office and, giving the name John F. Foster, stated that he had met and spoken casually with Guiteau in June. Guiteau—according to Foster-Morris—informed his chance acquaintance that he was a candidate for the consulship to Paris and that if unsuccessful, "he would get up the greatest excitement in Washington since 1865." Though the facts of the case seemed straightforward enough, dozens of such eccentric witnesses and numberless rumors had to be traced. It was exhausting work for the normally torpid District Attorney's office.

But they had little choice. No possibility of the assassin's escaping the gallows could be allowed. Corkhill and Attorney General Wayne MacVeagh were well aware of how embarrassing the proceedings might be; Arthur and the Stalwarts were anxious to have Guiteau expeditiously dispatched and thus banish the lingering memory of plots and faction. Corkhill and the judges of the District bench had another and perhaps even more pressing need to handle the case with skill and vigor; the fulminating scandal of the Star Route postal frauds was being handled by the same District Attorney and the same bench. With the suspiciously legalistic quashing of the indictment in that case, Corkhill must certainly have hoped that reformist criticism would be drowned in the furor surrounding the Guiteau trial. "It was too small a business," as one sardonic legal editor put it, "for the attorney general to prosecute a company of fellows charged with defrauding the government out of $3,000,000! the district attorney was probably too busy in interviewing Guiteau and arranging with the New York *Herald* for the publication of the assassin's biography."

Though there was little likelihood of any jury failing to convict, the government took every precaution to guard against this remote possibility. The major question, of course, was the adequacy of George Corkhill's legal skill for the management of an important state trial. The District Attorney was hardly a leading light of the District bar—and in 1881 the Washington bar was no more distinguished than that of a dozen other provincial cities. Attorney General Wayne MacVeagh immediately added a prominent local attorney to the prosecution as special counsel; he was Walter Davidge, the leader, most contemporaries agreed, of the capital's bar. One colleague recalled that in his day "there was scarcely any case of importance or difficulty in which he [Davidge] did not appear as counsel for one side or the other." Another Washingtonian described Davidge as resembling the Gilbert Stuart "George Washington"—but without the first President's stiffness.

The government turned then to the legal world of New York City. On October 22, the Attorney General wrote personally to Judge John K. Porter, explaining that "it had been felt that counsel should be associated with the District Attorney of this District, representing in as high a degree as possible, the learning and character of the profession"—and offering Porter a place in the prosecution.

He accepted enthusiastically. Born in Watertown, New York, in 1819, Porter had been for decades one of the state's most prominent trial lawyers. At twenty-seven he had served as delegate to the state's constitutional convention;

later he had been a member of New York's Court of Appeals, and then a well-known and prosperous New York attorney, having had his hand in a great many difficult and highly publicized cases. Henry Ward Beecher, for example, had hired Porter to defend him in the Tilton case. (Beecher had become involved in an extra-marital affair with the wife of Theodore Tilton, a long-time associate.) MacVeagh, with the authorization of the President and his cabinet, offered another place in the prosecution to Daniel G. Rollins, New York City's district attorney—"the President," as he explained it, "being solicitous that no slip shall in reasonable possibility, occur in any matter connected with the trial of Guiteau." Other commitments, however, forced Rollins to refuse the invitation.

While these distinguished men were being solicited, preparations for the trial moved forward. On September 28, Corkhill set in motion the procuring of an indictment and subpoenas were issued to witnesses. The District Attorney was anxious to complete the trial's time-consuming formal preliminaries. On September 27 he had informed Guiteau that the indictment would be returned on October 4. The prisoner immediately asked Corkhill to telegraph his brother-in-law so that the defense might begin its preparations.

The District Attorney was happy to comply. Each such step brought closer the beginning of the trial. Guiteau, he explained to a reporter, did not give his victim much of a chance to do anything but suffer and die; the protracted formalities of the law should not delay just retribution. On October 8, the presentment and indictment for the murder of James A. Garfield was filed. Three days later, the marshal certified that he had served a copy of the indictment, list of the jurors, and a list of the witnesses for the United States against the defendant.

The morning of October 14 marked something of an occasion for the assassin; it was the day of his arraignment, Guiteau's first public appearance in his new dignity of presidential remover. Despite rumors that he would be moved in the Bureau of Engraving's armored car, that he would be surrounded with several companies of troops, and that assorted bands of "avengers" lay in wait with dynamite bombs and rifles, the arraignment was conducted quietly enough. There was no public announcement and only the usual court regulars were aware of it, though a score of police and marshals were present. Guiteau left the prison at about ten-thirty, arrived in court shortly before eleven, and stayed for two hours of legal argument. It was his first trip outside the prison since the morning of the assassination. According to one report, Guiteau appeared pale and terror-stricken, crouched between the two marshals who brought him into the courtroom. After the reading of the indictment, legal arguments centered about the request of the defense for a continuance. District Attorney Corkhill asked that the trial begin forthwith on the morning of Monday, October 17. Scoville, sole counsel for his brother-in-law, asked for a continuance to prepare his case more effectively—and especially to collect witnesses. There would, he submitted, be two defenses, insanity and malpractice.* Judge Cox heard both arguments and decided to grant a continuance until November 7, three weeks from the Monday on which Corkhill had asked that the trial commence. In a proceeding of such gravity, he explained, the defense should have every opportunity to prepare its case properly.

The defense had, thus far, consisted of Guiteau assisting in his own cause and his brother-in-law, an experienced lawyer, but hardly a prominent one and completely inexperienced in criminal practice. The defense was, moreover, penniless. Scoville appealed for assistance to the profession generally and particularly to several prominent trial lawyers. Guiteau was especially enthusiastic about the possibility of

* Scoville and Guiteau both use the term "malpractice." The question of the role played by Garfield's medical care in bringing about his death would today be discussed under the general heading of "causation."

Chicagoan Emory Storrs joining in his defense. (Storrs lost no time in refusing indignantly to act as counsel for the "unmitigated scamp"—though several years later he did manage to find the moral fortitude to undertake the defense of the much-detested Mormons in the federal courts; the Saints, however, were reputed to have offered a very handsome retainer.) Scoville hoped to land Ben Butler. And Butler did show some interest in the task before refusing on grounds of inadequate time.

Unsuccessful in their attempts to find another John Adams, the defense turned to Judge Cox, asking that he appoint counsel from the District, provide for the expenses of defense witnesses, and authorize subpoenas. On October 26, he issued such an order, providing for twenty witnesses for the defense. On November 5, he issued subpoenas for twenty, and on November 15, thirty-five, additional witnesses. On October 26, Cox appointed Leigh Robinson, a young District of Columbia attorney, to serve with Scoville and in addition postponed the beginning of the trial to November 14. He was taking care that there would not be the slightest ground upon which the defense might base a successful appeal.

Throughout the trial, Guiteau served as assistant counsel, or at least believed that he did. The defense was, not surprisingly, conducted on two levels, one peculiar to Guiteau, the other corresponding to the perceptions of the other participants. It was the intricate interweaving of these two aspects, of the delusional and real, which gave the trial its quality of pathetic grotesquerie.

On the real level, Guiteau's defense began when his brother-in-law returned from Chicago in answer to the District Attorney's telegram. Scoville arrived on October 4 with his wife and immediately had a long and apparently amicable interview with Corkhill. He announced both to the District Attorney and to reporters that insanity would be their principal defense. "If I didn't think the unfortunate man was insane, I would not defend him at all. If he is not insane and cannot be clearly made to appear so, he ought to be hung." October 4 also concluded the grand jury hearings and the presentment of their findings, while the District Attorney had almost finished drawing up his indictment.

Scoville was studiously humble in his unaccustomed role of criminal lawyer. In a practice of thirty years, he had handled but two criminal cases and both of these, like Guiteau's, by accident. Within a few days, however, he was beginning to adjust to the peculiar tensions inherent in defending Charles Julius Guiteau. On the one hand, he was besieged by reporters and beset by threatening and lunatic correspondents. (One, for example, confided that Guiteau was a victim of the "telephone combination" and that he was undoubtedly being drugged by electric currents of air.) Like all family matters, moreover, Guiteau's defense had its inevitable areas of friction. John Wilson, for example, Charles's older brother had never gotten along well with his brother-in-law, or for that matter with Charles, and was violently opposed to any defense that might cast his father in an unfavorable light—any attempt, that is, to prove that the Guiteau family had been harboring a tendency toward hereditary insanity. But Scoville's problems with his brother-in-law John were minor compared to his difficulties with the defendant.

Guiteau considered himself the principal architect of his own defense and responded to any criticism of his strategy with untiring abuse and sarcasm. Soon after the President's death, Charles outlined his plans. First, he would appeal to the public, explaining his inspiration, detailing his pious life, and outlining the legal arguments that justified his acquittal. Guiteau's second line of defense was legal; he would establish his insanity and irresponsibility by proving that the Lord had stripped him of free will.

On October 6, Guiteau was exuberant; the first step in his defense had been taken. On this date, the New York *Herald* printed his "autobiography." With the public relations phase of his defense thus well under way, Guiteau now concentrated on its legal aspects. He deluged his brother with fragmentary notes, urging him to see the new president and have Arthur use his influence to stay the trial. "See him at once," he asked on the twelfth, "and get what time we want. He is bound to help me, and he will help me if you stick to him." Do not waste any effort, Charles's instructions continued, in trying to prove me actually insane. "It would disgust the court and jury. Legal insanity is all I claim."

But without funds and without influence, the defense proceeded slowly. Not until assured of financial support could Scoville confidently appeal to witnesses. Nevertheless, on October 19 he released to the public a circular letter asking persons who had encountered Guiteau in his evangelical metamorphosis and thought him insane to come forward. "Will they not," he pleaded, "in the interests of patriotism, justice, humanity, and mercy." But these efforts to prove him—and assorted relatives—insane met with an unenthusiastic response from the prisoner. "I spit upon such evidence," Charles said when asked by Scoville about relations who had, he understood, died in insane asylums. "If you waste your time on such things," the assassin wrote scornfully, "you will never clear me."

Far more important than any strained inventory of geneological psychopathology, Guiteau believed, was his laboriously written plea. He submitted it to the court on October 22 and it was widely reprinted the next day.

Its preamble was a bitter attack on those newspapers that had, Charles believed, unjustly vilified him. The ex-lawyer's argument was satisfyingly elaborate. It was God's act, he explained first, and not his own. Without free agency there could be no criminal intent and no responsibility; God, in choosing him for this task, had stripped him of his moral faculty. Second, Guiteau's plea submitted, the President had died not as a consequence of the wounds inflicted by his gun, but as a result of the surgeons' malpractice. Had they not stated categorically in July that the President would recover? Third, Guiteau argued in his awkward scrawl, the court itself was without jurisdiction, for the President had died not in the District of Columbia, but in New Jersey. His second and third arguments, Guiteau concluded triumphantly, were clearly based on providential dispensation; it was only fair to God and himself that he take advantage of them in his defense. Besides which, Guiteau noted aptly, all men die; General Burnside, for example, had suddenly passed away about the same time as the late unfortunate Garfield. Guiteau felt equally sorry to see both "excellent men go." Garfield died of malpractice and Burnside of apoplexy; "both were special providences and the people ought to quietly submit to the Lord in the matter." It was this document that W. W. Godding, Superintendent of Washington's Government Hospital for the Insane, characterized as "bearing the same relation to ordinary reasoning that the scenery and incidents of a nightmare bear to ordinary life."

On October 26, but a few days after the publication of his plea, Scoville abandoned one of Guiteau's cherished defenses. This was the question of jurisdiction. Scoville explained to Judge Cox that he would drop the matter; reading in the precedents had convinced him that the courts of the District did indeed have jurisdiction. He could never argue, Scoville assured reporters later, a cause in which he had no faith. It soon became apparent as well that the issue of malpractice would not be pursued. Legal authorities agreed that Guiteau's interpretation was quite specious; the prisoner had certainly shot the President and it was the wounds he inflicted that led to Garfield's death. Only suicide by the patient or a consciously—and demonstrably—felonious course assumed by Garfield's physicians could remove from Guiteau responsibility for causing the President's death.

While these routinely time-consuming preliminaries were completed Guiteau remained, of course, in prison—and in his jailors' opinions infuriatingly optimistic. Dr. Noble Young, the prison physician, and an elderly and respected member of the District's medical faculty, told reporters that the thought of hanging never seemed to have occurred to the assassin. (Dr. Young indignantly rejected the idea that the prisoner might be insane; he was simply feigning, for "there was too much method in his madness.") Indeed, as winter approached, Guiteau grew anxious about his lack of heavy clothing. On October 26, he asked that a suit of good Scotch woolens be ordered for him—and requested as well that his overcoat be redeemed from the tailors where it had hung since the spring; Guiteau had never been able to pay for the repairs.

As the trial drew closer, the government entered the final phase of its preparations. About November 1, Judge Porter traveled to Washington for a meeting with Corkhill. It was obvious that they would need expert medical witnesses, perhaps as many as a dozen. Their first decision then was to find some *cicerone,* some reliable guide to psychiatric men and ideas. Porter recommended John Gray, superintendent of New York's Utica asylum. Gray was in all probability known personally by Porter; certainly the New York attorney knew his reputation as the nation's stoutest defender of the M'Naghten rule and opponent of moral insanity. Corkhill agreed that Gray would serve perfectly as chief advisor to the prosecution.

Porter returned to New York City and telegraphed Gray. His answer arrived almost immediately and was, as Porter had expected, a favorable one. Gray placed the asylum's affairs in the hands of an assistant and left for New York, where he spent almost a week with Porter, planning the prosecution's strategy and interviewing prospective witnesses before continuing on to Washington. Gray was, as Corkhill put it after the trial, "in the most full and complete confidence of the attorneys for the prosecution." He performed services, the District Attorney recalled, which were asked of no other witness. Gray prepared a list of reliable experts to be called by the government and then followed the testimony day by day and witness by witness, sitting at the prosecution table and briefing its attorneys on the previous writings and personal foibles of the expert witnesses for the defense, making digests of their testimony, even preparing specific questions for use in cross-examination.

But this, of course, was all later. Gray's first and most important task was to examine the prisoner, to decide whether he was sane enough to stand trial. A defendant had to be sufficiently rational to understand and aid his own defense and it was within the District Attorney's power to order a pretrial psychiatric examination of any prisoner whose mental condition was in doubt. A report that the prisoner was incompetent could mean commitment to the Government Hospital for the Insane—and no trial. Not surprisingly, Gray was Corkhill's choice to make the pretrial examination.

On November 7, the Utica physician met with the District Attorney and left with a letter to Warden Crocker, admitting him to the defendant. When the assassin was led into the warden's office, where he was to be examined, Gray introduced himself casually as Dr. Gray from Utica. The prisoner's face immediately lit up as he asked whether he was *the* Dr. Gray, superintendent of the Utica Asylum. "When I was at the Oneida Community," Charles explained, "Victor Noyes, the son of Mr. Noyes, was a patient at the asylum and after he came back he told us a great deal about it." Gray seized this opportunity and began the interview by asking about life at the Community and the religious and social views of its leaders. Guiteau, the doctor noted approvingly, spoke clearly and intelligently, was indeed in every way respectful. Gray then guided the prisoner, happy apparently to have such an eminent listener, through the circumstances of his childhood and early life, his father's faith in Noyes and the Community, Guiteau's desire for education, his decision to leave Michigan for the brotherhood of the Community, his growing dissatisfaction with its leadership, and, finally, his abortive then irrevocable leave-takings. The prisoner maintained vigorously that he saw no differences between his abilities and those of Noyes and the Community's other leaders. Certainly none which justified the dictatorial control they exerted. Physically and morally, Guiteau felt himself in excellent condition; he had always eaten and slept well, he assured the psychiatrist, and had never tasted alcohol or used tobacco.

But marriage, he confessed, had been unfortunate. What exactly, Gray asked, did Charles mean by unfortunate? "Well," Guiteau explained,

it was as to the woman I married. I got her on my hands on very short notice; not over ten weeks. Then I proposed to her at ten o'clock in the morning and we were married at six in the evening. There were no agreeable relations between us. I made up my mind that I would not fasten myself through life to such a woman and I determined to get rid of her and the whole thing.

He explained, as well, the mechanics of his divorce. Charles had simply visited a brothel in Brooklyn, committed adultery, and then asked the woman (Clara, last name unknown) to take an oath to this effect. New York, he explained to the doctor, accepted no other grounds for divorce; it was not at all a question of morality or the lack of it.

An experienced interrogator in criminal matters, Gray gradually turned the conversation toward the events preceding the assassination. It soon became apparent that Guiteau had not really known any of the party's leaders. He had been merely one among scores of similar hangers-on, lounging in the lobby of party headquarters, reading newspapers, and nodding expectantly to the great as they passed. Between the election in November and March 5 when he left for Washington, Guiteau had shifted about in New York, spending some desultory time soliciting insurance business. "All this," Gray reported to Corkhill in summarizing his examination, "shows there was no change in him in any way. Certainly nothing suggestive of insanity, or of any interest in politics beyond looking out for himself."

The background had been sketched in: Gray turned their conversation to the events immediately preceding the assassination, to Guiteau's months in Washington. After reviewing Guiteau's persistent and unavailing attempts to gain preferment, Gray forced the assassin to admit that as late as the end of May he would not have shot the President had he received a favorable response to his requests for office. Guiteau matter-of-factly, and to Gray infinitely damagingly, explained how he had purchased and then practiced with the unfamiliar pistol. Equally damaging, as Gray interpreted his interview, was Guiteau's ability to make and then change plans, foregoing several opportunities to shoot the President. Gray's summary of his impressions was in every particular damning. "Whether he overestimated his qualifications, or his political services was quite entirely immaterial."

He made no claim for office on the ground of being inspired, either in the inception of the application for office or in pressing his appeals or in asking his friends for recommendations. . . . When Mr. Blaine rebuffed him he said it hurt his feelings. . . . He made no remonstrance, did not assail Mr. Blaine, either at the time or subsequently, by speech or menace; on the contrary discreetly kept quiet; did not mention this rebuff to any one of his friends; kept it to himself; showing what control he had over his *feelings* and *emotions. . . . He never went to the White House or called upon the President after the 18th of May,* but said he had addressed him two letters upon the subject, to neither of which did he receive any reply. After about two weeks thus deliberating and not getting a reply to his letters, he made up his mind to the killing. Here there was no *inspiration,* and

no *claim* of *inspiration* for the *inception* and development of
the deed. In my conversation in connection with *this point*
he never alluded to the *Deity* neither did he at this time or
covering this period allude to the political situation as forming
any grounds for the *inception* of the idea of killing the
President. Thus far it seems to be a mere matter of personal
motive from wounded vanity and disappointment, though he
afterwards referred to the political situation as a ground for
removing the President. . . . In connection with the *inception
of the crime . . . the essential starting point*—he not only
did not refer at this interview to the political situation or to
the Deity, but never alluded to praying to God or calling upon
Him in any way for counsel, advice or guidance.

The assassin, on the other hand, felt himself in an unassailable legal position; he had simply executed God's impera-
tive command.

   Gray naturally pursued Guiteau's somewhat individualistic view of criminal responsibility. What exactly, he asked
Guiteau, his pencil poised, do you yourself feel about your
insanity? "I do not," Guiteau replied, "claim to be insane
as a medical man would judge—what is ordinarily called
insane—but legal insanity."

A. It is insanity in a legal sense, irresponsibility, because
   it was an act without malice, . . . as I have shown in the
   New York *Herald* of October 6.
Q. How did you come to think of insanity as a defense; when
   and where did it occur to you?
A. I knew from the time I conceived the act if I could
   establish the fact before a jury that I believed the killing
   was an inspired act I could not be held responsible before
   the law. (He paused a moment and then added): You
   may add this, that the responsibility lies on the Deity,
   and not on me, and that, in law, is insanity.
Q. How can this appear in evidence as a fact?
A. I see that, but I think I can answer it. Suppose you take it
   down: That if the jury accepts this as my belief, and if
   the jury believes as I believe, that the removal of the

President was an inspired act, and therefore not my own
act, they are bound to acquit me on the ground of insanity.
I have looked over the field carefully.

. . . .

Q. I ask you again, can you state just when this idea of the
defense of insanity first came up in your mind.

A. I can't state just when it came up in form, but it was
latent as a part of my general knowledge on the subject.
I want you to put in the idea that it was the Deity, for this
is my only defense.

Of course, Guiteau admitted, there had never been any
doubt in his mind that the laws of society condemned assassination. But it was impossible to have withstood the
"pressure" to which he had been subjected by the Deity.
Inspiration, Charles explained, had been a constant theme
in his upbringing and experience. It was part of Luther
Guiteau's world view, part of the Community's faith; Noyes
and the other leaders of the Oneida Community presented
themselves, indeed, as agents of the Deity. "You see I was
brought up to the most orthodox views, even to a special
Providence."

Why then, Gray asked, did you change your mind so
frequently in choosing an occasion for the assassination?
Hesitate when some chance circumstance interfered? "I
wanted," the prisoner answered, "to make a sure thing of it."
But, Gray probed, what was the logic in your careful plans
to protect yourself from harm after the assassination? "I
thought it all over," Guiteau explained, "for I gave my mind
all up to it for a time." Why, Gray returned to his still
unanswered question, "did you not take chances if it rested
with the Deity?" "With a mob?" Guiteau was startled by
the physician's obtuseness. "I knew what a mob would do."

Before leaving that afternoon, Gray was careful to ask
Guiteau about his physical condition and general health.
For in the 1880's it was still assumed by most clinicians
that true insanity almost always coexisted with physical
disease and debilitation. Guiteau was able to assure him,

however, that aside from a brush with malaria, his health was excellent.

The next morning, November 8, Gray returned to the prison and continued his examination of the assassin, concentrating now not on the crime itself, but upon other evidence relevant to the prisoner's mental condition. They traversed a good deal of ground already familiar to newspaper readers: Luther Guiteau's peculiar religious notions, for example, and the alleged insanity of a paternal uncle and several cousins. But what, Gray interrupted sharply, of his mother's family? Had it produced insane offshoots? None that he knew of, Guiteau replied.

"From this statement," Gray explained in his formal report to the District Attorney, "there is no ground to infer heredity." The evidence in regard to Luther Guiteau was inconclusive; and fanatical religious beliefs were not inherited, but learned, the result of training and inquiry. Insanity in cousins, moreover, provided no evidence whatsoever of hereditary tendency to insanity; the susceptibility could only be inherited through the direct line. Gray emphasized as well that insanity as such could never "be transmitted—only a susceptibility of the physical organs to take on disease under the ordinary causes of such disease more readily than when the parents have not suffered from it; and this is only the occasional result, by no means the rule." Though remaining within the logical boundaries of contemporary medical theory, Gray was clearly assuming the strongest possible—and in the context of the 1880's a strained—antihereditarian position.

Turning from such comparatively remote influences, Gray sought to learn more of the prisoner's own life. After some questioning, Guiteau finally admitted that he had very strong sexual passions, that he had indulged them freely, and that in doing so had contracted a venereal disease. Again, Guiteau seemed to incriminate himself; sexual excess was undeniably a cause of mental illness and a deterioration in moral capacity. Yet the individual who had chosen to embark upon a course of dissipation must bear the responsibility for its ultimate consequences.

Another factor, of course, which might imply either insanity or simple lack of character was Guiteau's erratic course in life, his abrupt turn from law to theology, from theology to place-seeking. What, for example of Guiteau's forsaken law practice? If, as he said, he had been doing "first-rate," why abandon it? Guiteau pounced on Gray's matter-of-fact question: it had, he explained, an essential relationship to the question of his inspiration

because then I was doing well. I had a first-rate business which I left then and went into theology. You see I was restless and uneasy, like a woman in childbirth. I had something in me and had to get it out, so I left [the] law business and went lecturing but I had little reputation and I had but little success. People did not want to hear me.

Finally, after a lengthy recounting of Guiteau's career as theologian and lecturer, Gray brought the interview to an end, reading all his notes to the prisoner so that he might confirm their accuracy.

Gray's conclusions left no room for doubt; the assassin was perfectly sane. "I was unable," he summarized his two days' observations, "in these interviews, taking his whole life from his boyhood up, to discover the slightest evidence of insanity, nothing beyond simple desire for notoriety and self-consequence and for an easy way to make a living. . . . He appeared to be destitute of generosity of sentiment where his own personal ends and personal gratification were not concerned. His egotism cropped up at every point." Guiteau's character, Gray decided, had been particularly demoralized by his years of bitterness and sensual indulgence at the Oneida Community.

Whatever the religious fanaticism which brought him into the Community, it was there developed in the midst of sensualism, contentions and self-conceit and laid the foundation for the

after character of religious ranting, hypocrisy and his
dishonorable conduct. . . . Following up his whole history
given by himself, I see nothing but a life of moral degradation,
moral obliquity, profound selfishness and disregard for the
rights of others. I see no evidence of insanity, but simply a
life swayed by his own passions. He voluntarily abandoned
himself to the gratification of his passions and self-indulgence
in every way.

The circumstances of his crime made it quite clear that
Guiteau had been motivated neither by some uncontrollable
rage nor by the torrents of insane compulsion. He had
thought, reasoned, controlled his actions. Guiteau's claim
of inspiration, Gray argued, was simply a rationalization
demanded by his vanity *after* he had decided upon the crime;
revenge and a desire for notoriety were the true motives
for the assassination. Vanity, revenge, a desire for notoriety
—none of these were the symptoms or products of physical
disease.

Other physicians, however, examined Guiteau before
the trial and some came to very different conclusions.
Charles Folsom, for example, of Boston's McLean Hospital, found Guiteau's mental state

clearly one of weakness due, possibly, to some very early,
if not congenital, form of insanity, or to the dementia
produced by disease, mild if chronic, organic if acute, possibly
what some alienists would call the insane temperament or
partial (moral) imbecility. There was no incoherence, but the
want of connection in thought was very striking. The
weakness of judgment, reason, and reflection was as striking
as the quickness of perception, and in matters interesting
him, readiness of memory. When in the least opposed
his excitement was simply maniacal, but on indifferent subjects
he conversed calmly and amiably.

These two opinions, the contrasting diagnoses of Gray and
Folsom, reflected the differences in clinical orientation and
moral commitment that, as we have seen, already divided
the medical profession. The same division was to character-

ize the detailed testimony at the trial, the preparations for which continued vigorously while the exhilarated defendant entertained a constant stream of medical and journalistic visitors in his cell.

With the formality of Gray's examination completed, the trial could begin. There was little likelihood that Corkhill would have been swayed by even the most unequivocal report that the prisoner was insane; certainly he had had no reason to expect such a verdict from Dr. Gray.

In the weeks immediately preceding the trial, lawyers, editors, physicians, and articulate Americans generally, found the prospect of extraordinary interest. Partially it was the absence of other news to pre-empt the headlines, partially the significance of the crime, partially the recollection of other controversial cases that had turned on the issue of criminal responsibility. Legal and medical journals felt, of course, a particular interest in the impending process, but general and religious newspapers and magazines were equally concerned; they seemed alarmed by the possibility that Guiteau might succeed in using the insanity "dodge" to escape just punishment. The apparent cynicism of the assassin in advancing this plea merely seemed to dramatize the more general threat it posed to the administration of justice. At the end of September, for example, newspapers throughout the country reprinted a letter reportedly written by the late President Garfield in 1871, congratulating a Cleveland judge for his rejection of an insanity plea. "The whole country," Garfield had written, "owes you a debt of gratitude for brushing away the wicked absurdity which has lately been palmed off on the country as law in the subject of insanity. If the thing had gone much further all that a man would need to secure immunity from murder would be to tear his hair and rave a little, and then kill his man." As in so many other things, the late President had been able to express the opinion of his solid and thoughtful fellow citizens.

Few Americans, even in the first bitter weeks immediately following the President's death, doubted Guiteau's eccentricity and peculiarity of temperament. It was equally clear that he would hang. Most could have agreed with Nicholas Murray Butler when he conceded that the assassin was "unbalanced," but as well "the vilest assassin that ever cursed the earth by living on it." Common sense suggests that no American jury in 1881 would have dared vote to acquit Guiteau. The debate on insanity and criminal responsibility that filled the weeks between the President's death and the beginning of his assassin's trial had almost certainly little effect on his fate; it is nevertheless illuminating for the light it casts on American attitudes toward crime and criminal responsibility, heredity and mental illness.

To most editors and clergymen, the assassin's undoubted eccentricity was simply an inevitable consequence of his moral failings, failings that successive biographical revelations made only the more unmistakable. Guiteau seemed almost to exemplify that pattern of immorality we have already discussed—the criminal whose moral faculty was indeed paralyzed, but as the consequence of a lifelong series of immoral acts. If insane, Guiteau was, as one clergyman put it, a man "whose weakness was so saturated with selfishness as to silence the excuses of charity." "If Guiteau," the physician-editor of the New York *Medical Record* argued in similar terms, "had not debauched his moral sense and surfeited his vanity by constant self-indulgence, he could never have felt his 'inspiration.' " It might well be conceded that neither Guiteau's father nor mother had passed on to him a perfectly sound neurological make-up; but this did not constitute an excuse for his criminality. The assassin might well be compared to a person born with imperfect hearing; through proper training he might have been able to lead a normal, if not terribly outstanding, life. But his career of depravity, beginning with the pollutions of the Oneida Community, had atrophied his will to do good. This position was the one most commonly endorsed by physicians, lawyers, and educated laymen generally as they anticipated the trial. And in assuming this intellectual stance, Americans reinforced the social logic that lay behind the generally consistent support granted the M'Naghten test in medical as well as in legal circles.

Paradoxically, however, these discussions revealed at the same time a universal belief in the determining role of heredity in the causation of mental illness. Heredity, it must be realized, served in this generation to explain susceptibility to infectious disease, the occurrence of most chronic illness, and as well behavioral aberrations of all kinds. Everything from prostitution to alcoholism could be and was attributed to hereditary "influence." The *Nation* summarized the situation neatly when it pointed out that if Guiteau's defense could prove several members of the assassin's immediate family to have been insane, it "would do more to establish a doubt in the minds of an ordinary jury than all the testimony of all the experts in the country with regard to hereditary insanity."

In the camp of those physicians opposed to the conservative leadership of American psychiatry, there was a much greater and more deterministic emphasis upon the role of heredity in shaping human behavior. Indeed Spitzka, Kiernan, and a number of other Young Turks were beginning to accept the currently fashionable concept of "degeneration"—the idea that patterns of progressive and hereditary neurological degeneration lay at the root of much insanity, mental deficiency, and antisocial behavior. They were also, as we have seen, beginning to assume a related and somewhat derivative concept, the theory of Cesare Lombroso that criminality could be best understood as the "normal" behavior pattern of an instinctive criminal type. In these Lombrosian terms, Guiteau was a completely determined product of heredity, his behavior the consequence of a defective, structurally more primitive brain organization. Guiteau was, in the newly fashionable terminology, a throwback or atavism; that is, he behaved in the nineteenth century as man's more primitive ancestors had normally acted in the prehistoric savagery of the race. Few doubted that moral evolution was intricately dependent upon an underlying and increasingly complex physical development. It appeared then self-evident that morality would be the last mental characteristic acquired in point of time—and in the process of disease and devolution the first to be lost. "It was entirely consistent," as Dr. Folsom explained it, that Guiteau

should have quick perceptive faculties, a retentive memory, extraordinary acuteness, extreme self-will, an inordinate egotism . . . if this supposition is supposed to be correct, Guiteau is simply an anomaly in the fourth quarter of the nineteenth century and he is only a type of an earlier civilization than ours.

But heredity was, of course, only one issue discussed by concerned physicians. From their editorial strongholds, medical conservatives and liberals kept up a steady fusillade, pardoning or condemning Guiteau before the trial itself had begun.

And the medical issues provided only one facet of the debate; lawyers and editors found more than a few disquieting possibilities in the impending trial. The *Nation,* for example, like many other respectable journals, feared that with both court and counsel so weak, the proceedings might well degenerate into farcical confusion. A prosecution headed by an obscure political appointee and a defense conducted by an anonymous midwestern real estate lawyer could hardly be considered appropriate for the management of a major state trial. Even the news that Davidge and Porter had been added to the prosecution did not completely allay such fears.

Perhaps, the more farseeing and articulate agreed, the most significant aspect of the trial lay in the light it might cast on the relationship between psychiatry and the law—and, specifically, upon the usefulness of the M'Naghten rule as an intellectual vis-à-vis between these realms. Sophisticated editorialists were well aware that a radical discontinuity existed between legal and medical views of insanity. Many physicians—and some lawyers—agreed that the great majority of crimes committed by the mentally ill were in fact the work of persons aware of society's condemnation of their acts but yet unable to restrain themselves. Most legal writers, on the other hand, demanded not a discussion framed in terms of quality and degree of deviation from some theoretical standard of normal behavior, but categorical answers: was a particular individual responsible or irresponsible? As the physician's clinical knowledge of insanity grew more elaborate, however, his views of mental disease became increasingly complex, less and less amenable to the categorical demands of the legal process. There seemed to be no mutually consistent formal means, either institutional or intellectual, for bringing legal thought and practice in line with changing clinical pictures.

Even those jurists and lawyers unenthusiastic about the M'Naghten rule could see little in the way of a workable successor to it. To conservatives, on the other hand, the M'Naghten test had come to possess an almost sacrosanct quality. Proposals for modification of the rule seemed to imply a threat to the very foundations of individual morality. To emphasize control rather than knowledge, most jurists felt, would serve to undermine criminal justice, allowing room for the entry into American courts of that ancient enemy "moral insanity."

By 1881, the term had already become a label, a verbal cue with strong connotations of moral subversion and materialism. And moral insanity did clearly imply an interpretation of criminal responsibility that would, if adopted, become inevitably more open-ended, controlled increasingly by medical men and medical theory, decreasingly by the courts and men trained in the law.

Something of a solution to the impasse, in logical terms at least, lay in the doctrine of "irresistible impulse." This test might provide a strategy of compromise between the many psychiatrists convinced that emotional control was the key factor in determining responsibility and the need of the courts for some workable yet seemingly conservative rule. But there was a good deal of legal opposition to the irresistible impulse test (though by the 1880's it had been adopted by a number of states as a supplement to the M'Naghten rule). As early as the 1850's, a New York judge was quoted as saying that "If a man has an irresistible impulse to commit murder, the law should have an irresistible impulse to hang him."

There was, however, still another alternative. The jurisdiction of New Hampshire had in the early 1870's established a novel test of criminal responsibility. It was based on the assumption that the mental status of an accused criminal should be regarded as a question of fact, not law, to be determined by the weight of evidence, not by some formal legal test. The New Hampshire holding, following the conviction of its sponsor Justice Charles Doe, assumed that mental disease was in no essential way different from physical illness, that the central issue in determining responsibility lay not in whether the defendant knew his act to be forbidden, but in the relation between his crime and the mental illness from which it might possibly have sprung. If the crime was a product of mental disease, its perpetrator should not be held responsible. The spirit of this rule is clearly expressed in a phrase from one of the classic decisions in which the state's supreme court declined to endorse the M'Naghten test. The question, the decision held, of whether the defendant's killing of his wife was the product of mental disease was as "clearly a matter of fact as whether thirst and a quickened pulse are the product of fever." The decision would then rest largely in the jury's hands; the court need provide only a minimum of explicit guidance.

It was apparent to most legal writers well before the beginning of the Guiteau trial that the best hope of the defense lay not simply in pleading not guilty by reason of insanity and convincing a jury that Guiteau was in fact irresponsible, but, in effect, for the supreme court of the District of Columbia to explicitly reject the M'Naghten test and adopt the so-called New Hampshire rule. Unless this were the case, the court's instructions would have necessarily left the jury little option but to convict. Guiteau undoubtedly knew that his "removal" of Garfield was forbidden by law, certainly knew its nature and consequences, had stayed his hand and bided his time so frequently that his crime could hardly be seen as an "irresistible impulse." Guiteau could not hope to rely alone on his seemingly ingenuous plea of divine inspiration. Should the court follow the M'Naghten test, the President's assassin was as good as hung. The government need logically prove only that Guiteau understood that pulling the trigger of his revolver might have the effect of killing the President and that this act was forbidden by law (and that he was under the mitigating compulsion of no truly insane delusion).

Though there seemed little hope of Guiteau's acquittal, it was assumed by both defense and prosecution that the broadest kind of standards would be followed in the admission of evidence. Logically, as we have seen, a strict application of the M'Naghten rule would have precluded the admission of evidence bearing on matters other than the defendant's intellectual awareness. But practices governing the admissibility of evidence in insanity proceedings were very flexible, reflecting popular ideas concerning insanity more than they did the boundaries implied by the M'Naghten rule. As one authority put it, "every *habitual* and established expression of mental conditions becomes competent evidence." A short time before the assassination, Francis Wharton, probably America's leading expert in the field of legal medicine, neatly categorized the kinds of evidence ordinarily admissible in cases involving the possibility of criminal insanity. There were, he felt, three general kinds: first, prior insane conduct, second, "physical malformation and physical diseases likely to sympathetically affect the mental and nervous systems," third, evidence concerning insanity in near relatives. Though insanity could not, Wharton explained, be presumed to be absolutely hereditary, it was congenital in so many instances that evidence regarding the insanity of blood relatives was quite properly admissible. There could be little disagreement with standards so broad.

There was some disagreement, however, as to the burden of proof; did the defense have merely to provide evidence sufficient to establish a reasonable ground of insanity to justify acquittal? Was it the responsibility of the prosecution or defense to prove its case? An individual was presumed innocent yet presumed sane as well. But if he were presumed sane and pleaded not guilty by reason of insanity, then might he not in being presumed sane be presumed guilty? American jurisdictions differed widely in the 1880's in placing of the burden of proof in such cases. The prominence of Guiteau's victim made it clear, of course, that more than the ordinary amount of evidence would be needed to overthrow the presumption of sanity—if, indeed, any kind or amount of evidence could have done so. (The current of authority in 1881 did, however, seem to run in the direction of requiring the prosecution to establish the sanity of the defendant, especially in capital felonies, whenever any reasonable doubt had been cast upon it.)

The defense had, finally, to face an ingrained and bitter hostility to the insanity plea as such, a feeling quite common in legal circles. Adding to the ill-feeling that had already crystallized about the emotionally charged issue of "moral insanity" was a certain undercurrent of hostility between lawyers and physicians. The more self-consciously progressive in the medical camp tended to dismiss the law as precedent-ridden, formalistic, and essentially antagonistic to change. The law seemed particularly vulnerable to this charge in cases—like those dependent upon psychiatric judgments—where it seemed as though scientific truth would have little chance in competition with conventional rules. "Judicial instruction," as one alienist put it, "cannot make that true which is false in fact and contradicted by science." Lawyers were on their part often willing to return with enthusiasm the dislike and misunderstanding that some members of the medical profession entertained toward the bar. In the area of criminal responsibility particularly some attorneys did not hesitate in characterizing advanced medical views as materialistic, very likely atheistic, and certainly inimical to the welfare and stability of society. As the editor of New York's legal *Daily Register* remarked in discussing the impending Guiteau trial:

We are now to see pitted against each other in the arena at Washington, the doctrines of the common law and the diagnosis of the physicians . . . the only substantial question seems to be whether extreme recklessness, heedlessness, and indifference to moral obligations can amount, without disease of the brain or idiocy to incapacity for criminal intent.

Moral insanity, from this point of view, was simply a euphemism for unrestrained passion and selfishness. And, not unexpectedly, throughout the seemingly endless medical testimony that fills the transcript of the Guiteau trial, this sensitive theme reasserts itself again and again.

The trial itself could not be long postponed—enough perhaps to preserve the dignity of the law in providing Guiteau a formal hearing, but hardly long enough for popular resentment to subside. On November 10, Walter Cox, the presiding judge in the Guiteau trial, announced that the government informations in the Star Route case would not stand;* the indictment was quashed and Washington's legal world could, with a nervous backward glance, turn its undivided attention to the matter of Guiteau.

* The Star Routes were specially subsidized postal routes; a great deal of scandal had been connected with the awarding and performance of these lucrative contracts.

Meanwhile, the details of staging the trial proceeded apace; carpenters were busy putting the District's aged and undistinguished criminal court in readiness. They laid a temporary board floor in the space between the railing and the main entrance, about two feet above the main floor. As many chairs as possible were to be placed on this temporary flooring and when these were filled the marshal planned to allow no standees. Additional chairs and tables were being hired for the scores of newspapermen expected. For the first time in the court's history, strangers claiming to be reporters would be asked to show credentials before being allowed to enter. Others would be admitted on first-come, first-served basis. District Attorney Corkhill had been busy too, attending to the scores of last minute details of staging the trial. He had, for example, employed Mr. H. H. Alexander as stenographer at the rate of fifteen cents a folio for ordinary testimony and eighteen for argument or discussion. He was to receive twenty cents a page for expert testimony; it was clear that the trial would serve as a sounding board for a whole faculty of physicians. (Each afternoon, Mr. Alexander was to supply a copy of the day's proceedings to the printer so that a printed copy might be available for use the next morning.) On November 9, Judge Porter arrived in Washington, found rooms, and then met with his fellow counsel, Corkhill and Davidge. Dr. Gray joined them as they formulated the prosecution's strategy.

The defense too was readying its case. Scoville predicted that the trial would be no mere formality, but—contrary to many opinions—last at least a month, perhaps as long as three. On November 11, three days before the trial was to begin, Guiteau's sister Frances arrived with her daughter from Chicago to be with her husband and brother. A reporter meeting her train at the station dismissed persistent rumors that she was on the verge of insanity herself. She appeared, he noted, to be much aged by grief, however, resembling a woman of sixty-five more than one of forty-five, her actual age. Mrs. Scoville was reserved in manner, dressed without ostentation, and showed no hesitancy in discussing her special, almost maternal, relationship with her younger brother and the years of anxiety his wanderings and succession of morbid projects had meant for her. Charles's brother John also appeared in Washington. He seemed, moreover, to have changed his original impression that Charles was sane and responsible. "I have always," he told a reporter, "believed him 'crack-brained' or 'off his base' to use an expression of the day." John explained, however, that he had never really believed his brother to be insane until he reread the letters and other documents that illuminated Charles's life for the past few years. (But a few weeks earlier, John had written to his brother-in-law George Scoville that he held Charles morally responsible for the late President's death. "The crime," he explained, "was the legitimate ending of his former vicious life. I have always credited him with enough natural ability and a sound mind, except as it has become perverted by excessive egotism, wilfulness, lust and laziness.")

By a strange chance, another figure from Guiteau's past now appeared on the stage. This was John Humphrey Noyes. On November 4, the New York *Herald* reprinted the hostile circular Guiteau had distributed almost fifteen years before in an effort to have the Oneida Community destroyed. Scoville had provided the document. Noyes, on November 7, sat down at the writing desk in his Canadian home and prepared to answer this unexpected attack on himself and the now disbanded Community to which he had given his life. "I am seventy years old," he began his calculated letter to the prosecution, "and have long been disabled by laryngitis, and deafness, so as to be quite unfit for service as a witness. But I can write a little yet, and it is no more than fair to the memory of the defunct community to show that Guiteau's insanity had always consisted of vicious and irresponsible habits." Early in life, Noyes explained, Guiteau had destroyed his physical and mental health by frequenting brothels, where he had contracted both habits of dissipation and a venereal disease. He had, Noyes continued, "fastened himself to the Community as a lascivious hypocrite" and left it as a "pettifogging plunderer." "In other words," he concluded, "his wickedness was just as ferocious and versatile in 1867, when he issued from Scoville's office to plunder the Oneida Community, as it was in 1881, when he shot President Garfield." He did not mention the letters he and other leaders of the community had written Luther Guiteau in the 1860's, consoling him for his son's impious behavior with the reflection that Charles was insane and irresponsible.

Preparations for the trial were concluded on November 13, the day before proceedings were to begin. The District's criminal court—one reporter described it as an "old and insignificant building"—had been made ready, temporary flooring and extra chairs installed, and arrangements made for controlling the huge crowd expected. The room itself defied last minute remodeling efforts; it was rather small, somewhat cramped, and—again in a reporter's words —"might well be defined as dingy."

In Washington, hotel lobbies and barrooms were filled with groups discussing the imminent trial. The Washington *Post* reported the unmistakable consensus: Guiteau was a detestable villain and deserved immediate hanging. There was in addition some real anxiety that he might escape condign punishment through the "insanity dodge." Other less polite Washingtonians complained of the elaborate preparations that had been made for the trial, the making ready of the courtroom, the summoning of witnesses from throughout the country—when the proper treatment for Guiteau could quickly and inexpensively be organized by a vigilance committee.

The object of their attentions, quite unaware of such hostile sentiments, was joyous with anticipation. On the Sunday morning before the trial, the prison was filled with visitors and curiosity-seekers, including a large party of

"Christian women" who arrived to pray for the assassin's soul. Mr. and Mrs. Scoville and John Wilson Guiteau paid a family visit to the prison. With the completion of arrangements for the trial, Corkhill had relaxed his previously strict restrictions on visitors. The Guiteaus and Scovilles met in the warden's office, the highlight of this family reunion being John's presenting his younger brother with a new suit of clothes. Charles retired from the office and soon returned newly and neatly attired to explain his plans for the trial. He intended, the defendant explained, to make a dramatic opening statement to the court. "It will be a racy, stirring speech," he confided, "and I intend to light into Arthur, Conkling, and Grant for their cowardice in not coming forward and taking their share of the responsibility."

Garfield out of uniform, a handsome and imposing figure,
the picture of a President. *Photography by Sarony. The
Bettmann Archive, Inc.*

"The Tragedy at Washington," scene in the upper room at the
depot immediately after the shooting. The President rests on a
workman's mattress while Dr. Smith Townshend, the first
physician to reach him, examines the wound. Looking on are
the President's son, Secretary of State Blaine, and Dr. D. W. Bliss,
prominent Washington physician and Board of Health member.
Drawn by W. P. Snyder from a sketch by W. A. Rogers.
The Bettmann Archive, Inc.

Opposite. Advertisement for "Grand National Tableaux Representing the Assassination of President Garfield," detail from a
circus poster. The assassination and trial become a sideshow
attraction. The extent of commercial exploitation intensified
interest in the Guiteau affair. *The Bettmann Archive, Inc.*

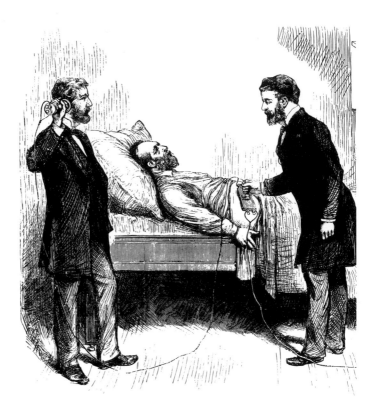

Ascertaining the location of the bullet. Several of America's
most prominent scientists, among them Simon Newcomb and
Alexander Graham Bell, were involved in attempts to use an
electromagnet in locating the elusive bullet. *From a sketch by
W. Shinkle. The Bettmann Archive, Inc.*

Opposite. The Long Death. Among those present, in addition to
the grieving Mrs. Garfield, were Colonel David G. Swain, an
intimate friend and long-time companion of President Garfield;
Dr. Susan Edson, a female homeopathic physician who often
attended the Garfield family and whose presence was something
of an embarrassment to the medical men; and Robert Reyburn, a
prominent physician, surgeon, and teacher of medicine, who
worked on the Garfield case throughout. *The Bettmann Archive,
Inc.*

John K. Porter arraigning the prisoner. *From A Complete History of the Trial of Guiteau.*

Guiteau on the witness stand. This sketch, by J. O. Davidson, suggests the crowding in the courtroom and the vehemence with which the prisoner customarily spoke. *From Harper's Weekly, December 10, 1881.*

"From Grave to Gay." Thomas Nast dramatized with bitter irony the contrast between the very real tragedy of Garfield's death and the bizarre antics of his assassin; the moral was apparent. *From Harper's Weekly, December 10, 1881.*

5

THE TRIAL BEGINS

By eight-thirty on the first morning of the trial, a substantial crowd had begun to gather in front of the courthouse. It was quiet and orderly, perhaps in response to the presence of numerous special marshals sworn in by the District's high sheriff. Ornate red badges in their lapels distinguished the deputies from the crowd surrounding them. Almost half the courtroom was reserved for lawyers, journalists, and "distinguished guests"; many waiting outside would not gain admission. By 9:35, all of the reserved seats had been filled and at 9:45 the crowd was allowed to occupy the few remaining chairs. These filled quickly and at ten, when the trial was to have begun, the aisles and rear of the room were tightly packed with the standees the marshal had hoped to avoid.

It was, on the whole, a respectable audience. But there were only nine women present aside from the prisoner's sister. And several of these, a reporter wryly noted, were boardinghouse keepers "beaten" by Guiteau. By ten the defense and prosecution tables were filled as well. Joining Judges Porter and Davidge at the government table were E. B. Smith, a prominent New York lawyer and former assistant attorney general and the youthful Elihu Root. The crowded room with its windows shut, and, like many American rooms, overheated, very soon grew extremely close—but as the defendant was led in the crowding and heat were momentarily forgotten.

Guiteau looked a bit more presentable than he had in his photographs. He was dressed in the new black suit his brother had bought for him and wore a clean white collar and black tie. His hair had grown out a bit and he no longer had the shaved look of a convict. Almost before the crier had time to open court, the prisoner rummaged in his pockets and located a manuscript. It was the plea upon which he had spent so many hours in his cell. Judge Cox refused, however, to allow its reading, despite Guiteau's persistent attempts to be recognized. Finally, Charles turned to the newspapermen and presented it to them; obligingly, they saw that it was widely printed. The defendant's plea concluded with a warning to the Court and prosecution counsel. "I beg," it ended, "they go slow in prosecuting this case; that they do no injustice to the Deity, whose servant I was when I sought to remove the late President. At the last great day they and all men will stand in the presence of the Deity, crying for mercy and justice. As they act here, so will be their final abode hereafter. Life is an enigma. . . ."

Formally, of course, the trial began with the presentation of the grand jury's indictment. Luckily for the spectators it was not read, for the document filled nine closely-printed octavo pages; obviously its drafters hoped to leave not the slightest chance for some technical objection. Despite its archaic inversions and redundancies the indictment's burden was clear enough. The said Charles J. Guiteau, the Grand Jury charged, "him the said James A. Garfield, in the manner and means aforesaid, feloniously, willfully, and of his malice aforethought, did kill and murder, against the form of the statute in such cases made and provided, and against the peace and Government of the United States of America."

The trial began with a moment of confusing surprise. Leigh Robinson, the counsel appointed by the Court to assist Scoville rose and—without warning either his colleague Scoville or the defendant—pleaded for a continuance so that more prominent, and presumably more competent, counsel could be found to assist in the defense.

Specifically, the young Washington lawyer asked Judge Cox to appoint a particular, though dramatically unnamed, counsel to assist them and an additional week to properly acquaint this prospective colleague with their somewhat peculiar problems. The additional time, Robinson argued, could also be used to bring more witnesses to Washington.

Guiteau was furious; *he* certainly needed no more time. "We are ready," he shouted, "to try this case now." District Attorney Corkhill was equally indignant. It had been almost a half year since the shooting of the President and no further dawdling should stand in the way of his assassin's disposal. The normally diffident Scoville was equally outraged at Robinson's suggestion—and for once found himself siding with the District Attorney. Robinson, he informed the court, had not bothered to consult with him for the past four days, and now, in this crowning act of arbitrary discourtesy, asked for a continuance.

Judge Cox was confused. He had, he confessed, hoped to leave no grounds for the reproach that Guiteau had been "hurried to the gallows without a fair trial." Yet, on the other hand, the Judge explained, he wished the trial to proceed without unnecessary delay. It was better, he finally decided, to err on the side of leniency—and was about to accede to Robinson's request when Guiteau protested. "I do not wish it," he burst out excitedly,

and my counsel does not wish it. I want to say emphatically that Mr. Robinson came into this case without consulting me; that I know nothing about him; that I don't like the way he talks; and I ask him to retire. I expect to have some money shortly, and I can employ any counsel I please. I want it understood that I am not a beggar or a pauper.

Scoville, with a rather studied wistfulness, added to Guiteau's words his request that Robinson at least tell him the name of the anonymous counsel he had suggested to the Court. This flurry of words decided the harassed Judge.

Cox ordered the trial to proceed and the bailiff immediately called the first member of the juror's panel, a Mr. B. Lewis Blackford.

Before any questioning began, however, the Court was careful to explain to the panel generally and to Mr. Blackford specifically that mere knowledge of the case, even an opinion in regard to the defendant's guilt or innocence, would not disqualify, only a fixed and immovable opinion. Turning then to Mr. Blackford, he asked whether he considered himself a qualified juror. Was there anything which prevented him from rendering a fair and impartial verdict? The prospective juror answered immediately that his opinion was "exceedingly" fixed. "So far as my present information on the case goes," he explained, "it would take testimony of a very extraordinary and unexpected character to shake it." And Mr. Blackford was more moderate than most of his fellow panel members in expressing his opinion. Unwilling to serve as jurors in what promised to be a long trial, most members of the panel felt no hesitancy in expressing their hostility toward the prisoner. One John Lynch—apparently his real name—answered, for example, "I think he ought to be hung or burnt or something else. . . . I don't think there is any evidence in the United States to convince me any other way." Joshua Green simply answered that "I think he ought to be hung; that is all I think." Jacob Boll was dismissed when he too explained that he would listen to no evidence—"nothing save the rope." Again and again such replies disqualified and on the first day only five jurors were accepted, on the second only four, and this despite the calling of a panel almost three times as large as that available the first day.

The defendant was prepared for them. Guiteau had formulated, in addition to his opening plea, a list of questions to be asked prospective jurors, a list that he pressed upon Scoville as the first member of the panel was sworn in. The defendant's questions were straightforward enough: "Do you believe in the Bible? Do you believe in the letter

of the Bible or simply its spirit? Are you now or have you
ever been a Christian? Do you believe in the inspiration of
Paul and the Evangelists?" Charles urged Scoville to pursue
the religious convictions of the prospective jurors, to ask
whether they believed in the story of the Creation, Noah
and the flood, Abraham and Isaac, the Hebrew children
and the fiery furnace. "Do you believe Martin Luther &
Dwight Moody to have been inspired? Do you believe the
prisoner could have been inspired by the Lord to remove
the President and are you open to be convinced of this?"

Defense and prosecution, however, pursued other points
in questioning those few witnesses who allowed that they
would at least listen to testimony. One was their attitude
toward capital punishment, another their view of insanity
and the plea of irresponsibility. The unbelieving were, of
course, sought out by the prosecution and immediately
excused, as were those who expressed doubts concerning
capital punishment. The matter of insanity provoked an assortment of interesting replies. A number of jurors simply
refused to answer when asked if there had ever been insanity in their immediate families. Some experience with
mental illness, if only casual, was common enough. Many
of the panel members had seen insane persons when visiting asylums through curiosity, others had neighbors, one a
wife suffering from mental illness. (The latter was peremptorily challenged by the government.) Drinking was the
most commonly assumed cause of insanity, testimony to
the thoroughness of temperance appeals. A number of
jurors, of course, stated categorically that the nature of
Guiteau's crime implied mental abnormality. Ralph
Wormley, colored, a plasterer for the Pension Bureau, expressed what must have been the consensus among Washingtonians—if among prospective jurors, an unspoken one
—when he said that "the man is partly crazy or something
of that kind, and it seems to me that no sensible man would
have done such a thing anyway."

Even in the trial's earliest stages, during the choosing of

the jury, Guiteau made it clear that he planned to play an active role in the proceedings. He was especially animated during the first day of jury selection, discussing tactics in a loud voice and giving constant advice to his legal colleagues, Scoville and Robinson. Not all was accepted. He asked, for example, that no Negroes be allowed on the jury and that they be challenged peremptorily. Yet Scoville did accept Mr. Wormley. (As a minor political appointee, Wormley was obviously not worth one of the government's challenges; and though he had said that Guiteau was certainly unbalanced he had also declared that any proven murderer should hang.) It was no easy task to find jurors; even those accepted asked to be excused while almost all those questioned expressed varying degrees of hostility toward the prisoner. It was not until Wednesday, November 16, after three days of selection, that the final juror was chosen. The first tale of twenty-five had been exhausted the first day, another of seventy-five the second day, and it was not until a third of seventy-five was called that the jury could be completed. It was a mixed and satisfactorily representative group. All, of course, were male, and one, as we have seen, was a Negro. There was one restaurant keeper, one retired businessman, one machinist, two plasterers, one iron worker, two grocers, a cigar dealer, and three merchants.

While the jury was being chosen, rumors and rumors of rumors spread with renewed vigor, perhaps stimulated by the publicity attending the opening of the trial. Guiteau was pictured as the cat's-paw in numberless hypothetical plots, while other widely circulated stories detailed conspiracies to assassinate the late President's assassin. The mood of the crowd outside the courthouse was outspokenly unpleasant as the prisoner was led through it, to and from the van that shuttled him between prison and court.

The atmosphere in the courtroom itself, however, changed a bit after the confusion of the trial's opening day.

As it became clear that order would be maintained, the trial became something of a fashionable diversion; the proportion of female spectators increased each day. Most were obviously ladies and had come to the trial dressed in new and stylish ensembles. They ate gingerly from lunch baskets during the noon recess, unwilling to chance leaving the room and possibly losing their seats.

On the second and third days of questioning prospective jurors Guiteau remained comparatively quiet, spending a good deal of time in making copies of a beseeching letter "To the Legal Profession of America." Charles explained in this appeal that the defense desperately needed the help of experienced counsel. He had no money at the moment for legal fees, but would soon have some as the result of public contributions, the sale of his book, and the settlement of an "old matter" in New York. When he finished composing this appeal, Guiteau immediately handed it to a reporter. Scoville, however, quietly urged the newsman to simply "put it in his pocket." Guiteau unfortunately heard his brother-in-law's whisper and became suddenly more disturbed than he had since the opening moments of the trial. His sister explained later to reporters that Charles was very much in earnest and would be most disappointed if several prominent trial lawyers did not respond to his appeal.

On Thursday, November 17, the prosecution was to begin its case. Before it could, however, Guiteau initiated the days proceedings—and titillated the audience—by clashing sharply with his brother-in-law and the court. Scoville had stated placatingly that there was no essential disagreement between Mr. Robinson and himself. Guiteau immediately sprang to his feet and objected to Robinson's mere presence in the courtroom, arguing that he was his own counsel and that the Court had thus no right to cut him off. "I intend to be heard in this case and I will make a noise about it." He sat down, managed to remain seated for few moments, then leaped to his feet. "One word," he shouted,

about the *Chicago Post* special that appeared this morning.
I want to say it is an absolute lie from beginning to end. . . . I
wouldn't trust my case to the best lawyer ever made. I
know my position and my views in this matter. One or two
blunderbuss lawyers constitute my entire defense, and I won't
allow it if I can help it.

Guiteau sat down abruptly, then after a momentary pause leaped up again before the proceedings could begin. "If your honor please," he shouted, "I came here in the capacity of an agent of the Deity in this matter, and I am going to assert my right in this case."

At last, the District Attorney was able to begin the government's case. His opening statement held no surprises. Corkhill began with an incantatory reference to Lincoln and the Civil War, and with praise for those American institutions which guaranteed even Charles J. Guiteau a fair trial. As the District Attorney recited the circumstances of the assassination and read a number of Guiteau's notes and letters into the record, the prisoner interrupted repeatedly—though reading a newspaper and attempting to appear elaborately unconcerned (finally causing Judge Cox to threaten Guiteau with removal if he did not maintain order). Concluding with an obligatory mention of the "bereaved wife and fatherless children," Corkhill ended his comparatively straightforward statement to loud and continued applause. The defense reserved its opening statement until after the prosecution had presented its direct testimony.

This testimony, which filled the next few days, was a thorough, on the whole stolid and unassailable, reconstruction of the crime. It documented Guiteau's purchase of the pistol, his relations with Washington landladies, his engagement of a hack before the shooting; even the details of the President's wound and his treatment and autopsy were elaborately presented. There were only a few lively moments. Among them were the appearance of notables like Secretary of State Blaine, another the amusing accent of Achille Barton, the Negro hackman, and Officer Kearney's rich brogue. The dramatic climax of the prosecution's presentation was reached on Saturday morning as the prosecution presented its final witnesses. One was Dr. D. W. Bliss, who had supervised the autopsy; during the course of his testimony, the District Attorney introduced several of Garfield's shattered vertebrae as evidence and passed the bits of bone to the jury "for identification." It was clear that the prosecution would spare no effort or effect in making its case irrefutable.

The most novel aspect of this essentially formal presentation was the submission and publication of the letters and papers Guiteau had left with the newsdealer at the Baltimore and Potomac Station on the morning of July 2. The package included a copy of his book, *The Truth,* Guiteau's several letters to the American people and to General Sherman, another to the New York *Herald* (suggesting that they print his book in one or two sections a day so as to spread the Gospel more efficiently), and a "Personal Mention" in which Guiteau provided a brief biographical sketch for the convenience of newspaper editors. In addition to his book, Guiteau included a lengthy summary of it and several notices that had appeared in Boston newspapers. "The book," Guiteau explained, "cost me trouble enough, and I have no doubt but it is official. It was written in sections, as I had light, covering a period of nearly five years. If it does not prove the existence of heaven and perdition, I submit they cannot be proved."

It was not only Guiteau's prose style that helped enliven the trial. He was proving a most peculiar counsel. When not reading the New York *Herald* or Washington *Post,* he followed the testimony carefully, leaping up from time to time to address comments to the court, to witnesses, or to the jury. In a trial in which suspense and uncertainty did not really exist, the defendant himself became inevitably a dramatic focus. When he entered on Friday morning, for example, the *Post's* court reporter observed at least fifty pairs of opera glasses belonging to the "fair sex" levelled at him. In addition, artists from several national weeklies were busily making likenesses of the prisoner and other important participants. When aware of being sketched, Guiteau sat rigidly in his chair and assumed a look of dignified earnestness.

When the defendant left the courtroom at the end of the day, however, he became the object of less welcome attentions; especially during the first week of the trial crowds gathered outside the court waiting for him, jeering and pushing against the line of police guards. One reporter noted that Guiteau always entered the van with a sudden jump, as though fearful that one of the spectators might take the opportunity to shoot him. Certainly there were enough threats. "We don't want any cursed foolishness in this trial," a Civil War veteran in the mob explained it, "and we won't have any. If they play malpractice and insanity the case will end damned soon." Another veteran, his sleeve dangling at his side, asked coolly to see the prisoner and when refused on the grounds that he might have a pistol, replied: "Well, I carry one, and a mouth full of tobacco juice for the damned dog." He left, threatening to end the case himself if there was any "damned legal sentimentalism about it." Guiteau's courtroom histrionics only sharpened the resentment of those who felt that he was fortunate to be alive at all and receiving the privilege of a trial. The *Evening Critic,* appealing to its lower-class readership, put the matter bluntly: "A few more such scenes as have been witnessed during the past week will to a certainty nerve the hand of some honest man to kill him."

On Saturday the nineteenth the prosecution arrived at the high point of their direct testimony, D. W. Bliss's account of the autopsy. The Washington physician took the stand, explaining that the wounds inflicted by Guiteau's revolver were necessarily mortal, outlining as he did the course taken by the ball after striking Garfield in the lower back. It was at this point that the portion of the President's spine—about five inches long—was submitted in evidence. Bits of rib were still attached. Ladies wept, one reporter noted, "while even strong men trembled." The day's testimony ended with this exhibit of gross pathology and Guiteau was led out to his van. The doors were closed and two guards climbed aboard, one riding in front with the driver, the other Perry H. Carson, a six foot six inch Negro, stood on the rear steps. Almost immediately the driver started his horses toward the prison. As they drew away from the court, a sorrel horse galloped past and a man mounted shakily on its back drew a pistol and fired at Guiteau through the bars. The shot missed but did leave a bullet hole in the prisoner's new coat. (The would-be assassin was quickly captured; his name was Bill Jones, a twenty-nine-year-old Maryland farmer and quite drunk.) This remarkable and almost successful exhibition of mounted, alcoholic marksmanship served as an appropriate end to the trial's first week.

On Sunday, Guiteau held court. He was exhilarated by the trial and by his narrow escape. (In the District, a defense fund for farmer Jones was already being organized.) The main corridors of the prison were filled with the curious—most of them well-dressed and eminently respectable. In midafternoon, Guiteau was led from his cell to be inspected by a group of socially prominent young ladies who had driven out for the afternoon. Charles spent a much longer time with reporters discussing plans for the trial. He began, however, by complaining to the *Post* reporter; their stories, he objected, always called him "the assassin" or "the fellow." The latter especially he considered a "low, vulgar appellation." Guiteau was particularly indignant at published reports that he had cursed his would-be assassin. "I did not," Charles explained; "I don't swear. I abhor profanity and vulgarity. I have only associated with high-toned people, Christians and politicians of high moral principles. Whenever you see an oath coupled with any expression purporting to come from me, you can put the expression down as a manufactured falsehood."

On Monday morning, the van—now provided with extra guards—arrived without incident at the court. The trial itself did not continue as smoothly. On Saturday, Robinson had cross-examined Dr. Bliss at length, obviously with the intention of accumulating evidence of malpractice on the part of the President's physicians. Robinson thus managed again to infuriate Scoville, for the Chicago lawyer had stated publicly and repeatedly that he would not resort to this defense. Unfortunately, Robinson had vanished over the weekend; whatever chance there might have been for the young Washington lawyer and Scoville to have compromised their differences ended on Sunday when Scoville aired his resentment to a number of reporters. Leigh Robinson began Monday's proceedings by asking the court for permission to make a statement. What, Robinson asked dramatically, was he to think when he found himself criticized—not in private as colleague to colleague—but in the columns of the morning newspaper? After Scoville and Robinson indulged in a bit of name-calling, the Washingtonian finally succeeded in having himself discharged from the case. Scoville and Guiteau were alone as they began their defense.

The older man opened with a careful hour and a half statement, begun on Monday and concluded on Tuesday. In a period given to perfervid oratory, Scoville's speech was calm, playing on the audience's natural sympathy for his difficult task—if not for the prisoner—and urging that the court endorse the broadest possible interpretation of criminal responsibility; it was very much, he argued, a part of the progressive spirit of the age.

It would come as no surprise, he told the jury by way of introduction, that they would have to do a good deal of thinking in the course of the trial, especially in regard to the prisoner's mental condition. One need not be an expert to realize that the mental processes of the insane differ greatly from those of normal persons; the problem lay in recognizing them. Both defense and prosecution would produce medical experts, Scoville warned. Those appearing for the prosecution, however, would be paid and—of course—this might be expected to influence their opinions; the prosecution witnesses, like other men, were not immune to such sordid considerations. The defense witnesses, on the other hand, he assured the jury, would not be paid a fee: "You will find them summoned here before the court, commanded to come, almost dragged here by the officers of the law, to give their testimony in a case in which it is almost abhorrent to their feelings to testify."

Perhaps the most important thing for the jurors to keep in mind, Scoville continued, was that there had been a tendency since the Middle Ages for the insane to be treated with gradually increasing understanding; the criteria by which their insanity was determined had in parallel fashion broadened consistently. This change, he argued, "is precisely like all other changes in society, in politics, in civilization. It is a change all the while progressing to a better state of things, to higher intelligence, to a better judgment." Only 250 years before, Scoville pointed out, the only acceptable insanity defense was one which proved an accused to have had no more reason than that possessed by a wild beast. This doctrine had been superseded by the acceptance of a test emphasizing knowledge, the ability, that is, to know and understand the difference between right and wrong. This position, embodied in the M'Naghten rule, had—Scoville argued—been modified and in a sense superseded as well by the introduction of a new criterion; this was the doctrine of "irresistible impulse." (In stating, as he did, to the jury that most American jurisdictions accepted this test, Scoville indicated an ignorance of criminal law, for this was not the case.) But the impulse test too, Scoville's preliminary argument concluded, was being challenged by a more enlightened doctrine. And here Scoville turned directly to the Court. "The whole question," he emphasized, "of the criminality of the accused depends upon whether the act was done by a man insane, that is whether it was the result of an insane mind or a deranged mind"— and this decision, like any other matter of fact, should be left to the jury.

"That," said Judge Cox interrupting, "is the New Hampshire doctrine." Quite right, Scoville conceded; and this indeed was the burden of his plea. It was time that the Court take this step forward, adopt the New Hampshire rule and with it a firmer and more progressive relationship between medicine and the law. "Now"—he turned again to the jury—"if the court leaves that to you, gentlemen, it will be for you to say, taking all the facts in this case that may be developed by the evidence, whether this crime would have been committed by the accused here if he had been of sound mind, judgment, and reason."

Central to the modern view of insanity, Scoville continued in his quiet and didactic fashion, was the recognition that it was a complex state, one which appeared in countless guises. Most of the insane did not appear overtly deranged; contrary to popular misconception, comparatively few were either delirious or completely irrational. Indeed, Scoville remarked with careful informality, one of the asylum superintendents sitting now as a witness in the courtroom, had recently told him that perhaps the most frequent and annoying question asked by asylum visitors was: "Why is he here? . . . they seem to talk as rationally as anyone else." It was not complete irrationality that ordinarily marked insanity, but rather a failure of reason and proportion, an acceptance of false premises and an inaccurate view of practical matters. Would such symptoms not explain Guiteau's quixotic publishing schemes? Might it not explain his inability to function as a lawyer, his erratic theological peregrinations?

The defense would prove, he contended, that an essentially consistent thread of madness ran through Guiteau's adult life; it would, moreover, trace this taint to its origin before his birth. The causes of insanity were complex, Scoville explained to the jury, but medical opinion agreed that heredity was perhaps the most general and important. And, as they hoped to prove, the taint of insanity was to be found abundantly in the Guiteau family. Though environmental causes might develop insanity in anyone—no matter how strong his nervous endowment—they acted with far greater malignancy if a taint of insanity were established in the blood. The exciting, that is environmental, causes of insanity were, of course, well known to the jurors—alcohol for example. But there were many others. "Epilepsy is a cause of insanity; gout may be; rheumatism may be; impure blood may be; excitement may be; strong emotion may be; love, hate, fear."

All of this might be readily conceded; but still the problem of insanity and its diagnosis remained an extraordinarily challenging dilemma for American courts. How, in individual cases, was this diagnosis to be made? How was one to decide which offenders were truly insane and hence irresponsible and which simply wicked? One clue lay in the area of motivation. "Of course," Scoville conceded defensively, "a person may be so depraved, his moral nature may be so perverted, he may be so lost to all sense of right and wrong, and as reckless of consequences that he will do an act without any adequate motive." Thus, for example, the case of the young cowboy Billy the Kid. He had casually murdered some twenty-five or thirty men before being killed himself, some weeks previously. In his case, Scoville argued,

you can trace it to his absolutely perverted, demoralized nature; caring nothing for human life; caring nothing for consequences; and he would shoot merely from a certain impulse or feeling that could not be accounted for or explained; yet he was not deranged, but bad, absolutely and totally depraved. . . . But, ordinarily, if a man who is otherwise a good man commits a crime, the first thing you inquire about is the motive. . . . And if you cannot assign a motive, I think these gentlemen will tell you that it is to some extent an evidence of insanity.

Appealing, then, to the presumably moralistic sentiments of the jurors, Scoville emphasized how dissimilar Guiteau's life had been from that of a Billy the Kid or a Jesse James. Piety had been one of Guiteau's hereditary endowments, piety in an intensity which seemed to exist frequently in connection with madness. His brother-in-law, Scoville claimed, had always been a gentleman. ("And," Guiteau interjected, "with no bad habits of any kind.")

He never [Scoville elaborated], left the Young Men's Christian Association rooms to go into saloons. He never visited saloons at all. He never smoked. He never drank spiritous liquors. He never used tobacco in any form. He never visited a gambling place and would not talk with a person who used improper or profane language a moment; he would turn away from them instantly. Now, what I have to say is that, having these traits, it was not difficult for him to introduce himself to business men. . . . But, at the same time, if any one conversed with him any length of time or became intimate with him at all, his peculiarities of religious belief and otherwise, and I must say it, his shortcomings of mind, his want of mental capacity would be manifest.

"I had brains enough," Guiteau interrupted jumping to his feet, "but I had the theology on my mind and this is the reason I did not go on in the law business. There is no money in theology, and I ran behind on that pretty badly and haven't got over it yet. I am out of the business now though."

Despite Scoville's surprisingly well-argued opening address, the audience's attention had been distracted throughout by the comments and interjections of his client and—

as Charles saw it—fellow counsel Guiteau. Spectators stared at the assassin, as one visitor put it, as though he were some exotic zoological specimen. Fashionably dressed ladies continued to make up a large part of the audience; indeed, on the second day of Scoville's opening address, more than half the spectators were ladies, many arrayed in purple and velvet. Mrs. Blaine and several of her close friends were among them; conscious of their relation to the President, they did not join in the laughter that swept through the courtroom at each of Guiteau's interruptions.

When Scoville was characterizing his brother-in-law's legal practice, for example, Guiteau broke in to say: "Just put it down that I gave up a $5,000 law practice to go into this theology business. . . . It was the same kind of business the Apostle Paul was in. He got his pay at last. I expect it from my book." Several times, however, he became furious at Scoville, especially when he lingered on the peculiarities of the defendant's legal practice. On a number of these occasions it took two guards to hold Guiteau in his seat; reporters described him as almost "foaming at the mouth" as he shouted objections. At the same time, his remarks were not always well calculated to increase the jury's possible sympathy. Despite the presence of a Negro in the jury box, for example, Guiteau remarked heatedly that he disliked being called by his middle name; it had too much of the "nigger about it."

In allowing almost complete latitude to the defendant, Judge Cox had made a decision that was to affect the conduct of the entire trial—and his own reputation as well. He had decided to follow the rather commonsensical notion that if Guiteau's mental condition were the principal issue, then the more opportunity he were given to display it, the more solidly founded the jurors' judgment. But this was an invitation to criticism from respectable editors who regarded the proceedings as a national disgrace, and from the less respectable who felt that Guiteau should have been hung some time before the trial's opening in November and certainly not allowed to wallow in the attention attracted by his buffoonish cavortings. Judge Cox was beset with crank letters threatening imaginative reprisals for his overly lenient direction of the trial.

On Wednesday, November 23, the defense began its direct testimony. The most important early witness for the defense was Dr. John Rice, of Waukesha County, Wisconsin, the physician called by Frances Scoville to her Beaver Lake summer home when Charles threatened her with an axe several years previously. Dr. Rice had at that time examined Guiteau and told Mrs. Scoville that her younger brother was clearly insane and should be committed. The reasons for his decision, Rice testified, were easily explained. First was Guiteau's suspect heredity and his history of erratic behavior. Perhaps even more important was his morbid emotionality, his tendency to sudden excitement with no apparent stimulus. "During these periods of excitement," the Wisconsin physician continued, "I thought I could detect more or less incoherency—incoherency of thought—and I thought I detected also an excessive egotism . . . and I thought he was also the subject of an intense pseudo-religious feeling." Rice was careful to explain his use of the term "pseudo-religious": one could not entertain true religious principles and talk, as Guiteau did, of Christianity and religion without following its moral principles; Guiteau clearly lacked something in the line of morality.

The theme of Guiteau's religion was reemphasized by the testimony of John Wilson Guiteau, the defendant's older brother. The religion of the Guiteau family had, as we have seen, been a rich mousse of pietism and adventism —evangelicalism pushed to its emotional and perfectionist end. In Luther Guiteau's cosmology, the earth, as John Wilson explained the doctrine his father had instilled in his children, was the scene of a bitter struggle between God and Satan. Since the fall of man, however, Satan had had much the better of things, controlling the souls of all "who were not absolute believers in the Lord Jesus Christ as a Savior."

. . . all evil, all sin, all disease, all deformity, all infirmity; was the result of sin or the permission of those who had the will to accept Christ and reject Satan, and that they were under the dominion of Satan or of an evil spirit or of other evil natures. That was my father's theological view; it is my brother's and it is mine. . . .

Thus, clearly, at some point in the past, Charles must through his own perversity and sin have allowed Satan to take hold of him, so that he "was under the power of Satan or of a demon."

The defense also—and, as we have seen, despite the opposition of John Wilson Guiteau—pursued in detail the issue of Luther Guiteau's mental condition. Scoville hoped, obviously, to prove his late father-in-law to have been insane; in the medical climate of the 1880's such proof would have strongly impugned his son's competence. Dr. Rice and a number of other witnesses, brought under attachment from Freeport, were questioned intensively in regard to the older Guiteau's psychological peculiarities. Rice, for example, testified that he had attended Luther Guiteau during his final illness, at which time the older man had confided that his sickness was his own responsibility, that he might have lived forever had he had sufficient faith and brought himself into the proper relationship with Jesus. Another Illinoisian, then a Chicago lawyer but some years earlier an assistant to Luther Guiteau as circuit clerk, stated that Luther had often explained to him his lack of belief in doctors. Sufficient faith, he encouraged his young clerk, would save him at once from theological error and the material ills of men. Luther Guiteau believed, as a logical consequence of these assumptions, that there were men living on earth—and he among them—who might never die. Several other witnesses told of disturbing incidents in which the older Guiteau had sought by faith alone to heal persons gravely ill.

While still documenting the alleged taint of insanity in the assassin's blood, Scoville began at the same time an effort to prove Guiteau's mental infirmity to have been a chronic and long-standing condition. His strange theological career was an obvious point of emphasis. After Dr. Rice left the stand, the defense called Mr. Frank L. Union of Boston. Mr. Union was a freethinker and active in the affairs of the Boston free thought society. He had made Guiteau's acquaintance, Union explained, in September of 1879, when the prisoner had come to his office, asking about the possibility of hiring Paine Memorial Hall to give a lecture. Two-thirds of the human race, Guiteau warned, were going down to perdition and he hoped to be instrumental in saving at least some of them. (Guiteau habitually referred to himself, Union recalled, as being in the employ of that great firm, Jesus Christ and Company.) His curiosity aroused, Union agreed to let him have a lecture room and also allowed the intense evangelist to postpone payment until he had taken a collection at his talk. About fifty listeners appeared, Union continued, on the night Guiteau was to speak.

The lecturer brought in a manuscript which he placed upon the pulpit, and after apologizing for a cold, which he seemed to have, or which he thought he had, he commenced by reading some half a dozen lines and then turned over perhaps half a dozen pages and then commenced and read some more. Then he read some more, and then he would turn over, and so on, without any connection whatever, to the previous part he had been reading. After some half an hour or so he evidently became disgusted with himself, and took his manuscript and immediately left the platform in a great hurry. . . . Mr. Damon who was formerly a Unitarian minister, arose and made some remarks, and during them I believe, the prisoner left the hall. After he had gone out, of course we had a conference meeting then, and we all, unanimously, voted that the man was crazy, as we called it.

Mr. Davidge assumed the cross-examination. Not surprisingly, his principal goal seemed to be that of impressing upon jurors and audience the lamentable infidelity of Mr. Union and his fellow freethinkers and that—if by some chance they had not noticed—the very hall in which Guiteau spoke had been named after that infamous atheist, Tom Paine.

Thursday the twenty-fourth was Thanksgiving and court did not convene. Guiteau spent a comparatively uneventful day in prison, visited only by his sister, his brother-in-law, and two psychiatrists. Frances prepared her brother's Thanksgiving dinner and ate it with him. Unquiet reporters were able to root up only one tidbit of news; this was the arrival in Washington of Guiteau's former wife, now Mrs. Theodore Dunmire of Leadville. Mr. Dunmire, who accompanied her, immediately informed reporters that he had in his possession a picture of his wife and Guiteau, showing clearly her haggard and abused appearance. He was thinking of having copies made; they would, he expected, sell briskly.

As the trial resumed on Friday and Saturday (with spectators now arriving with lunch baskets filled with mince pie and turkey sandwiches), the defense continued its array of witnesses, all attesting to Guiteau's erratic behavior and to the morbid symptoms displayed by several of his relatives. Perhaps the most telling testimony came from two Chicagoans, Charles Reed, for a dozen years Illinois State's Attorney, and Fernando Jones, a Chicago businessman and sometime trustee of the Jacksonville Asylum for the Insane. Reed was a man of some reputation in Chicago's legal world; though he could not recall the incident, he had been indeed one of Guiteau's casual examiners for the bar. Much more vivid was his recollection of Guiteau as a would-be trial lawyer. One case remained with particular clarity in his memory, for Reed himself had been prosecutor. Guiteau's client had been accused of petty larceny—apparently an open-and-shut case. Despite Reed's plea that the court was busy, however, Guiteau insisted on speaking, which to the dismay of his listeners he did for three-quarters of an hour.

He introduced all sorts of subjects into the case, that were foreign to it. He had some theology, I remember, in the case, which created somewhat of a smile in the courtroom. As I remember, the case was one of petty larceny, a small amount of property involved, and he talked about theology, about the divinity, and about the rights of man, &c., &c. , . It was a very wandering, rambling speech, full of vagaries and peculiarities.

Reed then described his several encounters with Guiteau during the spring of 1881. The Chicagoan had been in Washington on business when he ran into the defendant several times in the lobby of the Riggs House (at which Reed was staying when Guiteau was using the public rooms of the hotel as a kind of informal office). He tried, Reed explained, to discourage Guiteau's hopes for a consulship. Did you, Scoville prompted, notice anything odd in his appearance? Yes, Reed answered, "he looked very haggard and gaunt, and as if he was friendless. He used to be very neat in his personal appearance. I noticed his clothes . . . had become very much worn and had quite a seedy appearance." His requests for money had become pathetically importunate as well. The murder of the President came as a complete surprise, Reed continued, for Guiteau had always seemed a harmless, if eccentric, sort. Some time after the assassination, Reed visited the defendant in the District prison and found him to have deteriorated perceptibly since he had last seen him in the Riggs's lobby. Guiteau had been sick immediately before his visit, Reed explained, and throughout their talk lay on his bed, except when he sat up to emphasize some point. Reed asked immediately why he had done it, why he had shot the President. At once Guiteau became extremely agitated, sitting bolt upright in bed and shouting that he had not done it, that it had been the work of the Lord, that he was merely a chosen instrument.

I guess I staid there with him [Reed continued] half or three-quarters of an hour, I should say, and he made a long speech. It was a rambling, disconnected, incoherent statement, and at times he would be very violent, slapping his hands against the brick wall very severely, with great force, and then again he would relapse into a whisper and talk in a very low tone of voice.

Had he had much experience with the insane, Scoville abruptly asked? Yes, the Chicagoan answered, he had visited insane asylums on a number of occasions and as State's Attorney had prosecuted a number of men who had set up insanity as a defense. "I should say," Reed stated formally, "he was of unsound mind."

Walter Davidge, in many respects the ablest of the prosecution attorneys, was entrusted with Reed's cross-examination. He began by casually managing to establish that Reed had been a friend of Scoville's for twenty years. Davidge accused Reed as well of telling Corkhill some days before that, although he regarded Guiteau as unbalanced, it had never entered his mind that the assassin might lack responsibility before the law. No, Reed flatly contradicted his questioner, he had never said such a thing. As they awkwardly faced each other, Davidge quickly turned to a point he had been holding in reserve. Had he not seen the witness, Davidge asked, sitting at the defense table several days previously and suggesting questions to Mr. Scoville? Yes, Reed admitted, he had suggested a few questions to be used in cross-examination—and saw no reason to hide it.

But before Davidge could pursue this point the proceedings bogged down in a confused exchange between Reed and Guiteau. The defendant, though apologizing all the while that Reed was a "good fellow," had contradicted him on point after point, ignoring the Court's repeated warnings that he remain silent. "If there is no other way," Cox finally threatened, "of preventing this interruption you will have to be gagged; that is all there is about it. You must shut your mouth and not let us hear you again while this trial proceeds. I do not want to go to such an extremity, but it must be done if we can not find any other way to control you." These threats, and many others like them, had not the slightest effect on the prisoner—and with Judge Cox unwilling to take any chance on a mistrial, the proceedings continued in their somewhat erratic course.

Fernando Jones was another strong witness for the defense; like Reed, he was respectable and hence plausible. And, as we have noted, he boasted the added credential of having served for years as an asylum trustee. Jones admitted having known Guiteau for a time in the 1870's when they both took meals at the same boarding house. There was, he said, no question in his mind that Guiteau was abnormal. Friday and Saturday's defense testimony had thus sought to prove Guiteau overtly abnormal for years prior to the President's assassination. Other witnesses, equally numerous, had testified to the clouded mental status of Guiteau's blood relatives, especially his father.

Sunday was a busy day for Guiteau. Experts for both defense and prosecution queued up to interview him. "I certainly draw well," Guiteau observed; "The best doctors from all parts of the country and the reporters of the leading newspapers." Dr. Rice, for example, even joined the group of waiting physicians, anxious to reexamine the patient whom he had not seen since the summer of 1878. After speaking with Guiteau, the midwestern physician generously shared his insights with waiting reporters. He is as crazy today, he told them, as he was then, only not so excited. "I ascertained," he added, "one important fact: that the prisoner is subject to nocturnal emissions. There is undoubtedly a strong sexual factor in the case."

Of greater interest, especially to native Washingtonians, were the comments of W. W. Godding, superintendent of the Government Hospital for the Insane in the District. Washington was still a very small city and Dr. Godding had at least a nodding acquaintance with a good proportion of the community's respectable citizens. When asked about sex and the possible influence it might have in the causation of insanity—and specifically upon Guiteau's mental condition—he agreed in words that constituted in 1881 a simple truism: "The disorders and excesses that grow out of the abuses of the sexual organs are," he explained, "practically the cause of much insanity." There was no question in Dr. Godding's mind that Guiteau was now insane—whatever the role youthful immoralities might have played in the development of his condition. As superintendent of the government asylum, he pointed out to reporters, he had had a rich experience with what he called "presidential cranks." There were always some drifting into the city, perhaps three or four a month—though after the assassination, he estimated, the number had probably doubled.

Godding then volunteered a particularly deep felt observation. All experts he argued, inasmuch as they appeared as witnesses for defense or plaintiff in American courts, played a totally inappropriate role. Expert testimony should in its nature be neutral—provided by skilled court-appointed physicians, not "hired" by opposing sides. When there was any question at all, Godding suggested, as to a prisoner's mental condition, it should be evaluated before any trial by a commission of court appointed experts. In taking this stand, Dr. Godding was simply voicing a feeling quite general in psychiatric circles, but a position on the whole still unfamiliar to contemporary legal practice.

Monday afternoon, November 28, the defendant took the stand in his own behalf. Perhaps Guiteau's ebullience on Sunday had simply reflected his anticipation. And for the public as well, the assassin's appearance was to be the highlight of the trial. The largest crowd to attend any session besieged the courthouse and Washington police and deputies were hard pressed to keep the unwashed from forcing their way into the building; judge, experts, and counsel had to fight their way into the courtroom. Those fortunate enough to gain admittance were not to be disappointed.

Guiteau's direct testimony and cross-examination lasted from late Monday, November 28, through Saturday morning, December 3. In print, it fills almost two hundred crowded octavo pages. The defendant was extremely nervous on the stand and spoke with an almost impenetrable rapidity. Yet Scoville quietly and methodically led Guiteau through a rehearsal of his life, the years in Freeport, Chicago, Ann Arbor, and the Oneida Community, and his legal career in New York and Chicago. Even a brief Chicago stay at Bell's Commercial College in the winter of 1857 was, for example, carefully detailed through Charles's youthful letters; misspelled and pathetically distraught, they begged again and again for money. (Luther Guiteau would not send any unless his son supplied periodic accounts of each penny he had spent.) Guiteau interrupted continually as Scoville read such letters—the materials of Charles's biography—into the record. Even when simply called upon to identify the handwriting of particular letters as his own, Charles seized the opportunity to make his characteristically informative pronouncements: "This does not look like my present handwriting." "There is a decided improvement shown here." "This is as fine as steel plate."

Scoville documented Guiteau's Oneida years with particular care—for there could be no doubt of a jury's willingness to assume the Community's influence upon the young man to have been a baleful one. (And hence, as well, the prosecution desire to show that Guiteau had entered the Community already dissipated, entered it only in search of further sensuality.) Guiteau's own rejection of the Community was expressed in the "Circular" attacking it, which he sent to newspapers and public officials after leaving—and which Scoville read into the record. "Whereas," it began

the Oneida Community is among the most spiritual and social despotisms of the nineteenth century; and whereas in social matters they are constantly violating the most sacred laws of God and man; and whereas nightly, innocent *girls* and innocent young women are sacrificed to an experience easier imagined than described; and whereas the founder of their "delightful" system is said to cohabit with his own flesh and blood; and whereas for the sake of these ruined and oppressed women, and for the good of society at large, said community ought to be "cleaned out."

After such whereases what forgiveness; Guiteau demanded that the Community be destroyed completely. Scoville emphasized (in addition to the sexual peculiarities of the Oneida Community) its attitude toward inspiration; Guiteau had, he argued, lived since childhood in surroundings in which inspiration was assumed to be commonplace. The Community, as Charles explained it on the stand,

looked upon Noyes as God's prophet upon earth, and everything was under his active control in the community. . . . Everybody there, as I said, looked upon John H. Noyes, the founder of the community, as especially inspired to introduce the kingdom of God on earth, and the community was the kingdom of God, as they looked at it. . . .

Thus Scoville covered in some detail every facet of Guiteau's life and experience.

Finally, his story reached 1880 and the immediate background of the assassination. For three or four months, Guiteau explained, he haunted the lobby of the Fifth Avenue Hotel, headquarters of the Republican National Committee. He knew and chatted with all the party's leaders. What, Scoville interrupted his witness, exactly was your relationship with these men? "Always very delightful," Guiteau immediately replied, "and pleasant in every way.

They treated me well, and seemed to think I was a good fellow at that time. I used to be on free and easy terms with them. I used to go to General Arthur and talk just as freely with him as I would with anybody." Unfortunately Guiteau explained, they uniformly failed to appreciate the campaign speech he had written—nor did they provide him with the speaking assignments he was so eager to fulfill. "They didn't want a man without any reputation," he explained. So great was his zeal for Garfield's cause, Guiteau continued, that he had had the speech printed at his own expense, then gave or sent copies to men of influence in the party. During the spring of 1881, Guiteau became, as he explained it, increasingly alarmed at the dangers threatened by the Stalwart–Half-breed split in the Republican party. Each day's editorial columns only increased his distress. "I wrote the President several notes . . . in which I told him that he ought to do something to pacify the Stalwarts; if he did not, the Republican party would go to wrack and ruin, and there would be terrible trouble here in this country. He never answered the notes at all. He paid no attention to it whatever." Then, on June 1, he continued, his inspiration possessed him. The next few weeks, he explained to the court, he spent in prayer, hoping that the Lord would grant him some confirmatory sign, some proof that his inspiration was divine, not diabolical. But why, Scoville asked, was it necessary that the President be removed? If the party had continued as it was, Guiteau explained patiently, the Democrats would have taken control of the government and, by their inevitable mismanagement of the nation's finances, would have precipitated another civil war. The safety of the nation depended upon the Republican party maintaining unity and dominance.

The Democratic party and the rebel element were not yet sufficiently civilized, to use a term, to take possession of the national finances. That was the idea put into all the stump speeches and into all the newspapers during the canvass.

Such chances could not be taken; the Republican party must not be allowed to split, must not be allowed to lose control of the national government.

Throughout the defendant's testimony, Scoville kept emphasizing Guiteau's belief in inspiration, in the habitual interposition of Providence in human affairs. Charles was happy to document this point; he had survived a collision at sea in which many other passengers had died, had survived a jump from a speeding train—and, Guiteau concluded, been shot at three times and still lived.

> . . . it did not disturb my equilibrium any [Guiteau explained
> to the court], I thought the Lord would take care of me.
> I want to say right here in reference to protection, that the
> Deity himself will protect me; that He has used all these
> soldiers, and these experts, and this honorable court, and these
> counsel, to serve Him and protect me. That is my theory
> about protection. The Lord is no fool, and when He has got
> anything to do He uses the best means He can to carry
> out His purposes.

And, Charles claimed, he was not only protected from physical harm by divine providence, but had been divinely inspired on at least four occasions. The first was when he entered the Community, the second when he left for New York to establish the *Theocrat*. His third true inspiration commanded him to leave a successful law practice and begin lecturing for the Lord; the fourth bade him remove the President. He had never, the defendant explained, felt any malice toward Garfield, but simply carried out the Divine Will—and in doing so saved the nation from a second dreadful civil war. "Some of these days," he snapped, "instead of saying 'Guiteau the assassin', they will say 'Guiteau the patriot'."

On Wednesday afternoon, after two days of direct examination, John K. Porter began the government's cross-examination. The former judge was the most prestigious of the attorneys at the prosecution table, a courtroom lawyer of the old school, fond of rhetorical flights and moralistic set pieces, and—surprisingly for a man past middle age—still almost tireless. His strategy was confidently direct. The government would attempt to show that Guiteau had excellent control of his memory and reasoning power if perhaps a somewhat exaggerated view of his own abilities. Most important, Porter intended to hammer away at Guiteau's flaws of character, seeking to prove that he was no pitiable madman, but an habitual petty swindler and sensualist. Porter planned as well to emphasize the methodical care devoted to the crime, detailed preparations far beyond the capability of a disordered mind.

Porter retraced Guiteau's checkered career with the defendant, arguing at point after point that what the defense had claimed to be the symptoms of illness were in reality the consequences of sin. Had he, he asked Guiteau for example, been "strictly virtuous" at the Oneida Community? ("Mostly virtuous as a matter of fact," Guiteau amended his earlier statement.) The experienced cross-examiner forced Guiteau to admit repeatedly that he expected the President's assassination to increase the sale of his book—clearly a motive for the crime. Similarly, Porter sought to show how the details of the shooting implied conscious design, not inspiration. "Who bought the pistol," he asked, "the Deity or you?" "I say the Deity inspired the act," the prisoner answered excitedly, "and the Deity will take care of it." Porter ploughed on relentlessly: "Were you inspired to buy that British bull-dog pistol?"

I do not claim [Guiteau answered impatiently] that I was to do the specific act; but I do claim that the Deity inspired me to remove the President, and I had to use my ordinary judgment as to the ways and means to accomplish the Deity's will.

"Did it occur to you," Porter asked sarcastically, "that there was a commandment, "Thou shalt not kill'?" "If it did," Guiteau answered, "the divine authority overcame the written law."

And so on and on. Porter was a most persistent questioner, Guiteau a picture of frustration, unable to explain the simple truth of his inspiration to the older man. Thus Porter sought to identify Guiteau's inspiration with blasphemy: what else was the prisoner's habitual reference to being in the employ of Jesus Christ and Company? But why had you, Porter asked accusingly, been chosen among all men for this task? How could you be sure that it was God, rather than the Evil One, who inspired an act normally so repugnant to men of religious principle?

I claim [the prisoner explained] that I am a man of destiny. I want to tell you and the public that I am a man of destiny. You spoke of Napoleon. Napoleon claimed that he was a man of destiny, but he was on a very different kind of work from me. I claim that I am a man of destiny as much as the Savior, or Paul, or Martin Luther . . . the Deity never employs a fool to do His work; . . . He put the inspiration into my brain and my heart, and let me work it out in my own way.

Porter delighted as well in ridiculing Guiteau's theological pretensions—quoting Noyes's *Berean* to prove that the defendant had simply plagiarized his religious ideas from the Oneida Community's founder.

It became clear by the second day of cross-examination that Porter also intended simply to wear Guiteau down, and to do so by covering each point in mindless detail. With fatigue, he must have felt, Guiteau's true mental condition would manifest itself. By noon on Thursday, with another full day of cross-examination still to come, both questioner and prisoner were exhausted; even the indefatigable Porter had to take a seat. And Guiteau became increasingly bitter and indignant throughout the day as Porter probed those aspects of his career in which Guiteau took least pride. Charles began to broadly imitate Porter's overblown manner in his answers, to lean forward and glare at the New York lawyer. At one point, he asked Porter to stop shaking his bony fingers in his face; it was well known, he shouted, that Porter was the meanest and hardest man in the New York bar. After Thursday's testimony—at Guiteau's request, the court adjourned a bit before three—the defendant was visibly exhausted. He appeared gray and haggard, by afternoon unable to arouse even his usual indignation at Porter's baiting questions. "Can't you see, Judge," Mrs. Scoville said to Porter as they left the courtroom, "how rapidly he is burning out." She begged him not to extend the cross-examination. It was not until late Friday, however, that he excused the witness.

It was, indeed, so late in the day that Scoville had time to call only one witness before court was adjourned. This was Dr. Alexander Neil, a Columbus, Ohio physician. Neil explained that he had spoken with Guiteau several years before when the prisoner tried to sell him a theological pamphlet. There had been no doubt in his mind that the itinerant evangelist was insane. On Saturday morning, the defense finally managed to bring Emory Storrs to the witness stand; Storrs was a prominent lawyer, an influential Illinois Republican, and one of the men with whom Charles identified intensely. (Storrs, it will be recalled, was Guiteau's original choice for the management of his defense.) Like Charles Reed, Storrs had known Guiteau in Chicago, but casually as he knew scores of other beginners in the law. What, Scoville asked, did he as an experienced attorney think of Guiteau's mental condition? "I shall not," he answered warily, "express any opinion whatever as to Guiteau's sanity or insanity, or as to the character of any mental difficulty under which he might be laboring. My impression was that he had an illy-balanced mind, and that he did not have what the average man calls common good sense." Whatever support Storrs' oblique testimony might have given the defense was soon undercut: Walter Davidge, who cross-examined Storrs, played the prosecution's strongest logical card. Have you ever seen anything in the prisoner, he asked, which might have suggested that he lacked the capacity to distinguish between right and wrong? "No," Storrs replied immediately and decidedly, "I have never seen anything in Mr. Guiteau which led me to believe that he could not distinguish between right and wrong."

After a quiet Sunday, the court met an hour late on Monday morning, at 11:08. The defense immediately called their first important expert witness, Dr. James G. Kiernan of Chicago. Kiernan was a man of character, and a zealous and evangelically righteous disciple of positivistic science. Like Spitzka, he was a German-oriented neurologist opposed personally and intellectually to the established leadership of the asylum superintendent's association. Kiernan was born in New York City in 1852 and graduated in 1874 from the College of Medicine of the University of the City of New York. After graduation, Kiernan worked as an assistant physician and apothecary at the Ward's Island asylum until 1878, when he was dismissed by the hospital's superintendent, A. E. MacDonald. There were two reasons for his dismissal, Kiernan charged at the time, and neither reflected any discredit on himself. First was his refusal to sign a death certificate stating that a patient had died of some innocuous infection when he had, as a matter of fact, been beaten to death. Secondly, Kiernan explained, he had had the poor judgment to comment favorably at a meeting of the New York Neurological Society on one of Spitzka's papers attacking the leadership of the asylum superintendents' association. Soon after his dismissal, Kiernan left New York for Chicago where he began a long and distinguished career as a medical writer, teacher, psychiatrist, and would-be reformer of the state's notoriously corrupt asylum system. (A task in which he was not only threatened, but on at least three occasions assaulted physically.) By mid-1881, the hardworking young man had already established himself in Chicago. In February of 1881 he had assumed the managing editorship of the *Chicago*

Medical Review and a bit later in the same year had begun to lecture on nervous and mental diseases at the Chicago Medical College.

Kiernan was still a staunch, indeed embittered, opponent of the psychiatric establishment. In an editorial on "The Early Treatment of the Insane," in the *Chicago Medical Review* for July 20, 1881, for example, he endorsed the idea "that long residence in an insane asylum has a deteriorating effect on a mediocre mind. That such effect is exerted is shown," he could not resist adding, "by the occurrence of insanity among superintendents." Unfortunately for Guiteau, Kiernan's youthful zeal outweighed his caution; he was to prove a most indiscreet witness. Even as he grew older and more experienced, Kiernan never lost his reputation as a whimsically ineffective expert witness.

There was a good deal of interest in the courtroom as the youthful physician was called to the stand; he was the first psychiatric expert in a proceeding that promised to revolve about the testimony of many such specialists. After stating Kiernan's qualifications, Scoville immediately disclosed the strategy he was to follow in handling expert testimony; he chose to elicit Kiernan's opinion by asking him a hypothetical question. It was, contemporaries agreed however, even less illuminating than most specimens of what was considered a generally unfortunate genre. It was only to be expected, of course, that an attorney would frame a hypothetical question in his favor; Scoville's question, however, not only assumed as true each of the defense's many contentions, but was so strongly worded that, as several observers noted, it asked in effect whether an insane man were in fact insane. The wording of the question leaves no doubt of this criticism's validity. "I wish," Scoville began,

to propose to you this question: Assume it to be a fact that there was a strong hereditary taint of insanity in the blood of the prisoner at the bar; also that at about the age of thirty-five years his mind was so much deranged that he was a fit

subject to be sent to an insane asylum; also that at different
times from that date during the next succeeding five years he
manifested such decided symptoms of insanity, without
simulation, that many different persons conversing with him
and observing his conduct believed him to be insane; also that
during the month of June, 1881, at about the expiration of
said term of five years, he honestly became dominated by the
idea that he was inspired of God to remove by death the
President of the United States; also that he acted upon what he
believed to be such inspiration, and what he believed to be
in accordance with the Divine will, in preparation for and in
the accomplishment of such a purpose; also that he committed
the act of shooting the President under what he believed to
be a Divine command which he was not at liberty to disobey,
and which belief amounted to a conviction that controlled
his conscience and over-powered his will as to that act, so that
he could not resist the mental pressure upon him; also that
immediately after the shooting he appeared calm and as
one relieved by the performance of a great duty; also that there
was no other adequate motive for the act than the conviction
that he was executing the Divine will for the good of his
country—assuming all these propositions to be true, state
whether in your opinion the prisoner was sane or insane at the
time of shooting President Garfield?

A. Assuming those to be true, I should say the prisoner was
insane.

Q. Would you have any doubt about it?

A. No, sir.

Mr. Scoville. Take the witness, gentlemen.

Thus abruptly—and as he must have thought, with an air
of triumphant elegance—Scoville turned his witness over
for cross-examination. His direct examination had taken
no more time than that required to identify the witness and
read to him this omnibus hypothetical question.

"What is your age?" Davidge asked as he abruptly began
his cross-examination. "I shall be thirty," Kiernan admitted,
"on the 18th of next June." "Do you," the Washington attorney quickly added, "believe in a future state of rewards
and punishments?" "No, sir," Kiernan replied without

hesitation. For many of the jurors, Kiernan's testimony could, from that moment, be disregarded. The experienced cross-examiner next established that Kiernan's editorial and professorial positions were recent acquisitions and that he had, indeed, been dismissed from his assistant physician's post at the Ward's Island Asylum. (Dr. Gray's preparations had been careful.) He forced Kiernan to admit, moreover, that he had acted for a time as apothecary as well as assistant physician—without mentioning that such duties were often a part of a junior staff member's tasks at such institutions. Then, insinuatingly, he asked, whether Kiernan had ever had anything to do with a drug store (which, of course, the young man denied).

Unwilling to concede even the smallest point to the defense and sensing an opportunity to use Kiernan's own inexperience to discredit the position he endorsed, Davidge kept the young man on the stand for a lengthy cross-examination. As with most of the expert witnesses who were to follow Kiernan to the stand, the first explicitly psychiatric questions addressed to him sought to elicit a definition of insanity. One element in the Chicago neurologist's definition which particularly attracted his questioner's interest was Kiernan's statement that insanity could exist without "delusion, hallucination, or illusion." (At the time, of course, no more than a truism.) Kiernan next conceded that he did believe in what many writers called "moral insanity." This did not mean, Kiernan amended his statement, as was often assumed, that he believed a man's moral nature might be diseased while his mind remained sound. "The mind I regard as an entity," he explained, "when the moral nature is diseased, the mind is diseased." But what then, Davidge asked, if a man claimed to be inspired yet acted not as a maniac, but "all through as a vulgar and wicked criminal?" Should this not constitute presumptive evidence against the genuineness of his inspiration—or madness? Kiernan had to confess that this was true. ("There is nothing vulgar about this case;" Guiteau interrupted, "it is all high-toned.") Davidge then quietly returned the witness for redirect cross-examination.

Scoville again—and it would seem unwisely—returned to the subject of his witness's religious views and to his feud with MacDonald at Ward's Island, reinforcing, of course, the impression that Kiernan was a youthful hot-head. "I am," he answered Scoville, "like a great many other scientific men, what is called an agnostic. I do not accept the possibility of a future state of rewards and punishments," he explained patiently to the jury, "because I have no positive knowledge of it"; but for the same reason, Kiernan continued, he did not categorically reject such a possibility. He would simply not commit himself without more definite knowledge. Scoville then turned his youthful witness back to the attentions of the prosecution's cross-examiners.

District Attorney Corkhill now assumed this role and almost at once began questioning Kiernan in regard to his psychiatric doctrines, covering and sometimes even repeating exactly points brought up in Davidge's original cross-examination. Kiernan almost immediately criticized traditional—and legally hallowed—definitions of insanity for their emphasis upon a distinct behavioral change invariably marking the onset of mental illness. There was, Kiernan maintained, an innate form of insanity, one which the German psychiatric association had agreed several years previously to call *primäre Verrücktheit*.* That is, he explained to Corkhill, primary or original insanity. ("Is that the same as original sin?" Corkhill asked facetiously.) No, Kiernan elaborated his somewhat unfamiliar point, I did not mean idiocy or imbecility—the two forms of mental illness traditionally accepted as congenital—but simply individuals born insane, individuals whose behavioral characteristics did not essentially change during life. They were born insane and would die insane, though at certain periods of life—as puberty—their symptoms often intensified. These patients

* This diagnosis was a clinical predecessor of paranoia.

were easily irritated, unable to tell right from wrong, prone to embark upon visionary schemes. "They have not," he elaborated the sensitive point, "in a strict sense of the word any conscience. They are guided purely by utilitarian matters in connection with their ideas of right and wrong." He then explained to the District Attorney, and in his most patient manner, that this had to be considered a teratological problem; the "originally insane" person was born with an asymmetrical skull, one half invariably larger than the other, "the asymmetry of the skull [being] identified with the asymmetry of the brain." But skull shape, Kiernan cautioned, was not in itself absolute proof of insanity, only a symptom to be considered in connection with other such signs in reaching a final diagnosis. Not only, Kiernan continued, could one correlate behavioral symptoms during life with this asymmetry, "but after death we find in these cases certain conditions of the brain that must have existed from birth, certain deficiencies." The legal implications of the Kiernan view were unmistakable: what could be salvaged of traditional concepts of free will and individual responsibility should heredity thus underlie antisocial behavior—indeed, make it quite impossible for the criminal to act other than as he did?

The cross-examination then turned to the problem of simulation. How, Corkhill asked, could the physician detect malingering? It was ordinarily no problem at all, the witness replied; in fact the simulator was usually much easier to detect than the person genuinely insane. The most common belief among simulators, Kiernan explained, is that the insane lose their memory and are completely unable to relate to the world around them. ("My memory is remarkably good," Guiteau crowed in interruption; "there is no simulation about me. I go straight.") But then Kiernan was maneuvered into making another admission damaging to the defense. He conceded that the insane might well be motivated by the same emotions as normal persons. "The asylums," he admitted, "are nearly all run on the principle that an insane man is guided by ordinary motives in life. I myself have had patients whom I have paroled upon conditions that they would not stray from a certain place or indulge in certain demonstrations." The implication was clear enough: the insane too might be responsible, responsible that is in the sense of being amenable to the threat of punishment. Thus another argument for the utility of the M'Naghten rule—or so at least it seemed to many editorialists and some physicians.

Kiernan had thus far made no really disastrous statement after his opening confession of agnosticism. It was too good to last. Walter Davidge, who had again assumed the role of cross-examiner, now artfully managed to conclude his questioning of the Chicago alienist on a note of comforting ridicule. It was clear, he began innocently enough, that standards of insanity varied widely; according to your experience, he asked Kiernan, what proportions of persons not already in asylums would you say were insane? Kiernan, in his usual earnest fashion, replied without hesitation:

A. ... I have not any exact statistics, but I know that probably out of twenty-five people in ordinary life, you would be apt to meet five who were insane, and sooner or later would become inmates of insane asylums.

Q. That is that one man or woman in every five, either is insane or is going to be?

A. Well, I would not put it that way exactly.

Mr. Davidge. That is a liberal and most encouraging prospect for all of us. (Laughter) ...

By Mr. Scoville. Q. Will you explain a little further what you mean by saying one man in every five is insane—if that is it?

A. I meant to say simply this: That if I went into ordinary business, or was talking with twenty-five men in ordinary life, I should probably find five insane men. ...

By Mr. Davidge. Q. Even among business men?

A. Yes, sir; among business men I might find that number.

Of course, Kiernan relentlessly expanded his disastrous explanation, among the dissipated, among persons with no regular occupation, "floating in the world," the proportion of insanity would certainly be higher. It was almost as though Kiernan had said to the jury: "I am a rash, impractical, almost ridiculously earnest young man." Davidge was more than pleased as he allowed the youthful neurologist to leave the witness stand.

After Kiernan's testimony, Scoville called to the stand seven more psychiatrists. In each case, however, he contented himself with putting to his witness the same hypothetical question asked Dr. Kiernan. Each of the seven answered that the person described must certainly have been insane; Scoville then simply dismissed each witness. Wisely, the prosecution waived cross-examination of the seven, content simply to emphasize that these diagnoses were based upon the assumed truth of the numerous circumstances presented in Scoville's ponderous hypothetical question. Legal observers agreed that Scoville had, in effect, squandered his expert witnesses. This was clearly unfortunate in the case of W. W. Godding, who as superintendent of the government asylum was well known to Washingtonians. A number of the defense experts were, in addition, far more experienced and better known than the hot-tempered Kiernan—Charles H. Nichols, for example, superintendent of New York's Bloomingdale Asylum, or Charles Folsom of Harvard and the McLean Asylum in Boston. His failure to examine Nichols in detail may well have been Scoville's most serious mistake. Nichols had been superintendent of the District's asylum for a quarter-century and was known for his piety and approachability; Godding, indeed, thought it likely that Nichols knew every juryman personally.

Probably more influential with the jury than this abortive succession of medical witnesses was the testimony of two laymen, Richard Hinton, a Washington editor, and Charles Farwell, representative from Chicago in the House and one of the men whom Guiteau had hoped would back his *Inter-Ocean* venture some years earlier. Colonel Hinton was questioned about Guiteau's political career and especially his speech, "Garfield versus Hancock." "On reading the speech," Hinton replied, "I regarded it as an ill-jointed and utterly inconsequential production and remembered at the time—the day after the assassination—distinctly, that this man used to be around headquarters and that he was the laughing-stock where he was not an annoyance to everybody about the room." Guiteau was furious; his speech, he shouted,

was very highly spoken of by the best men in the nation. Mr. Scoville had no business to put you on the stand either, and he must not put any more of this expert fool business on the stand. I don't take any stock in this kind of business because I am not a fool. I would rather be hung as a man than acquitted as a fool.

But Guiteau's faulty estimation of his political abilities did not, of course, prove him insane.

Farwell's testimony was far stronger, coming as it did from a successful man of affairs, who had, moreover, known Guiteau years before Charles undertook his political career. The prominent Chicagoan explained that Guiteau had some years previously approached him in regard to the purchase of the *Inter-Ocean*. He had found his way into Farwell's office and handed him a sheaf of lengthy and disconnected editorials—samples of those which were to appear in the paper. Charles promised that if Farwell lent him $200,000, he would make the Chicago merchant President of the United States. Farwell recalled as well having seen the assassin twice in Washington during the spring after Garfield's election. (Guiteau maintained a tenacious grasp on even the most casual acquaintance.) On both occasions the bedraggled office seeker importuned him for letters of endorsement to the State Department and President. "I never," Farwell stated firmly, "thought him a sane man from those two interviews." Davidge did, however, retrieve some ground by forcing Farwell to concede that he never thought Guiteau so insane as to be unable to distinguish between right and wrong.

The defense concluded its direct testimony with a reading of passages from Guiteau's book, *The Truth,* and from handbills Charles had had printed advertising his books and lectures. "Just out," one read,

A book for every one to read. 'The Truth: A Companion to the Bible.' By Charles J. Guiteau, lawyer, theologian, and lecturer. Read it, and get some new and important ideas. It is handsomely printed, and contains: 1, a reply to recent attacks on the Bible; 2, an oration on Paul, the apostle, presenting an enlarged view of this wonderful character, and giving a vivid account of his life, sufferings and great work for the Master. . . . 4, a review of Christianity from the destruction of Jerusalem to the present time, presenting among other things a condensed view of the great work of Luther, Calvin, Wesley, and Messrs. Moody and Sankey; 5. Some thoughts on the final judgment. Price, 50 cents. Orders from the trade supplied by the Western News Company.

Before turning to the prosecution's testimony in rebuttal, Scoville asked permission to call later on Dr. Edward C. Spitzka; he had, he explained, telegraphed the New York neurologist asking him to testify but had not as yet received a reply. This was late Tuesday, December 7.

When Spitzka did not answer the bailiff's call on Wednesday morning, Scoville rose and asked the judge for an attachment, explaining that he had written and telegraphed his prospective witness three or four times during the past few days. Judge Cox granted the defense its attachment before the prosecution began its testimony in rebuttal.

The government produced dozens of witnesses, relentlessly accumulating almost eight hundred pages of testimony before concluding its presentation. Almost all was dedicated to proving Guiteau an example of depravity, not mental illness. Corkhill began with General William Sherman and continued with witnesses from every part of the country and all walks of life. They chronicled in detail a life of unalloyed vice and selfishness. The prosecution sought as well to show that those members of the Guiteau family pictured by the defense as insane, were in reality quite normal.

They called, for example, the Reverend R. S. McArthur, pastor of New York's Calvary Baptist Church. The clergyman's testimony established not only that Guiteau had borrowed money under false pretenses, but that he had taken his wife's wages and spent it on prostitutes, thus contracting a "vile and loathsome" disease—all of which Guiteau had admitted and as a consequence of which he was expelled from Dr. McArthur's church. Scoville, of course, objected that such testimony was irrelevant and prejudicial and should not be allowed. Corkhill replied vigorously: "We are showing this," he explained to the court, "to settle the question that what the defense calls insanity is nothing more than devilish depravity." ("Great applause," the court's stenographer noted.) The judge failed to sustain Scoville's objection; in general, he conceded, Scoville was correct—one could not prove a charge against a defendant by proving another one to be true. This, however, was an atypical case. The defense had probed exhaustively into all phases of the prisoner's life in an effort to prove him insane; the prosecution should have an equal right to explore his past in the hope of proving his actions a consequence of moral depravity rather than mental incompetence.

The most spectacular among the prosecution's numerous witnesses came as a complete surprise to the defense. He was one D. McLane Shaw, a marginal lawyer from whom Guiteau had rented office space when he first began practice in New York. Shaw seemed quite nervous, as one reporter described him, with a weak face, flushed inside a fringe of dark whiskers; his facial muscles twitched constantly.

Shaw testified that he had, some years before, rented a suite of offices at 59 Liberty Street and in 1871 had sublet one of the rooms to Guiteau. A year or so later, Shaw continued, he had asked the Chicagoan to find another office, for he disapproved of his tenant's questionable business practices. Guiteau had, for example, boasted of passing off a burnished brass watch as gold so as to cheat a pawnbroker, just as he had boasted of borrowing money from his minister with no intention of repaying it. "From the first I knew him," Shaw testified, "I knew that he was vain and egotistical, and had a desire to be in the prints; a desire for publicity." Once, in fact, he had said that if he could not get a reputation for good he would get one for evil—that he would imitate John Wilkes Booth and shoot some of our public men, even if he were to hang for it. ("You are a liar," Guiteau shouted, unable any longer to control himself, "a low, dirty, liar. . . . It is a falsehood from beginning to end. . . . A man with a face such as that to come here and lie about me! It is enough to make anybody mad, you lying whelp!")

Several days later, it might be noted parenthetically, the defense was able to show that Shaw had not long before narrowly escaped conviction—and a jail sentence—for perjury in a New Jersey court.

Shaw's testimony closed Saturday's proceedings and provided reporters with leads for their Sunday stories. Monday morning, however, was a bring a new and even more significant witness; Dr. Spitzka had arrived on Sunday in response to the court's attachment. The prosecution, as they had agreed, interrupted its procession of witnesses and allowed the New Yorker to take the stand.

6

ENTER DR. SPITZKA

It is not hard to understand Scoville's insistence that Spitzka appear. The outspoken immigrant's son was not only a most vocal foe of John Gray, of the leadership in the asylum superintendent's association, and of the M'Naghten rule, but had made abundantly clear his opinion of Guiteau's mental condition well before the beginning of the trial. In the New York *Medical Record,* in the *Chicago Medical Review,* in the *New England Medical Monthly,* he had declared vigorously that Guiteau was—in so many words—as mad as a hatter. Spitzka had, for example, written in the October 29th issue of the *Medical Record* under the signature "Philalethas":

There is not a scintilla of doubt in my mind, that if Guiteau with his hereditary history, his insane manner, his insane documents and his insane actions were to be committed to any asylum in the land, he would be unhesitatingly admitted as a proper subject for sequestration. . . . A thorough study will convince an impartial and competent jury of medical examiners, before whom such a case should be laid, that Guiteau is not only now insane, but that he was never anything else, that his crime was the offspring of insanity, and that in every act he will betray the characteristic features of querulent monomania. They will also conclude that, inasmuch as his insanity is not the result of his own vices, but based on a defective organization inherited from a diseased ancestry, anything like responsibility, complete or partial, is out of the question. . . .

It would be a great misfortune if the case ever came before a jury, Spitzka concluded. And should Guiteau be hanged

—as it appeared he must—it would be nothing but a formal lynch process, a permanent reflection on American jurisprudence. It was no secret in neurological circles that Spitzka and Philalethas were the same and psychiatrists friendly to the defense soon warmly recommended Spitzka to Scoville. The young neurologist remained, however, unwilling to appear until Scoville obtained the court's attachment. (As late as November 2, Spitzka had written to the New York *Times,* denying reports that he would be a witness in the case and pointing out that he had declined invitations from both defense and prosecution.)

Though the same age as Kiernan, Spitzka possessed a good deal more self-assurance and courtroom experience. He made, as well, a reassuring appearance, blonde and open-faced, his cheeks fringed with sandy whiskers. Scoville began the examination of his witness by eliciting Spitzka's qualifications: that he had studied for several years in Vienna, that he was a specialist in nervous disease, that he frequently appeared as an expert witness—and that an essay of his on the somatic etiology of insanity had won a prize of a hundred guineas in a competition sponsored by the British Medico-Psychological Association.

Scoville had obviously been convinced that it would be unwise to depend exclusively upon his hypothetical question. He asked Spitzka instead whether he had examined the prisoner. Yes, the witness conceded, and he would state his diagnosis, "if the court compels me." The result of his examination, Spitzka then answered, was easily stated: he had found the prisoner to be unquestionably insane. But, Scoville explored, what sort of insanity did the prisoner exhibit? What were his characteristic symptoms? "I may say," Spitzka replied,

that would be very difficult for me to render clear to any jury not composed of experts. I can simply say that the marked feature of this man's insanity, is a tendency to delusive or insane opinion, and to the creation of morbid or fantastical projects; that there is a marked element of imbecility of

judgment, and while I had no other evidence than the
expression of his face, I should have no doubt that he was also
a moral imbecile, or rather a moral monstrosity.

The most conclusive evidence, Spitzka continued, lay in
the prisoner"'s eyes and general appearance: "I concluded
that I had an insane man to deal with on sight, before I
asked him any questions. He has got the insane manner as
well marked as I have ever seen it in an asylum." Guiteau's
retentive memory and quick replies were, on the other
hand, no evidence for or against insanity. Only now did
Scoville revert to his hypothetical question (which Spitzka
at first refused to answer on the ground that the results of
his own examination had not been included in it). After
some fumbling, Scoville finally reached the crucial question: "Was he insane on the 2nd day of July last, at the time
he shot the President?" "I should say," the witness answered,

that the prisoner, whom I examined, had been in a more or
less morbid state throughout his life, and that he was
probably insane at the time you mention.

Take the witness, Scoville concluded.

Walter Davidge, entrusted with the cross-examination,
seemed at first uncertain of the best means of handling this
self-assured witness. He began by attempting to reaffirm
the logic of the M'Naghten rule, having Spitzka define insanity, then forcing him to admit that there were degrees of
insanity which rendered a person irresponsible, while
others did not. But even the inexperienced Scoville objected immediately, an objection sustained by Judge Cox;
it was a question of law, not fact. "I hold," Judge Cox
explained, "that a medical expert cannot say whether a
man may be responsible or irresponsible in the law."

With this tentative thrust parried, Davidge turned to the
more serious task of undermining the witness's credibility.
First, he asked Spitzka whether he had ever applied un-
successfully for asylum positions and forced him to admit

having made inquiries on three separate occasions. On
another occasion, Spitzka claimed, A. E. MacDonald,
superintendent of New York's Ward's Island Asylum—
and at that moment sitting at the prosecution table—had
solicited his application for an appointment as special
pathologist. Then Davidge blandly asked whether Spitzka
had ever been a professor in a medical college. No, Spitzka
admitted, but he had served as professor of comparative
anatomy at the Columbia Veterinary College. Davidge
pressed forward, exploiting what seemed a vulnerable point:

Q. What sort of a college is that?

A. It is a college where physicians are instructed in the art
of treating the lower animals.

Q. Horses mainly, I suppose?

A. Yes, sir. The branch I taught is one taught in medical
schools.

Q. Yes?

A. The branch that is pursued by such men as Thomas
Huxley, by Baron Cuvier, by Haeckel, and other of our most
eminent scientists. I have no reason to be ashamed of it.

Mr. Davidge. I do not say you need be ashamed of it.

The witness. The question has been asked me before or
suggested from a special quarter. I know this comes from the
same quarter now, and I have expected it, and it is done
with the purpose of casting a reflection upon the witness.

Q. All the celebrated gentlemen whose names you have
mentioned belong to what are called horse doctors?

A. I never have treated any other animal but the ass, and
that animal had two legs, and therefore, I could not consider
myself a veterinary physician, but a human professional.

Q. You are a veterinary surgeon, are you not?

A. In the sense that I treat asses who ask me stupid
questions, I am.

The laughter of the courtroom was directed now at Davidge
and the older man quickly dropped the subject. Are you,
he abruptly asked Spitzka, what is known as a professional
witness? Certainly not, the young neurologist answered, in
the currently accepted meaning of the term—a physician,

that is, who would sell his testimony to the highest bidder; he would, however, accept an appropriate fee for appearing in court and testifying to the truth as he saw it. "As to the value of my services in this case," he added acidly, "I do not receive enough to take me to Jersey City." And now Spitzka once again turned the cross-examiner's insinuations against the prosecution. "If I had desired to sell my services," he continued, "or to sell my conviction, I would be sitting by you as one of the experts for the prosecution." Judge Porter—at Davidge's insistence, Spitzka now swore to the incident—had visited him in his office on October 31 and asked whether he would be available to serve as a prosecution witness. Spitzka declined, explaining to Porter that he would appear for neither side, but that he certainly could not appear for the prosecution as he was firmly convinced of Guiteau's insanity.

On what grounds, Davidge asked, quickly shifting the emphasis of his questioning, could you have founded so fixed an opinion without having examined the patient? "Upon the man's insane documents," Spitzka answered,

the insane expression in a good picture which I saw, and his hereditary history as stated in the papers, and the almost unanimous interpretation made by the laity at the time and shortly before and after the crime of his mental condition.

Of course, Spitzka then explained, my present position is more defensible, for it is now based on an examination of the defendant.

The prosecution counsel were furious at Spitzka; in a day when a flair for personal abuse constituted important equipment for a trial lawyer, the young physician had beaten a number of experienced attorneys at their own game—and in so doing increased his own credibility. Spitzka's cross-examiners were, as we have seen, driven to extremes of innuendo; on at least three separate occasions, Judge Cox had had to defend the witness. The prosecution was, however, unwilling to allow Spitzka to leave the stand without forcing him to elaborate his somewhat controversial psychiatric views. They began by insisting that Spitzka reconstruct his entire interview with the prisoner, explaining what had taken place and why he had reached the conclusions he had.

Spitzka began his narrative confidently. In order to reduce the possibility of dissimulation, he explained, he had introduced himself to the prisoner as Professor Brown, the well-known phrenologist, placed atropine in the assassin's eyes, and then examined the shape of Guiteau's head. (He commenced with his examination of the prisoner's head, Spitzka explained, assuming that the prisoner would interpret it as a "phrenological dodge." And what, Davidge asked quizzically, was a phrenological dodge? "Phrenology is not a science," Spitzka lectured, "it is charlatanism; and all the procedures of a charlatan are dodges.") After some discussion of the assassination's political background, Spitzka continued, Guiteau became uncontrollably agitated, shouting as he discussed the trial and especially the injustice of the prosecution which had hired perjurers to blacken his name. "And so on," Spitzka concluded,

through a regular farrago of the kind that is familiar to those who visit the wards of a lunatic asylum. That will about comprise what I found of his mental condition; I found his memory good; I found that he had the legal attainments, as far as I have a right to pass an opinion, of a third-rate shyster of a criminal court; he displayed a certain amount of judgment certainly; he parried questions to answer those he preferred to answer, and betrayed great egotism in everything he said.

Had you drawn any conclusions, Davidge asked, about his knowledge of right and wrong? Of course, Spitzka answered, since he had been a lawyer I had no doubt that he was aware of the usual legal consequences of criminal acts—but, of course, Spitzka quickly added, he could not accept this as a test of responsibility.

What had impressed him most, Spitzka continued, was the prisoner's "tendency to insane delusion, morbid projects, and . . . delusive opinion." "Well," Davidge interrupted, "do not give me too much to carry. You found tendency to insane delusions and what else?" "Delusive opinion," Spitzka continued in his lecturing manner,

I mean a phenomenon frequently exhibited by those having the insane constitution, a tendency to misinterpret the real affairs of life, especially those of a complex nature, and to interpret those affairs in some way as having connection with themselves, the starting point being the exaggerated self-feeling of the morbid egotist in this case.

These delusive and extravagant opinions, Spitzka continued, manifested themselves—as every man sitting in the court room was aware—in the formation of morbid projects. Guiteau's life had been a succession of such projects; they could not and had not ceased with the assassination—only death would bring them to an end.

He told me [Spitzka continued], as positively and sincerely as a man could, that when he got out of the jail he felt firmly convinced that the American people would never allow him to die a disgraceful death in consideration of what he had done for them, and he would go to Europe for three or four months, and then he would come back and lecture, and he expected to make a great success at lecturing. That was a morbid project in anticipation of the future. I became convinced, in my examination of him, that the crime for which the man stands indicted was the result of a morbid project rather than of a delusion strictly speaking—delusive opinion entering into the crime.

Of course—Spitzka stopped diplomatically to explain his somewhat technical terminology to the court—the shooting of the President could be explained as the result of a delusion, only if one defined delusion quite broadly; it was more immediately the result of Guiteau's tendency to form such morbid projects, projects based on delusive opinion. "I did not find anything which I would call in the strictest and narrowest sense a fixed delusion."

And now Spitzka emphasized a point to which he was to return again and again. The morbid quality of Guiteau's mental processes had existed since birth. The defendant had not a diseased brain, but an imperfect one. "He was," Spitzka continued his exposition, "to use a very good popular term, a brain monstrosity, a congenital malformation of the brain, presumably, as far as we are entitled to form an opinion as to what the condition of the brain here is."

Davidge, however, returned the questioning to Spitzka's emphasis upon Guiteau's propensity for the formation of morbid projects. It was the word morbid he objected to and its implication of mental disease; why, he challenged, were they not simply depraved, criminal, projects? Depravity, morbidity—Davidge now pressed the point—how could one tell the difference? How could one assume that it was illness and not sin which motivated the President's assassin? There were no general answers to such a question, Spitzka explained; one had to consider the circumstances of any particular case. Guiteau's behavior was clearly the result of sickness. "Taking depravity as I understand it," Spitzka amplified his point, "criminal depravity, a man who had committed this crime from criminal motives would be only to glad to hide his head somewhere and not be seen again, if he were sane." Similarly, Guiteau's plan for lecturing to a grateful American public after a few months in Europe was not uncharacteristic of a certain class of lunatics—but hardly of the depraved criminal. These plans demonstrated his complete inability to evaluate the world of reality. Spitzka's testimony had now lasted all morning; the court recessed from twelve-thirty until half past one.

When they returned to the court room, Guiteau, who had been increasingly annoyed by newspaper treatment of the trial, leaped to his feet before the cross-examination could begin. "There are a good many poodle dogs in the newspaper business," he shouted,

and I want to express my utter contempt for some of those poodle dogs. I am glad to notice that the high-toned, conscientious press of the nation are saying, almost with one voice, that it will be a stain upon the American name if a jury should convict any man in my condition on the 2d of July, when I was precipitated upon the President.

"Shoot him now," a voice shouted from the front of the audience before Guiteau could be quieted and order finally reestablished.

With calm restored, Davidge turned immediately to what seemed the weak link in Spitzka's testimony, his reliance upon external, physical signs in confirming his diagnosis. He reminded Spitzka of his brash observation that one glance was sufficient to establish a diagnosis, that the defendant's face and expression were those of a moral imbecile or moral monstrosity. Spitzka did not equivocate, but strongly reaffirmed the validity of his reliance upon the defendant's appearance in making a diagnosis. He conceded, as well, that what he termed moral imbecility was a condition termed moral insanity by some authors. But, Davidge objected with elaborate sarcasm, the unsophisticated jurors, lawyers, and audience had still no idea what the learned physician meant by the term "moral monstrosity"? "By a moral monster," Spitzka explained.

I mean a person who is born with so defective a nervous organization that he is altogether deprived of that moral sense which is an integral and essential constituent of the normal human mind, he being analogous in that respect to the congenital cripple who is born speechless, or with one leg shorter than the other, or with any other monstrous development, that we now and again see.

There were a good many physical stigmata, Spitzka continued, which indicated Guiteau's peculiar mental status. One was the shape of his head and face, another defective innervation of the facial muscles, a third facial asymmetry and pronounced deviation of the tongue to the left. All these characteristics were easily seen, the young neurologist argued, in Guiteau's peculiar lopsided smile, a characteristic of a large proportion of "primary monomaniacs."

"Those," Spitzka concluded, "were the evidences that I found that he was born with a brain whose two sides are not equal." The presence of any one of these symptoms would not alone prove a man congenitally insane, but taken together and evaluated in conjunction with his pattern of behavior and the evidence of insanity in near relatives, they were quite conclusive. "I am inclined strongly to believe," Spitzka concluded vigorously, "and to affirm, as positively as science permits us to come to a conclusion, that it was a congenital moral defect."

Davidge then turned to a dissection of this tough-minded physician's clinical observations. Did Guiteau not reason logically, he pressed the New Yorker? Was it odd that a man on trial for his life should become excited and attack his accusers as liars? Every aspect of Spitzka's interview could be explained in terms of normal—if stress-distorted —behavior. True enough, Spitzka conceded, but Guiteau's excitement was not the normal excitement of heightened emotion, but rather a morbid excitement, indescribable in words, but easily demonstrated to any insane asylum visitor.

Spitzka remained calm throughout his endless cross-examination, despite the calculated badgering to which he was subjected. He had a foot ailment and had, for example, to overcome Corkhill's strenuous objections before he was allowed to take a chair. Throughout, of course, Spitzka was aware that his personal and professional enemies were sitting at the prosecution table, methodically prompting the government counsel in their questions. Finally, at one point, when Corkhill was unwilling to let him be seated on the ground that he would not then be able to see the witness's face, Spitzka ironically suggested: "You might move a couple of experts, and then I think Mr. Corkhill will be able to see my face."

Corkhill finally assumed the cross-examination; his tactics differed little from those employed by Davidge. Was it not true, he asked Spitzka, that he had once, when engaged to appear for one side in a case, taken a larger fee from the opposition, then changed both allegiance and opinion? "I am a witness and under attachment," Spitzka turned indignantly to the court, "I appear here unwillingly. I am asked questions that have no basis, and no earthly object but to run me down in the lowest fashion conceivable. There was no basis for that question. I would dare any one to make the assertion upon which that question was based." Certainly, Judge Cox reassured Spitzka, your answer is conclusive; the prosecution had no right to pursue such questions. Guiteau too was outraged at Corkhill's insinuations. "He has studied all over Europe and knows all this entire business of insanity," the defendant shouted scornfully; "He has studied in all the high-toned colleges of Europe, and then for him to come here and be insulted by this little bit of a scamp. Why, Corkhill, he wouldn't spit on you outside, among all his high-toned acquaintances; he wouldn't condescend to go to that extent."

The District Attorney then turned to Spitzka's ventures in medical journalism, to those articles written before the trial in which the New York neurologist had flatly declared Guiteau insane; Spitzka had clearly had a well-formed opinion before seeing the prisoner. The high point in Corkhill's cross-examination came when he read a passage from one of Spitzka's articles discussing the probable conduct of the trial. "Did you say this," the District Attorney asked:

Sane or insane, the narrow-minded official conducting this trial, whom Judge Hoar has already censured for his intemperate zeal, that has carried him on more than one occasion beyond the legal limits in this case, will find experts who will be only too willing to chime in with the public against what public prejudice stigmatizes as the insanity dodge.

A. Decidedly.
Q. To whom did you refer there?
A. I refer to you.

"Sensation," the court reporter noted; Spitzka was indeed a worthy antagonist. "I have repeatedly made the assertion," he finally explained sharply, "that in my opinion, and from my point of view the expert who would pronounce this man sane, positively, is either not an expert or not an honest one. That is my opinion."

And again, as Davidge had previously when cross-examining Dr. Kiernan, Corkhill brought up the question of religion, asking Spitzka whether he believed in God. "I refuse on principle," Spitzka replied, "to answer such a question; it seems to me impertinent in a country that guarantees civil and religious liberty." ("Irreligious liberty," Davidge intoned dramatically.) Later in the trial, whenever an opportunity presented itself, the prosecution counsel would refer to Spitzka as that "horse doctor," or atheist, or phrenologist. Such abuse implies at least some apprehension that Spitzka's strong testimony had made an impression on the jury. Guiteau enjoyed Spitzka's performance immensely, especially Corkhill's periodic discomfiture. "It is the unanimous opinion of the American people," he finally cackled, "that you are a consummate jackass, Corkhill, and if you had any self-respect you would go out West and go out digging."

Each of the three prosecution counsel had felt the sting of Spitzka's tongue and all were obviously furious with the quick-witted and confident young man. Perhaps indeed it would have been wiser for the prosecution not to have extended its cross-examination and thus increased Spitzka's opportunity to impress his views upon the jury. In any case, as soon as he had left the stand, the prosecution's strategy became unmistakably clear; they would drown his testimony in a sea of prestigious diagnoses—all agreeing upon the defendant's perfect sanity. Though originally scheduled to appear later in the trial, the prosecution immediately called one of their star medical witnesses to the stand vacated by Spitzka.

This was Fordyce Barker of New York. Dr. Barker was a man of commanding presence and a pillar of America's medical establishment. A professor of medicine for more than thirty years and in practice more than thirty-five, Dr. Barker bore the added dignity of serving, in 1881, as president of the New York Academy of Medicine; he had, moreover, he confessed just returned from London, where he had acted as vice-president of the recent International Medical Congress. The New York physician had, he explained, studied "mental disease almost constantly, practically on patients." Female patients he might have added, for Dr. Barker was a gynecologist, a fact which, oddly enough, did not come up in his direct examination.

The prosecution began by asking Barker to define insanity—a procedure which they were methodically to repeat with each succeeding medical witness. It was, Barker answered, a departure from the healthy condition of the organs or tissues of the body, "or a departure from the functions or healthy performance of the duties in that individual of those organs." Pressing this point, Judge Porter asked whether one did not always find in insanity either some verifiable organic change or marked alteration in behavior? One always found such changes, Barker affirmed: "we always find either one or the other, or both. It is not insanity where it does not exist." Porter hoped, of course, to reaffirm, in Barker's authoritative words, the traditional definition of insanity, especially its emphasis upon the necesary appearance of some tangible—often abrupt—change in behavior previously normal. Porter obviously sought to discredit Spitzka and Kiernan's contention that mental illness might be congenital.

Could insanity, Porter asked, ever be a hereditary disease? "There is," Barker replied without hesitation, "no such disease in science as hereditary insanity." There was, of course, Barker quickly amplified his position, a hereditary tendency to insanity; one could be born with a defective "nervous organization." One might, that is, succumb to environmental stress that would leave no psychological scars in those of normal mental endowment. Does the insanity of parents or grandparents, Porter continued, prove an individual to be more than ordinarily prone to mental illness? No, Barker replied, it does not necessarily prove it —although it may make it more likely. Does insanity, Porter pushed doggedly on, in an individual's brother or sister furnish any evidence as to his sanity? "It does not," Barker answered with wary ambiguity; "it may furnish some evidence of the constitution and temperament of the individual, but it proves nothing as to the individual." Barker's ingenuous testimony was to bring him criticism from medical contemporaries—for it constituted undeniably a strained attempt to minimize the importance of heredity in the etiology of insanity at a time when neither physicians nor laymen doubted its significance for a moment.

On the issue of moral insanity, Barker assumed an even more strained and arbitrary position. The New Yorker conceded, however, that insanity could exist without delusion. "A person," Barker explained,

may have the exercise of all the mental faculties, but by disease have his emotions and instincts so perverted, so changed from the normal or healthy action of those emotions or instincts as to destroy the power of the will to regulate his own conduct.

Porter, alarmed at this trend in his own witness's answer, quickly interrupted, asking whether this was the moral insanity so much discussed during the course of the trial. Of course not, Barker answered; moral insanity was quite different. "Moral insanity," Barker lectured,

is wickedness. It is a term which in medical science is not found as describing a form of insanity. It is a term loosely used to excuse or palliate conduct which on any other theory is indefensible.

Moral insanity, a controversial issue in American medical circles since at least the 1840's, had, as we have seen, lost almost all precise meaning; it had become a catchword, an emotion-tinged label for moral subversion. Dr. Barker's testimony shows clearly his willingness to accept the possibility of insanity primarily affecting man's emotional and volitional faculties—yet his refusal to accept the same concept if called moral insanity.

Judge Porter then turned to the analogously controversial problem of irresistible impulse. Was it too a form of insanity, he asked? No, Barker answered, it was merely a symptom, a kind of behavior which might or might not be present in the insane. But to return to the case at hand, Barker continued, Guiteau's ability to postpone Garfield's "removal" for a more appropriate occasion, as well as his ability to explain and rationalize the assassination, were evidence that his crime was the product neither of uncontrollable impulse nor of insane delusion. Dr. Barker's standards, however, were ultimately moral, not clinical ones. (Standards which the moralistic defendant could join in applauding: "I have always been a Christian man," he told the court, "I do not smoke or chew or drink or run with lewd characters at any time.") There was, Barker felt, a vital difference between irresistible and uncontrollable impulses. "Irresistible impulse," he argued,

is where the emotions are so perverted—of insane people I mean—or the instincts are so perverted as to destroy the person's power of acting otherwise. Uncontrollable impulses may exist in perfectly sane people as a result of bad habits. . . . Passions, and so forth. A man who is in the habit of using tobacco or opium, perhaps, may not be able to break off, and that is an uncontrollable impulse; but that is not insanity, it is vice.

Consistently enough, Barker denied that boasting of intimacy with great men or of wielding influence and power when one did not were evidence of insane delusion: "It is a result of vanity and self-conceit and love of notoriety, and these are vices and not diseases." The distinction between sin and the symptoms of disease was a vital one; it could not be narrowed or qualified.

With the dismissal of Dr. Barker, the prosecution returned to its planned list of witnesses. They added, bit by bit, to a picture of Guiteau as a plausible and habitual petty criminal and swindler, a man whose well-established pattern of life could easily culminate in an act of murder. Where witnesses might have been in doubt, their testimony was carefully prepared. This was true, for example, in the case of one L. Spencer Goble, an agent in New York for the Mutual Benefit Insurance Company. Guiteau had done some soliciting for the company and had, at one point, borrowed twenty-five dollars—unreturned—from the unfortunate Goble. In this gentleman's original deposition taken at the District Attorney's office, he explained that in October John W. Guiteau had called on him and asked whether he intended to testify. "I said," Goble recalled, "I would swear positively that he was insane.'" Yet when Mr. Goble took the stand for the government he testified positively that it had never occurred to him that Charles might have been insane. "Extraordinary shrewdness and judgment," was the opinion of another business associate when asked to describe Guiteau's *Inter-Ocean* scheme, "of the Colonel Sellers stripe, 'millions in it.'"

Even the elderly prison physician Dr. Noble Young was called to the stand and asked his opinion of Guiteau's sanity. He replied without a trace of hesitation: "A perfectly sane man, sir; a perfectly sane man; as bright and intelligent a man as you will see in a summer's day; bright, quick, and intelligent. I never saw anything about him that savored of insanity."

Throughout the prosecution's methodical presentation, Guiteau's interjections provided a welcome diversion for the audience. Time and time again his bizarre and irrelevant comments halted the proceedings. At one point, for example, Guiteau informed the courtroom of his magnanimity in rejecting the suggestion that he charge twenty-five cents for each signature—though he had given thousands of autographs since the beginning of the trial. His financial backing should, he explained, not come from this source.

There were many who ought, in justice, to support his defense.

I want to say that there are certain office holders in this city, and throughout the Government, who have been benefited by my inspiration. They now hold fat offices and they would never have gotten them if it had not been for my inspiration. I ask them, as men of liberality, as men of conscience, to respond that justice be done in this case. We want money. If they don't do it, the next time I am going to call their names right out in meeting. . . .

Guiteau was most likely, however, to interrupt the proceedings when he felt his morality or legal and intellectual abilities impugned.

On Friday, December 16, the prosecution began its full-scale medical onslaught. From that day until Wednesday, January 4, a succession of "insane experts" appeared for the government; only a handful of non-medical witnesses interrupted this learned procession. All, of course, vigorously denied the possibility that Guiteau might be insane.

The first witness called was Allen McLane Hamilton, a prominent New York alienist and direct descendant of Alexander Hamilton. Unlike Barker, Hamilton, though still a young man, was genuinely a specialist in the treatment of mental illness, having served as consulting physician at a number of insane asylums and even having written a text on the subject. To the end of his long life, Hamilton never doubted Guiteau's sanity. The presidential assassin, he wrote immediately after the trial and repeated in his autobiography forty years later, "is only a shrewd scamp, with the plausibility of an Alfred Jingle in swindling his boarding-house keepers, and evading the payment of his debts; the visionary enthusiasm of Micawber or Colonel Sellers; the cant and hypocrisy of Aminadab Sleek or Uriah Heep." Guiteau's crowning offense, Hamilton wrote immediately after the trial's conclusion, "was the culmination of uncontrolled wickedness, and his conviction and sentence the natural result of the failure of his last desperate scheme."

The prosecution turned almost immediately to the question of heredity, asking Hamilton whether there were any such thing as hereditary insanity. Only a tendency toward insanity could be inherited, Hamilton assured the District Attorney. Though the "primary insanity" mentioned by Dr. Kiernan did exist, it rarely manifested itself in acts of cool deliberation, but rather in violent explosions of temper and impulsive acts of violence. "I believe," Hamilton concluded precisely, "the man to be sane, though eccentric, and to be able to distinguish the difference between right and wrong, and to know the consequences of any act he may do."

Scoville began his cross-examination—almost certainly at Spitzka's suggestion—by asking Hamilton to clarify his views in regard to the physical signs of insanity, hoping to show inconsistencies in the prosecution expert's delineation of congenital mental illness. Yes, Hamilton conceded, there were bodily indications of insanity, especially of the congenital forms. Hamilton quickly doubled back, however, and in answering Scoville's questions elaborated the view that insanity was *not* congenital in any absolute sense, only the tendency to it. Hamilton did concede, however, that in certain conditions a mere glance at the patient's face could justify a diagnosis; certainly this was true in idiocy and imbecility and in the "developed insanities" as well—in dementia, in mania, and in general paresis. "All of these things present evidences that are exceedingly strong and well marked." ("I don't take much stock," Guiteau interrupted to record his clinical position, "in this subject of heads and examinations: It is the spirit that goes back into a man and drives him to do or not to do anything. Get acquainted with spiritology; you will get more sense than you will on craniology.") The connection between well-marked physical signs and hereditary causation, Hamilton cautioned, was no simple or inevitable one. General paresis, for example, though clearly marked by external signs, was only partially dependent upon heredity. "Usually it is a disease that comes from a prolonged strain, overwork, dissipation. We find it in broken-down merchants," Hamilton explained, "people who have had financial cares, and persons who have dissipated a great deal."

Assuming then, Scoville continued, for the sake of argument, that the role of heredity lay largely in weakening, in predisposing the patient—what exactly were the exciting causes in the environment? "Intemperance, sir," Hamilton answered without hesitation. Other exciting causes were "over-worry, hard work, insufficient food, venereal diseases." Before dismissing the witness, Scoville pressed him on one more point, the issue of moral insanity. What, he asked, were his views of the writings of Isaac Ray, Henry Maudsley, and other psychiatrists who had championed the view that insanity could be marked by an inability to conform to the dictates of morality? Yes, certainly, Hamilton conceded, Ray, Maudsley, and Balfour Browne were all authorities of unquestioned reputation, but all, he felt, took an extreme position on the issue of moral insanity. "I do not believe in moral insanity at all," Hamilton explained; "I believe that the term used by Maudsley and by a great many others, is a convenient term for the excusing of acts committed as the result of ungovernable anger and lust."

An almost uninterrupted stream of medical witnesses followed Hamilton to the stand; all were asylum superintendents. They included Dr. Samuel Worcester of the Massachusetts Homeopathic Asylum, Dr. Abram Shew of the Connecticut Hospital for the Insane, Dr. Jamin Strong, superintendent of the Cleveland Asylum for the Insane, S. H. Talcott, superintendent of the State Homeopathic Asylum for the Insane at Middletown, New York, H. P. Stearns of the Hartford Retreat, Orpheus Everts of the Cincinnati Sanitarium—and a half-dozen others. The government had combed the United States producing experts from everywhere, homeopaths and regular physicians, to refute the defense arguments. They filled the days until Christmas with their testimony and it was not until after the holidays that the government produced its star witness, John Gray. It was, as Spitzka implied, something of a government-sponsored rump convention of the more conservative wing in the asylum superintendent's association.

Though the longest and most elaborate examination was to be reserved for Gray, the prosecution's pattern of emphasis was unmistakable; indeed the examination of each expert soon assumed a numbingly repetitive quality. Insanity was a physical disease and depended upon the development of some physical change, some lesion in the brain. (Sane persons, as Dr. Shew explained it, might suffer from delusions—but not insane delusions; only by deciding whether it were a direct consequence of disease could one decide whether it were truly an insane delusion!) Certainly these lesions were difficult to locate and define. But this did not mean that somatic phenomena did not underlie the manifestations of insanity; the lesions of tuberculosis had been equally elusive until clarified by pathological investigations. Ultimately, most felt, a similar exact knowledge of insanity would be gained in the pathological laboratory. A present inability to demonstrate gross anatomical lesions did not disprove the existence of finer lesions. More elaborate means of investigation would assuredly disclose them.

Even when "moral" factors—fear, let us say, or business anxieties—played a central role in the causation of mental illness, they could only exert such influence through somatic mechanisms, by their effect on the nutritive quality of the blood or through the "electrical currents" in the cerebrum. These were functional changes, but which if long continued might ultimately bring about physical lesions in the brain. The prosecution experts rejected almost out of hand—with the exception of Hamilton and the grudging comment of a few others—the fashionable emphasis of Kiernan and Spitzka upon the significance of head shape in the diagnosis of mental illness. Moral insanity, of course, they unanimously condemned as a mere rationalization for vicious behavior.

Insanity, the prosecution's experts agreed with equal unanimity, could not be inherited, only the tendency or predisposition to it. A man could not be born insane; it was a logical impossibility, for then insanity would not be disease. Analogously, an individual born with an abnormal number of fingers might never have normal use of his hand—yet it could not be said that the hand was diseased; it had always been imperfect and was, therefore, not the consequence of a disease process commencing after birth. The logic seemed inescapable: insanity was a disease, disease a result of processes taking place during life. Thus insanity could not be hereditary.

The prosecution experts were a good deal less unanimous in their discussion of a more specific point—the diagnosis of Guiteau's behavior in the courtroom. Some, as the defense counsel noted sharply, felt that the defendant was shamming, others that he was simply acting out his normal characteristics. Dr. Shew, for example, was convinced that Guiteau was simulating, Dr. Everts that he was merely exaggerating to some extent his own character traits, "egotism, smartness, sharpness, vulgarity, ingratitude." (Everts denied during cross-examination that "intense egotism" was often a sympton of insanity; it could be considered as such only when it was a symptom of general paresis, and this, he explained, was ordinarily a fatal disease.) Guiteau's grandiose schemes, especially his two planned ventures into newspaper publishing, were dismissed as either religious fanaticism or mere impracticality. Though annoyed by Guiteau's interjections, the prosecution experts moved stolidly to their conclusions, interrupted only by the defendant's comments and the applause that greeted each opinion that the prisoner was sane and responsible.

While this cornucopia of medical dicta numbed their

critical faculties and the prospect of a juryman's lonely Christmas depressed their spirits, the jurors were treated to yet another unpleasant incident on Friday morning. Almost since the beginning of the trial, Charles Reed, the defense witness and former State's Attorney in Illinois, had been sitting at the defense table, advising and prompting Scoville. This morning, December 23, Scoville formally asked Judge Cox to add Reed to the defense; he had already testified and there was a growing undercurrent of criticism for the somewhat ambiguous role he had played.

The defendant himself, bursting with the news, intro-duced the subject even before court had been called to order. After the prosecution counsel entered the courtroom, Scoville explained that he had tried desperately, but without success, to find other lawyers willing to assist him, and had only then turned in despair to Reed, finally and with diffi-culty overcoming his reluctance to appear as counsel at a trial in which he had also served as witness. Magnani-mously, Corkhill disavowed any objection to Reed's assist-ing in the defense and commiserated with Scoville's peculiar dilemmas. Bitterness was apparent in the District Attorney's ironically elaborate politeness as he denied any intention of criticizing either Reed or the defense. Davidge did not even bother to conceal his indignation at what he considered the double role Reed had played. Indeed, Davidge was far more short-tempered and voluble than usual that morning, his anger exacerbated from time to time by verbal run-ins with the defendant. (When Guiteau maintained, for exam-ple, that he was perfectly sane—though insane on July 2— Davidge turned and told him to behave properly if he were sane. "I come here as my own counsel," the prisoner snapped back, "and I have just as good a right to talk as you have. You are altogether too talky this morning. You are worse than a boar with the diarrhea. You had better go home.")

The defense was no longer as pathetic as it had been: Reed was an experienced trial lawyer and assumed much of the burden of cross-examination and summation in the trial's latter stages. Christmas and New Year's, however, provided the first real break in the bitterly contested proceedings.

7

INTERLUDE

As expert witnesses higgled and evaded, the trial ground on through all of December. Correspondents and participants looked forward with pleasure to the break in routine which Christmas and New Year's promised.

Still, Americans outside Washington showed few signs of boredom with the case. Newspapers, magazines, legal and medical journals continued to cover the trial with unflagging zeal. Journalists and physicians continued to visit Washington in undiminished numbers, hoping to see Guiteau and spend a few days in the courtroom. In some cases a prison interview might even be arranged. "There seems," a correspondent for an influential Methodist weekly wrote on December 1, "to be as great a desire to see Guiteau as if he were some rare wild animal on exhibition for the first time in the United States." Although it had begun in mid-November, the Guiteau trial continued to rank as a coattraction with the sessions of Congress; as usual, the boarding houses and hotels were filled with legislators and lobbyists, office seekers and bureaucrats, sightseers and businessmen. The assassin, a closely guarded and shadowy figure until the opening of the trial, could now be inspected at close hand, his mental condition discussed and evaluated.

Few who had seen Guiteau's courtroom performance doubted his eccentricity; fewer still, however, questioned his responsibility. Perhaps not completely normal, he was certainly "sane enough to be responsible." This was the reassuring and almost unanimous verdict rendered by the editorialists and reporters who had had the opportunity of evaluating Guiteau's courtroom behavior. By common-sense standards, Guiteau's actions were clearly not those of an irresponsible maniac.

He remembers the most trivial circumstances from his earliest childhood, and often gives his counsel and witnesses, when they are at fault, the dates—day and year—that they have forgotten. Guiteau's character is compounded of vanity, egotism, self-conceit, ambition, a thirst for notoriety, and laziness.

Coherent speech and a sound memory seemed inconsistent with severe mental illness. Depravity, not insanity, was the indicated diagnosis.

Guiteau's physical appearance, on the other hand, seemed quite innocuous. There was nothing peculiarly brutal or diabolical in the slight man's features. He seemed, in the words of Charles L. Dana, "a puny, white-faced, insignificant little fellow, with a peculiar look in his eyes, and a rather anxious expression on his face." His smile, a somewhat nonplussed clergyman reported, was "pleasant and ingratiating." Oddly enough, the reverend doctor continued, two very popular and much respected ministers in New York City greatly resembled the assassin. It was hard to believe that an individual capable of such an atrocity would not—must not—somehow betray gross beastiality in his features.

The clergyman taken somewhat aback at the prisoner's mild appearance was James Buckley, editor of New York's widely read *Christian Advocate* and one of those visiting dignitaries fortunate enough to have arranged a long personal interview with Guiteau. Once the trial had begun, District Attorney Corkhill and Warden Crocker were as generous with access to the prisoner as they had been unyielding before. Dr. Buckley's impressions were typical of those gathered by other observers successful in arranging interviews with the assassin. Similar evaluations, copied and recopied, were to be found in local newspapers throughout the country.

The most important thing, Dr. Buckley realized, was the genuineness of the prisoner's inspiration; for on this point turned the diagnosis of his mental condition. "It was a feeling," Guiteau explained earnestly,

that I *must* do it. It pressed harder and harder, never let up, and in less than two hours after it was done I was wonderfully relieved. You never saw anybody as much relieved in your life.

And not for a moment since, Guiteau continued, had he felt a twinge of remorse; like Abraham he had been "predestined" to commit the act for which he was now imprisoned. But, Buckley asked somewhat ingenuously—recalling, of course, the testimony of Kiernan and Spitzka—did Guiteau think that his hereditary makeup or head shape somehow predisposed him to the experience of divine inspiration? For the first time, Guiteau smiled a bit as he answered:

I take no stock, as the common way of saying is, with hereditary insanity, shape of head, etc. It might come on you or anyone else. My free agency was destroyed. I had to do it. That's all there is about it. I'd rather take Spitzka's than Gray's testimony, for Spitzka has been through all those high-toned schools in Europe and everywhere, while Gray has been shut up there in the asylum; but I don't care anything for any of them. What I say is spiritology, a spirit coming into you, and taking possession of you, and you had to do it.

Though surprised by Guiteau's inoffensive appearance, Dr. Buckley regarded the assassin's guilt as unquestionable. He was lucid and rational, certainly responsible in terms of the standard established in the M'Naghten decision. Guiteau's motive was obviously a thwarted desire for office—a temptation he had *"voluntarily"* embraced, just as a criminal might choose to steal, forge, or murder.

There is nothing new in this case. St. James understood it, and every principle involved in it. "Let no man say when he is

tempted, I AM TEMPTED OF GOD; for God cannot
be tempted with evil, neither tempteth he any man; but every
man is tempted when he is drawn away of his own lust and
enticed.

When lust conceiveth, the New York clergyman concluded,
it bringeth forth sin, and sin, death. The prisoner should
be executed with a minimum of discussion and sentimental
logic-chopping.

The almost universal intonation of such confident and
pious opinions only intensified—and in a sense helped
justify—the determination with which Spitzka and his
circle defended their position. To these defense partisans,
the conduct of the trial—and especially the testimony of
the prosecution's medical experts—had served thus far
largely to dramatize the moral and intellectual bankruptcy
of the Gray camp. Spitzka threw himself with new vigor
into the fray; before his appearance on the stand, he had
limited himself to characteristically bitter and aloof de-
nunciations of the asylum superintendents—pointing out,
for example, that a number of prominent asylum officers
had pronounced the assassin unquestionably sane without
benefit of an examination. Even a reading of Guiteau's unmistakably pathological letters had not deterred these pious
diagnosticians. Spitzka derived a certain moral satisfaction
from the scientific indiscretions of his opponents.

On December 22, Spitzka wrote to Scoville, carefully
citing passages from eminent European authorities to support his diagnosis. "I trust," he cautioned, "you recognize
. . . the further necessity of asking questions exactly in such
order that the 'bad' four are convicted as liars and ignorami
out of their own mouths." (The identity of the "bad four"
is not perfectly clear; Gray was certainly one, and the
others were probably MacDonald, Kempster, and Hamilton.) Spitzka noted in conclusion that he had received two
hundred letters of commendation, three anonymous threats,
and "two letters from lunatics."

Even medical writers outspoken in their disagreement

with Spitzka's diagnosis—and often shocked as well by his overly self-confident manner—were indignant at the "gross indignities" to which he had been subjected. "It is difficult," the editor of the *Medical Record* explained, "to feel great sympathy for a witness who is often so inconsiderately aggressive as Dr. Spitzka. Yet every fair-minded man will share in the feeling of contempt for the mean attempts made by the prosecution to hurt the private character of the witness." Other medical men, not clearly, or at least avowedly, committed to either camp, were a bit sceptical of the strained denials by prosecution experts of the role of heredity in the causation of mental illness. Perhaps, the determinedly fair-minded Charles L. Dana suggested, this might be an involuntary consequence of the pervasive hatred for Guiteau that suffused Washington; such sentiments could easily warp scientific judgments.

A handful of physicians, firm in their allegiance to Spitzka and the values he represented, were much blunter in their criticism; the prosecution experts, they argued, had methodically prostituted science to the voracious appetites of popular passion. Charles H. Hughes, for example, editor of the *Alienist and Neurologist,* wrote later of Fordyce Barker's testimony that it was not strange that

our gynecological friends should sometimes have psychical misconceptions. This is clearly an extra-uterine mental foetation, speaking gynecologically, one of the 'higher revelations' of the speculum, perhaps, but not of the clinical study of psychiatry.

But such defense partisans were clearly a minority, within as without the profession. Most physicians, like most lay-men, assumed a position far closer to that expressed by the unbending Dr. Buckley. Indeed, among Americans of na-tional reputation only Wendell Phillips publicly and out-spokenly called for Guiteau's acquittal. "This pitiable and misbegotten wreck," he wrote of Guiteau in the December *North American Review,* "could not probably be proved the direct cause of the President's death, to the satisfaction of any jury assembled one year or twenty months hence." History would record Guiteau's hanging "as one of the most lamentable instances of temporary madness, or as evidence how much of actual barbarism lingers in the bosom of an intelligent and so-called Christian community." But Phillips, sometimes hero of the abolition crusade, had through his post-Civil War advocacy of radical causes already placed himself outside the pale of respectable opinion; his endorsement could hardly benefit the assassin's cause.

The new-model notions of mental illness pronounced by the defense seemed to many articulate and responsible Americans dangerous in the extreme—a deterministic apology for willful wrong-doing and a threat to civil tranquility. The *Independent,* one of America's more influential weeklies, argued sternly that Spitzka's interpretation of mental illness "would put into the category of insanity men who by long-continued habits of wickedness and vice have acquired an extremely gross and depraved moral character, and indeed become monsters in iniquity." But such men could not be considered insane and irresponsible, the editor continued: "They are of all others the men who can be influenced and restrained from criminal actions only through their fears. . . . The law must punish them or lose its power to protect society." Editorial columns of every political and theological tone varied little in the verdict they pronounced upon the defense testimony. The position of Spitzka and Kiernan was dangerously deterministic; not heredity, but the habitual satisfaction of base appetites was the essential cause of criminal behavior. Explanations less emphatic in their reliance upon human choice and responsibility clearly threatened social stability. Many responsible Americans saw the arguments of the defense experts as a culmination of decades of increasing materialism and misguided "liberal sentimentality." As one editorialist put it:

No doctrine has been so fruitful of sophistries that deceive the very elect; it steals the livery of mercy to serve the devil in. Its advocates are ever attempting to decide questions of desert by a phrenological examination or by the results of a moral diagnosis, rather than by the Christian law of personal accountability.

Guiteau's marked eccentricity was undeniable; but it was hardly severe enough to remove him from the ranks of those responsible for their acts. He was no dumb brute, and must be punished.

Many Americans in the 1880's already considered physicians a generally impious, mercenary, and cynical lot; the seeming materialism of the Spitzka position added a not unexpected bit of evidence dramatizing the profession's dereliction of moral duty. The bitterness and near unanimity of respectable opposition to the defense experts' arguments imparted a somewhat defensive tone to medical writings generally; even those physicians vigorously disassociating themselves from these ideas often did so with warnings that an endorsement of such deterministic views would only further deterorate the profession's already flawed public image.

The striking discordance in medical testimony similarly underlined disquieting failings in the status of the profession. It inevitably exacerbated a chronic cynicism—shared by both laymen and physicians—with regard to the expert witness. No matter what the cause, accepted wisdom assumed, grave experts would be produced by each side—all explaining with appropriately learned references the correctness of their employer's position. Logic implied that law should not contradict the verifiable data of science, but could medical science make demands upon the law when it seemed clearly unable to settle disagreements within its own camp? (And, it was assumed, when financial, not scientific, considerations ordinarily determined testimony?) In no area was this more sharply illustrated than in that of insanity and criminal responsibility.

But physicians were not the only professional men embarrassed by the Guiteau trial; lawyers, too, found it an awkward and cynicism-provoking event. The somewhat Hogarthian quality of the courtroom proceedings created both pious horror and professional indignation. Porter and Corkhill were well cast as supporting players in a Gilded Age genre piece, harsh and bitter, posturing and declaiming, accusing as much as arguing. Porter especially was conscious of being a large frog in Washington's small legal pond; he could be as grandly condescending to the court as he habitually was to opposing counsel. When, for example, Cox had had the temerity to sustain a defense objection to one of his statements, Porter noted acidly that he had been in practice far longer than the judge. The more fastidious found prosecution attacks on the professional and religious views of the defense experts particularly offensive as they anticipated the reaction of Europeans to reports of the trial. "Only two men," Corkhill had remarked at one point, "in this country that dare go upon the stand and say that this man is insane were two spawns of the profession unable to say that they believed in a God."

The defense too was not without sin. Particularly shocking to the respectable was Scoville's practice of lecturing to miscellaneous audiences outside the courtroom during the course of the trial. The *Nation,* which tended in any case toward a chronic moral pet, regarded the practice as grossly improper—though Scoville's lectures, they reported indignantly, contained enough vulgar tidbits to make admission cheap at five dollars.

Judge Cox's failure to enforce a fitting decorum upon the courtroom seemed questionable—to some positively disgraceful. He was, many editorialists believed, pursuing a dangerous course in allowing so wide a range of testimony to be introduced. Certainly, many Americans felt, the prisoner's disruptive behavior should somehow have been curtailed; the garish quality of the trial was a rankling embarrassment to the sensitive. (Apparently, the more alarm-

ist accounts of a circus air in the courtroom were somewhat
exaggerated. It was true, however, that Guiteau did spend
a good deal of time when he was not scanning the daily
newspapers in signing pictures and cards helpfully passed
him from the audience by court attendants.) But Cox did
have his defenders in legal circles, for his dilemma seemed
at the time almost insoluble. "Guiteau appears in the case
as defendant," the editor of the *Washington Law Reporter*
explained, "as defendant's counsel, and as the defendant's
witness. He cannot be punished for contempt, he is already
in jail. He cannot be disbarred, he is not a member of this
bar; and being his own counsel, the court is compelled to
endure his insufferable egotism, arrogance and insolence."
And, of course, to gag or otherwise restrain the defendant
would imply a judgment by the court and necessarily
prejudice the case.

It was not only the "informal" quality of the proceedings
that attracted so much adverse attention, but also the manner in which Guiteau had become a tourist attraction, a
living exhibit from Madame Tussaud's. *Harper's Weekly*
was typical in its bitter comment: that Guiteau, they editorialized,

should be placed on exhibition by his guardians, exposed to the
gaze of the idle crowd, and allowed on the Sabbath day to
display his cheap antics like a half-tamed chimpanzee in some
wandering menagerie, is a thing so hopelessly vulgar, wicked
and disgusting that it makes one doubt the reality of the
progress in social refinement of which our age and our land are
wont to boast. We may seek to console ourselves with the
reflection that this unseemly occurrence would have been
impossible in any of our larger cities, and that it is due only to
the whim of a set of careless officers in what is really a
community below the average in decency. . . .

The prisoner, unaccustomed subject of so much flattering
attention, made no protests; *he* was not concerned with
defending his privacy.

Charles found the holiday excitement particularly exhilarating. "I had a very happy New Year," he informed the court as it opened on January 3. "I hope everybody else did. I had plenty of visitors; high-toned, middle-toned and low-toned people. That takes in the whole crowd. Public opinion don't want me hung. Everybody was very glad to see me. They all expressed the opinion without one dissenting voice that I would be acquitted." Charles had found time as well to compose a grandiose Christmas appeal and greeting to the American people—emphasizing the extent to which they were in his debt. Even if they came as lobbyists or office seekers, Washington visitors tried not to miss Guiteau. To many he was worth the trip in himself.

8

THE TRIAL ENDS

John Gray was the final prosecution witness. The government had carefully saved him to conclude and summarize their case. Gray was a man of national reputation and experience, a dignified, indeed magisterial, witness. The mere recital of his credentials was overwhelming, emphasized as it was by the Utica physician's grave and didactic manner.

Gray had served as superintendent of the Utica Asylum since 1850 and, during these three decades, had diagnosed and treated some twelve thousand insane patients. He had as well, Gray conceded, been frequently commissioned by New York's governor and supreme court justices to act as adviser in cases where a defendant's sanity was in doubt. President Lincoln had also been among those calling upon his expert services. The witness had served as editor of the *American Journal of Insanity* since 1855, and had held honorary memberships in British, French, and Italian psychiatric societies. The jurors must have been almost mesmerized by the time Gray finished this recital of honors and responsibilities. (His appearance, on the other hand, was familiar to courtroom regulars; Gray sat each day at the prosecution table a few feet from the jury box.)

The Utica superintendent had enjoyed as well an excellent opportunity for interviewing the prisoner and for coming to a well-reasoned diagnosis. None of the two-dozen other physicians who examined Guiteau had had at their disposal even a substantial fraction of the two full days Gray spent with the assassin. And, Gray added firmly, *he* had not stated any conclusions or made any diagnoses on the basis of published sketches and documents before actually seeing the prisoner. The implied criticism of Spitzka was clear enough.

Though familiar with his appearance and almost certainly impressed by his formal credentials, few among the jurors could have been fully aware that Gray was, as we have seen, the most prominent American defender of a narrow interpretation of criminal responsibility and in general a staunch upholder of religion, social order, and traditional morality. The Utica alienist was a member of the theologically orthodox Reformed Church and regarded mental hygiene as in significant measure a problem of religious education. Gray saw no possibility of real conflict between science and religion—except in the case of that "puffed-up" science which presumed to explain God's moral world in terms of force and matter. His values and those accepted by Kiernan and Spitzka could not have been more opposed.

Gray had, from the first, been alarmed by the moral implications of the Guiteau case; the deterministic arguments of the defense only confirmed his suspicions. There was nothing, he argued, uncommon or incredible in the assassin's autobiography.

in our days, under the system of extreme liberty, not to say license, both of opinions and conduct allowed by the institutions of modern civilization; and the free play given to almost every possible form of education and belief to try their experiments in the formation of individual character. In an age when almost all authority is disregarded as to religious belief and social conduct, it is not extraordinary to find even the most destructive principles as well as the most transparent impostures brought under the cloak of religion, until society is almost forced to inquire how far the "rights of conscience" are to be respected when the good order and peace of the State begin to be imperiled.

Mormonism, lax divorce laws, "Guiteauism," were— equally—consequences of America's social instability.

Gray's faith in the omnipresence, the inevitability, and the vigor of evil provided the basis for his analysis of Guiteau's personality. Doctors, Gray suggested, need not search long for a motive in President Garfield's assassination—"when a sufficient reason can be found in that depravity of the human heart which knows neither nationality nor clime, but is everywhere the same whenever man yields to his baser passions." Immoral acts were a normal dimension of man's existence, his heritage from Adam.

The most dismaying aspect of the Guiteau trial, Gray reflected after its conclusion, was the attempt by a new and irresponsible school of alienists to explain all human conduct, not insanity alone, on the basis of heredity and evolution. In this, Gray asserted, lay the ultimate significance of the Guiteau case—not in the fate of the insignificant assassin, but in the possible faithlessness of the medical profession in its duty to society. "It is high time, therefore," Gray argued in the *American Journal of Insanity*, "for medical science to declare whether she is willing to be dragged beyond her legitimate sphere, and to become the mercenary abettor of the criminal and revolutionary elements of society." Gray made no distinction, nor could he, between criminality, innovation, materialism—and his critics.

And Gray did not hesitate to make his views known from the witness stand and in the editorial columns of the *American Journal of Insanity;* his testimony alone fills almost one hundred of the trial transcript's closely printed pages. By the time he stepped down from the witness stand on Tuesday, January 3, the government was ready to rest its case.

Gray began his direct testimony—as had previous witnesses—with a definition of insanity. It was, he explained, "a disease of the brain, in which there is an association of mental disturbance, a change in the individual, a departure from himself, from his own ordinary standard of mental action, a change in his way of feeling and thinking and acting." Like any physical disease, mental illness had, that is, a specific material basis, a discrete onset, and characteristic course. Thus Guiteau's long and consistently criminal life proved his assassination of Garfield to have been perfectly in keeping with his previous character—essentially normal, if reprehensible. Gray's testimony was then, in general emphasis, no different from that presented by the dozen prosecution experts who had preceded him to the stand; it was simply more massive in detail, more impressively magisterial in delivery.

Insanity, Gray patiently continued, was generally classified according to its principal clinical manifestations. The most common was mania, a condition characterized by incoherence, delusions as to grand schemes or plans, or as to the individual's greatness. There were many forms of mania: chronic, paroxysmal, acute, and subacute. Another major class among the insane were those suffering from melancholia, an ailment in which delusions were accompanied by "depression in every direction." Even laymen were familiar with the third and final category of mental illness; this was dementia, profound cases of either mania or melancholia. Certain cases of epilepsy and delirium tremens, as well as general paresis and some classes of idiocy, were also accepted for admission by mental hospitals. These discrete categories, Gray concluded in a tone of decided finality, "embrace all the possible manifestations of insanity." Guiteau interrupted indignantly: "You are," he shouted, "a very learned man, doctor, but you have forgotten the Abrahamic class. That is the class I belong to."

But Gray would not be distracted; he had arrived at the dramatic contrast which he hoped to make between "normal" depravity and the well marked types of insanity he had just described. Gray paused now to emphasize the contemporary assumption that sin, habitually indulged in, could itself produce insanity. This, however, was only a kind of moral aberration, Gray explained, uncontrollable though it might gradually become; true insanity, that implying irresponsibility, was always the direct consequence of a disease process. There was a "profound distinction" between mere demoralization of character and true disease of the mind.

In the first place, insanity is in all instances the offspring of disease, and when a person who is insane manifests evidences of depravity, so to speak, in his acts or speech, that is a mere offspring of disease, whereas the other is the offspring of education in vicious lines of thought and conduct and from the indulgence of passions. A man may become profoundly depraved and degraded by mental habit and yet not be insane. Such a man may become insane in the midst of his depravity, or afterward, but without such preceding disease it is only depravity.

In his thirty years at Utica, Gray emphasized, he had never seen a case in which insanity manifested itself through viciousness, depravity, or immorality alone; "that would be in direct antagonism to the very idea of insanity. That is vice and wickedness, there being no disease."

Moral insanity had been a lifelong dislike of Gray's and now seemed the appropriate time to dismiss this insidious concept. It was, he explained to the jury, a hypothetical condition in which the moral faculties were alleged to be perverted while intellectual abilities remained intact. But, Gray argued, there could be no physical action unaccompanied by some intellectual operation. "I look upon man, in his mental condition, as being a simple unit; that his mental being consists of his intellectual and moral faculties so united that everything he does must spring out of them jointly. Disease is a thing of the body; a sickness of the brain, if it is insanity. No physical sickness could reflect itself through a man's moral nature only."

After a luncheon recess, the District Attorney turned his questions more specifically to the case at hand. Corkhill first asked Gray to describe his pretrial interview with the

defendant. And for well over an hour the psychiatrist reconstructed his conversations with the assassin. The Utica
physician emphasized the prisoner's rationality, his ability
to answer questions, the care and precision with which he
planned the assassination. Perhaps most revealing, Gray
suggested, was Guiteau's failure to claim inspiration at the
inception of his plan—only after he had decided irrevocably
upon it. Gray did not doubt for a moment that Guiteau
was sane and responsible. He displayed reason, judgment,
reflection, and self-control, all indications of sanity, not
lunacy.

Guiteau indeed proved his own sanity by claiming to be
insane, by submitting his inspiration as proof of legal irresponsibility. "No man who has such a delusion and is
insane, recognizes himself as anything but sane, or recognizes that delusion as anything but an evidence of his
sanity." Even in the courtroom, Gray argued, the prisoner
consistently played a part, feigning in hopes of impressing
judge and jury with his erratic behavior. ("You are talking
about cranks," Guiteau suddenly interrupted; "Talk about
Abraham and the thirty-eight cases in the Bible where God
Almighty directed people to kill.")

With practiced confidence, Gray pushed his testimony to
the limits of medical logic. (His critics felt a good deal beyond it.) Heredity of mental disease, for example, Gray
simply dismissed out of hand. "The transmission of a susceptibility of any of these tissues, or any parts, as the nervous system, the lungs, and so forth, to take on disease under
certain exposures, is accidental and of rare occurrence; not
the law." The idea of inheriting a cerebral lesion from an
ancestor was perfectly ludicrous; "it is impossible," Gray
explained, "just as much so as that your ancestor could
give you a cough or a pain in your side."

As might have been expected, however, Gray's direct
testimony emphasized most strongly his rejection of moral
insanity, of any hint that some discrete physical or physiological mechanism did not underlie any symptom of true

mental illness. (There was a somewhat irrelevant quality to this argument, however, since proponents of moral insanity were equally firm in their somaticism; it was not pathology so much as symptomatology—with its social policy implications—upon which disagreement rested.) And hence, Gray argued, kleptomania, dipsomania, pyromania—those hated diagnostic neologisms—were simply nonsense, "makeshifts to secure from punishment for crime." The proper term for kleptomania was thieving, for dipsomania, drunkenness, and for pyromania, incendiarism.

Certainly, Gray conceded, moral influences played a significant role in the etiology of insanity, but they could not, he reiterated, without the intervention of some physical mechanism. There was little controversy as to the more important moral influences: "They are religious influences; they are hopes, fears, griefs, anxieties, and all difficulties and troubles incident to life." Gray admitted that many of his distinguished psychiatric predecessors had believed that a moral influence such as grief might pass directly into a state of melancholia without the intervention of any physical illness. But his own experience, he recalled, had proven to him that in every such instance

the person was sick previous to the appearance of the insanity
. . . that those moral causes so operated as to prevent them
from getting the necessary amount of sleep, the necessary
amount of food, the necessary amount of rest; and from those,
failing in their bodily health, the insanity was developed,
and therefore it had a physical origin, and the moral influences
were only the remote causes to bring about the development
of the physical disease, as the real cause of insanity.

Gray even suggested the precise mechanism. In most cases when moral influences produced insanity, he explained, they did so by altering the quantity or quality of blood supplied to the brain and thus leaving it "poorly nourished."

The defendant grew increasingly restive during this somewhat academic presentation. He finally shouted in interruption: "The idea that a man cannot be insane without he has got a diseased brain is all nonsense, according to the Savior. Read what he says in the New Testament about spirits and spiritology. There is no brainology in this case, but it is spiritology. Spirits get into a man and make him do this and that thing, and that is insanity."

Signs of physical disease could be found both during the course of mental illness and after death; Gray continued methodically, his dignity unruffled by Guiteau's periodic interruptions. During life the lunatic's affliction manifested itself frequently in poor nutrition, in bad skin and general debilitation; in other cases it was associated with tuberculosis or other constitutional ills. Post-mortem findings were equally characteristic: "I have never examined any case, after death," Gray asserted, "where there was not evidence of disease." Gray referred, of course, to gross cerebral lesions; again he had made a statement which would have been questioned by many psychiatrists of his generation. Even Spitzka, a dedicated student of cerebral pathology, had argued on a number of occasions before the assassination that discernible lesions at autopsy were very much the exception in most forms of insanity. Gray, however, was adamant and restated this conviction several times; insanity was a physical disease, its characteristic lesions readily located.

Gray spoke with unwavering assurance. An experienced witness and practiced casuist, he had little difficulty defending his position. At only one point during the cross-examination did he seem a bit embarrassed. Scoville introduced statistics published in several of the Utica asylum's annual reports; all casually reported the number of admissions presumed to have a hereditary basis. Of course, Gray conceded, the statistics were correct; he had never denied absolutely the role played by heredity in the etiology of insanity. It was simply that psychological attributes were ordinarily inherited less directly and inflexibly than their physical counterparts; the illusion of their unvarying inheritance was often the result of parents' influence in shaping the child's early environment. Again, Gray's position, somewhat strained in the context of his generation's psychiatric thought seems—in form at least—much closer to mid-twentieth century formulations than do the hereditarian emphases of his self-consciously progressive opponents.

John Gray was finally excused by the defense and the prosecution rested its case. The trial was drawing to a close. The defense had only a half-dozen witnesses in surrebuttal and then opposing counsel would present their legal arguments to Judge Cox.

On Wednesday, January 4, Scoville petitioned to be allowed to introduce new witnesses; George M. Beard, a well-known New York neurologist was called to the stand, but prevented from testifying when Cox sustained a technical objection by the prosecution. Scoville did, however, manage to introduce one significant bit of evidence. It was a letter of Luther Guiteau's in which he expressed the unhappy conviction that his youngest son was insane. As might have been expected, the son in question was furious. "What," he shrieked at Scoville, "was the object of reading that letter, to show that my father was a crank, or that I am? You are the biggest jackass, Scoville, I ever saw. If you can't learn any sense, I shall have to rebuke you in public."

This concluded the evidence in the trial of Charles Julius Guiteau; the jury and audience had now to sit patiently through the comparative tedium of legal arguments before the traditionally pyrotechnical concluding addresses by counsel to the jury.

Walter Davidge immediately rose for the prosecution. He obviously saw no need for delay; the government's prayers for instructions to the jury were simple and forthright. Based squarely on the M'Naghten rule, their position seemed almost invulnerable. Davidge summarized it neatly in four clearly phrased points which he asked the judge to adopt.

The first was the most important. Davidge asked that the ability to distinguish between right and wrong be re-affirmed as the legal test of criminal responsibility. That is, the defendant must be considered guilty if he were aware of the nature of his act and knew it to be forbidden by law. (As Davidge explained later, if the defendant in this case knew "that the bullet propelled by that powder would enter the body of a human being and would or might pro-duce death.") Davidge's second point was equally straight-forward. Even if an individual believed that in committing a crime he was carrying out a divine command or producing some public benefit, this did not constitute a defense against that crime, no matter how sincerely he held this belief. Thirdly, Davidge urged that the only kind of insanity that could be recognized in a criminal court was, by definition, the behavioral manifestation of a mind organically dis-eased. The law, Davidge explained helpfully, "recognizes no disease of the moral nature independent of disease of the mind." The "modern doctrine" of moral insanity was "unknown in courts of law and unrecognized by them." Finally—and by now in a sense redundantly—the Wash-ington attorney urged that the jury be instructed to disre-gard the sincerity of Guiteau's own belief in his inspiration; this did not constitute a defense unless the inspiration were proven to be an insane delusion.

This was Wednesday afternoon. After listening to this terse preliminary outline of the government's legal position, Scoville requested a respite till Saturday so that the defense might prepare its arguments. Judge Cox acceded and adjourned the proceedings until Saturday morning when Davidge resumed his plea.

He proceeded with relentless confidence, conscious of the weight of precedent endorsing his position. Davidge's argu-ment, as we have seen, rested upon the M'Naghten rule—

a test that, in the Washington attorney's words, expressed perfectly the truth of common sense and human nature. "Ask a child, ask an ignorant man," Davidge questioned rhetorically, "when responsibility begins? He will tell you it begins when the party has sense enough to know the difference between right and wrong." The wording of the M'Naghten decision was clear and unequivocal. Human beings differed widely, Davidge conceded, from Aristotle to an idiot, from the murdered President to his assassin, yet neither weakness nor eccentricity need imply irresponsibility in criminal law. Society had in the interest of self-preservation to draw an arbitrary line; if an individual understood the nature and quality of his acts he was responsible for them, though "the same man might not even be competent to make a contract, might not be competent to make a will; the same man might even be eccentric, peculiar, partially insane."

The polished dignity of Davidge's presentation was shaken only momentarily by Guiteau's repeated interruptions—particularly strident when Charles felt moved to applaud Davidge's characterization of the defendant as shrewd and intelligent. Of course I am no fool, Guiteau crowed, "The Lord does not employ fools to do his work." I do not pretend to be any more insane, he explained to Davidge, than yourself—nor have I been at all abnormal since July 2. "It was transitory mania that I had; that is all the insanity that I claim."

The legal arguments of the defense seemed pathetically flimsy in comparison with the precedent-embroidered position of government counsel. Reed, despite a good deal of rhetorical agonizing at the prospect of hanging a poor mindless lunatic, was able only to suggest that in the absence of a real motive nothing more serious than manslaughter could be proven. Scoville seemed to be showing signs of wear; he dissipated much of his argument in a sarcastic personal attack on Judge Porter—even to mocking the older man's elaborate mannerism of voice and gesture. (Porter alone among defense and prosecution counsel, for example, followed the traditional practice of bowing to the jurymen upon entering the courtroom.) Scoville did however—and with a good deal of logic— argue that insane criminals often knew the difference between right and wrong; that indeed, the frequent secretiveness of their schemes was a means of avoiding detection. This awareness did not make their crimes any the less irrational. Scoville urged as well that the plea of insanity be granted the benefit of a doubt whenever sufficient evidence had been presented to question in the slightest a defendant's sanity. Legally, Scoville argued, such a situation should be treated precisely as though doubt had been cast upon the facts of the crime itself.

The audience, still filling the courtroom each day in the trial's ninth week, sat quietly as the defense presented these legal arguments and with equal impassivity through the replies of Davidge and Corkhill. Most were anticipating the dramatic voice and manner of Judge Porter, the final speaker for the prosecution.

They were not disappointed; even Porter's legal arguments had their attractions for the connoisseur of rhetoric. Furious at Scoville's jibes, the older attorney assumed an air of lofty gravity, his sepulchral tones seeming at once to defend and embrace the foundations of social order. Moral insanity was Porter's opening text; it was a doctrine insidious in its implications, yet momentarily plausible in its explicit content. Its ultimate meaning was all too clear.

Whether [as Porter phrased it] there can be malice where there is intense depravity; whether wickedness to such an extent as to control a man's actions and redden his hands with murder and his conscience with the guilt of incendiaries and forgeries and burglaries, whether in those cases the Father of us all has interposed a shield so effective that when malice is so intense it ceases to exist; that when the will is mastered, in the language of the old indictments, by the instigation of the devil, a divine shield of protection is thrown over the criminal.

Perhaps, Porter continued with heavy irony, the antique M'Naghten decision, like his own oratory, was not adequate to this new generation, to the spirit of progress and Guiteauism. Porter began as well quite consciously to attack Scoville, giving better than he got in the clash of personalities; Guiteau became Scoville's "student" and "disciple," Scoville accomplice as much as counsel. More to the point of his legal task, Porter sharply emphasized that malice need not be proven, but could be presumed from the crime's premeditation; positive proof would be needed to offset this presumption.

"That is not the issue," Guiteau interrupted. "The issue is, was my free agency destroyed. I was overpowered. That is what the jury is to pass upon. It is a question of fact." Porter turned now quickly to the matter of inspiration, once the defendant had himself raised it. As a defense it was perfectly grotesque; to accept Guiteau's inspiration as genuine would imply a perfect faith in the defendant's veracity—to barter the late President's life for the word of a habitual liar and petty swindler. Could even the defendant himself believe that the Almighty Father of us all had deliberately chosen to remove the President and then

had gone to the Stalwart committee-room in the city of New York to hunt out some worthless vagabond like him . . . and that on examining him found that he had qualified himself for that mission by a life of imposture and of swindling and of beggary and of breach of trust and of wrong and of adultery and of syphilis, and that he selected him in the interests of the great Republican party of which he would represent the firm to which he claims to belong, Jesus Christ & Co., as being the responsible heads, and that to the junior member of that firm had been committed by divine authority the power and the duty of midnight murder, church murder, depot murder, murder everywhere.

"He will feel soon," Porter concluded with practiced assurance, "what he never has felt before; a divine pressure, and in the form of a hangman's rope."

Judge Cox's opinion on these legal arguments was as straightforward as it was predictable. He agreed completely with the prosecution's contention that knowledge of right and wrong was the cardinal point in the determination of criminal responsibility. No matter how sincere Guiteau's belief in the selflessness of his "removal," he must still be held responsible for it. Unless, of course, he were insane, suffering, that is, from disease of the brain. It was not a question of intelligence or ability. "Even if a man be deficient in intelligence it does not follow, you will agree, that he shall thereby be commissioned to commit murder or any other crime." The judge's personal commitment was unmistakable:

When [he explained] you come, however, to consider . . . such a crime as we have here—murder most foul and unnatural —the law requires a very slight degree of intelligence indeed.

Not emotion but understanding was the central element in the determination of responsibility. Even a casual reading of these instructions underlined the hopelessness of the defense cause.

The traditional climax of the trial was at hand. Counsel were to make their pleas to the jury. On Thursday, January 12, Walter Davidge began to present the government's case. (Corkhill did not speak, allowing the burden of argument to be borne by his fellow attorneys, both far more experienced in such grave causes.) Though the legal pleas had not been without a certain spice, both sides had clearly withheld their full rhetorical fire.

Davidge commenced with an elaborate verbal bow to the jury; their attentiveness and patience had been admirable. After so many weeks of testimony, he continued, there could be no doubt in their minds as to the one issue upon which the trial would be decided: had the defendant acted in response to a delusion produced by disease of the brain? Had he, in other words, been so lacking in intelligence as to be incapable of distinguishing between right and wrong? (And, as Judge Cox had explained so clearly, the amount of intelligence needed to make one responsible for so vicious and cowardly an act was small indeed.)

Yet Guiteau was by no means an idiot. On the contrary, Davidge assured the jurors, he was a man of excellent parts, a lawyer, lecturer, author, a conceiver of grand and imposing schemes. He was, for example, quite well aware of the principles governing the operation of American political parties; hence his skill and assiduity in "tickling" the executive and state departments, his deft pledging of future support for present preferment. Guiteau's memory too was remarkable. He was, in short, not the imbecile pictured by Scoville—"but on the other hand . . . a man of uncommon ability," though "of a most depraved moral nature."

And, though all men were equal before the law, the position of the victim must be taken into account in evaluating Guiteau's intellectual capacity.

A man may not have intelligence enough to be made
responsible, even for a less crime; but it is hard, it is very hard
to conceive of the individual with any degree of intelligence
at all, incapable of comprehending that the head of a great
constitutional republic is not to be shot down like a dog.

Responsibility, as Davidge presented his case to the jury, hinged solely on the possession of what he repeatedly called "intelligence." He also warned portentously of the lamentable social consequences that might follow a verdict of innocent by reason of insanity. "I would regret a result of that sort as tantamount to inviting every crack-brained, ill-balanced man, with or without motive, to resort to the knife or to the pistol, and to slay a man for party purposes, or, it may be, without any purposes whatever." Washington would become inevitably the scene of casual assaults and murders without number; men of position and attainments would be at the mercy of any ill-intentioned individual with the price of a pistol.

But in any case, Davidge continued, the defense could not hope to rely upon the absurd contention that Guiteau lacked mental capacity. His own actions in the courtroom belied it each day. Obviously an alternative was needed. "Hence," Davidge continued, "he had his cherished invention, to wit, the so-called inspiration."

It was a perfect fraud. The crime was a product of greed and egotism, of love for notoriety, of frustration at failure to gain office. The prisoner admitted that May 18 was the day on which he had first thought of "removing" the President. This decision was accompanied by no sensory hallucination. No hand had reached down from Heaven, no great light or burning bush had appeared to confirm the truth of this inspiration. How rarely, Davidge remarked with grim emphasis, "does it happen that we have portrayed to twelve men the initial point when the devil enters a human soul and suggests the propriety of committing an act of wickedness. And yet we have it here. He was in bed." It was an idea Guiteau had originated and decided upon himself—and then, of course, only after realizing that he stood no chance of winning office from the Half-breed administration.

But still, Davidge continued, the defendant was uncertain of his inspiration. Five days later, on May 23, Guiteau wrote to Garfield warning that Blaine was a wicked man; if he did not immediately ask for his Secretary of State's resignation, "you and the Republican party will come to grief." Throughout this period of indecision, as the defendant himself conceded, he had sought confirmation of his inspiration in newspaper reports; had there ever been such a madman? (But I was praying all the while, Guiteau interrupted; "If you prayed more," he suggested to the Washington lawyer, "you would be a better man than you are.") Then, Davidge continued, Guiteau admitted that his mind was not finally made up until June 1—at which time he wrote immediately to Boston for a copy of his book, *The Truth*. He would need a new edition for the readers created by his planned removal of the President. "I grant his egotism; I grant his unprecedented love of notoriety; but I think it will be difficult for counsel on the other side to convince you, that because a man is egotistical, he ought to have the privilege of slaying another."

The unifying theme in Guiteau's behavior was egotism, not insanity. All that seemed irrational in Guiteau's behavior could be seen as a consequence of the insatiable demands made by his hypertrophied ego.

Such is the indescribable egotism of this man that he put himself on the same plane as the Savior of mankind and the prophets. There you have the explanation of his applying for the mission at Paris. For this man, in his indescribable egotism, seems to have thought all along that there was nothing in the world too high for him.

Egotism seemed to have dwarfed all the defendant's better faculties; certainly he was lacking in personal courage.

And in this very cowardice, Davidge argued, lay another proof of sanity. Guiteau's fears for his life were hardly consistent with the feelings of a madman convinced of divine inspiration. Thus the absurdity of the defendant's picturing himself as having to screw his courage to the sticking point before carrying out Garfield's "removal"; could a genuine lunatic feel such qualms? Equally revealing was Guiteau's cringing fear of the mob. A mob, Davidge suggested, "is simply the outward expression of the best passions and sentiments of our nature. I am no mob man, but I never yet knew the mob, however much to be reprehended that had not behind it the highest forms of human passion and human sentiment."

Davidge turned then from Guiteau's alleged inspiration to his previous character, to that pattern of vicious actions which prepared him for this crowning infamy. Heredity could not explain him; the elder Guiteau, for example, was a respectable, God-fearing man—though an idealistic supporter of the Oneida Community, he was ignorant to the end of its licentiousness. His son, on the other hand, had proven himself an adulterer, liar, and cheat, had swindled and decamped his way across the United States. Before the assassination and during his adult life, no one had ever questioned Guiteau's sanity. He was simply lazy, unwilling to perform the honest work that could alone bring success in life. Even in small things this was apparent; Guiteau's constant and indignant affirmations that he was always "high-toned," always traveled first-class, illustrated the defendant's belief that honest poverty was in itself a sin. Such contemptible beliefs served only to dramatize the purity of character and height of achievement reached by the innocent victim of his "removal"; James A. Garfield's life proved his assassin's moral bankruptcy.

The dignified Washington attorney abruptly halted his examination of the defendant's checkered biography. The details of Guiteau's life, he explained, need not be explained in detail—for the judge's charge had made it clear that only "intelligence," only the defendant's ability to discern right from wrong was involved in determining his responsibility. Even that agnostic physician, Dr. Spitzka ("A young man with plenty of cheek," Davidge described him, "plenty of audacity"), admitted that Guiteau knew the difference between right and wrong. Were Spitzka's the only medical evidence presented the defendant must still be held responsible.

"But let me call your attention," Davidge continued with ingenuous casualness, "to some strange things in the evidence of Dr. Spitzka, simply as indicating the absolute hopelessness of their defense." The prosecution seemed wary of Spitzka, alarmed at the possibility that the assured young man's testimony might have influenced even one of the jurors. (Indeed, a rumor to this effect had made its way through the courtroom. The wife of one juror, the story ran, was insane and her grieving mate planned to vote for acquittal.) Spitzka had, for example, argued that Guiteau's skull shape was asymmetrical, rhombo-cephalic. Yet this was simply not true; Spitzka may have conveniently forgotten his instruments but Dr. Hamilton had remembered to bring his and had found no such results. And, Davidge warned, even if such asymmetry were proven to exist, mental illness could not be presumed.

The prosecution had also turned for help to a prominent firm of Washington hatters; their craftsmen employed a device called a "conformateur" to record the head shape of regular customers. Davidge introduced the head tracings of some two dozen prominent Washingtonians made on this device; not surprisingly, a good number proved more asymmetrical than that of the defendant. Equally irrelevant was Spitzka's contention that the deviation of Guiteau's extended tongue indicated a pathological mental condition. This was a perfectly normal phenomenon. At a recent meeting of the prosecution, Davidge pointed out, six of the government experts had extended their tongues and only two of the six were able to do so without some degree of deviation. ("A bit tonguey," the irrepressible defendant chortled.) Ironically enough, and despite the instinctive sympathy of the mid-twentieth century reader for the defense, the crude attempts of the prosecution to discredit Spitzka's views were, in a schematic sense, quite pertinent, foreshadowing later efforts to discredit such uncritically mechanistic explanations of mental illness and antisocial behavior.

Guiteau, who had been rather harsh with Davidge, did relent somewhat on Friday morning, January 13. "I find," he remarked, "that Davidge is a high-toned Christian lawyer, and I withdraw any injurious remarks I made against him. I still maintain my opinion of Corkhill." When Davidge was delivering his peroration, however, Guiteau seized the occasion to interrupt and urge those sending him checks to be sure that they were good; the previous day he explained exuberantly, he had signed 25 in the sum of $15,000. Popular sentiment was shifting each day in his favor.

It was now the turn of Charles Reed, first speaker for the defense. His was no enviable task, for Davidge's picture of the defendant had been one of perfect iniquity. Reed's strategy in replying was simple enough: his client was insane and had been so for years. No other explanation could account for his chronically bizarre behavior, his attempting, for example, to establish daily newspapers in New York and Chicago with neither capital nor experience. His understanding of American political realities was equally delusional. Who but a madman would expect the Stalwart leaders, men as diversely eminent as Grant and Sherman and Conkling, to come to his aid? Reed, of course, was in the awkward position of having to deny the validity of the judge's instructions to the jury—arguing that Guiteau was, as a simple matter of fact, insane and absolutely irresponsible, the M'Naghten rule to the contrary notwithstanding. Reflect, Reed asked the jurors, if at some other time you had been shown Guiteau's letter outlining his plans for the *Theocrat* and his relations with his employer, Jesus Christ and Company. Would you not have immediately presumed its writer insane? Reed was careful to cite only incidents from Guiteau's life before his decision to remove the President; none of these eccentric acts could be dismissed as deliberate attempts to create an illusion of irresponsibility with which to excuse the act of murder. There was, in truth, Reed argued, no really rational motive for the assassination; even the most cold-blooded hoodlums in New York and Chicago did not shoot men down without some motive. Perhaps most telling were the parallels Reed drew between Guiteau's crime and those of other insane regicides, particularly the resemblance between Guiteau and Richard Lawrence, the would-be assassin of President Jackson. Lawrence, Reed reminded the jurors, had in this very same jurisdiction been judged insane and placed in a mental institution.

A prisoner of his generation's moral logic, Reed had also to argue that Guiteau had, in fact, not been a chronic sinner—but, on the contrary, was remarkably pious. What could be more admirable than his intention of living on $225.00 a year in Hoboken—so close to New York, that Sodom of North America—subsisting on a diet of lemonade, dried beef, and soda crackers? "Were not his ideas of frugality and economy worthy of emulation by any other young man? And recall his confession—"it burst forth," as Reed put it, "like a rocket"—on the witness stand that he had been immoral on three occasions at the Oneida Community; only a madman would admit such a discrediting fact when on trial for his life.

Common sense attested again and again to Guiteau's pathetic condition. The obfuscation of twice as many medical witnesses could not make this obvious lunatic sane. His appearance alone provided unmistakable proof of his condition; no sane man, Reed argued, ever had that vacant, wandering glance. His brain was rapidly deteriorating. On any subject other than his inspiration, Guiteau was completely irrational and placed in an institution, he would become a driveling idiot within a short time. (Guiteau laughed uproariously at this absurdity.)

Could the formalistic testimony of the government physicians contradict the decisive verdict of common sense? The prosecution had been unable to agree among themselves as to whether Guiteau were simulating or not; eminent surgeons had been ludicrously misguided in their diagnosis of Garfield's wound. "Will you twelve men," Reed challenged, "send a man to the gallows on the opinion of doctors?" It would, the Chicagoan concluded, be a permanent reproach to American jurisprudence were an individual in Guiteau's mental condition executed; Christ would have healed, not destroyed such a pathetic misfit. (Reed found time as well to chide Davidge for his praise of the mob instinct. It had, he reminded the jury, been just such a mob that had called for the Savior's life.) Despite such rhetorical flashes, however, Reed was very much on the defensive, arguing what his experienced legal mind must have known was an impossible cause.

Scoville felt as little hope, but a great deal more bitterness. On Monday morning, January 16, he began an address that was to last for five days—one of the longest ever delivered in the District's criminal courts. His remarks were a mosaic of the trial's personal frustrations interspersed with a number of perceptive and—logically at least —quite telling points. Scoville was, of course, furious at the prosecution counsel and experts—at what he bluntly characterized as their conspiracy to hang Guiteau, a conspiracy headed by the District Attorney and his fellow counsel and actively abetted by the four experts, Gray, Kempster, Hamilton, and MacDonald. They had, he argued, formulated in concert the emphases of their expert testimony, had distorted evidence, had rehearsed witnesses —had in Corkhill's case even mutilated and destroyed pertinent documents. (Scoville referred to several of Guiteau's letters; it is not clear whether this charge was justified.) To the much-beset Scoville, moreover, Porter's melodramatic asides and elaborately theatrical gestures had —as we have noted— come to seem grossly and mockingly insincere. "Back of it all," Scoville complained bitterly, "is the fact that Judge Porter has come here to Washington and prostituted his talents, his high attainments for money to hang an insane man."

The prosecution counsel chose not to ignore Scoville's barbs. Again and again they interrupted with icy and ironic condescension. One reporter counted 147 such interruptions by government counsel between Monday and Friday.

Much of Scoville's week of summation was spent in a detailed review of the evidence. First, however, he hoped to clarify a point distorted in Davidge's opening remarks; he had never called his client an idiot or imbecile, but rather insane. The two conditions were not at all the same; true madness might coexist with acute intelligence. Like Reed, Scoville pointed to actions of the defendant that no normal man could have performed, his bizarre note to General Sherman, for example, or his speech, "Garfield vs. Hancock,"—the latter "the passport that he took with him from Boston to New York, to anything he might choose to ask of the Republican party." Could either of these documents have been composed by a sane mind? Guiteau's political speech was particularly revealing. Its three pages had been written while Charles still hoped for Grant's renomination; when Garfield was chosen instead, Guiteau decided simply to rewrite the speech. Only half a page of the refurbished version, however, concerned Garfield, the rest of the text was unchanged, an anthology of clichés praising Grant and his accomplishments. If his victim had been obscure, Scoville charged, Guiteau would have been placed in an institution without a second thought; he would never have seen the inside of a courtroom.

In his tireless review of the testimony, Scoville did score one particularly telling point against the prosecution's expert testimony. They had with confident uniformity defined insanity as disease of the brain, then stated unequivocally that Guiteau suffered from no brain disease and was, therefore, sane. Yet, they conceded that in no case could a final diagnosis be made on a living person and that even at autopsy it was sometimes difficult to locate a discrete lesion. "And yet here," Scoville argued, "is a living man whose brain they cannot see, and yet they tell you with all confidence that the brain has no disease. Why gentlemen the proposition on the face of it is absurd." ("Those experts," Guiteau added sarcastically, "hang a man and examine his brain afterward.")

Scoville, like Reed, urged acquittal on humanitarian grounds as well. Such a verdict, both argued, would assure Europeans that America's political institutions spawned no assassins, while hanging a man in Guiteau's state of incompetence would constitute a permanent discredit to American courts. In contrast to Reed's appeal to the jury, the tone of Scoville's remarks was consistently acid, flirting again and again with shrill indiscretion. He was, for example, seduced by his resentment into the mistake of rhetorically indicting the Stalwart leaders for moral complicity in the tragedy. They had, he charged, labored valiantly to create a suitable atmosphere of hate and distrust.

Guiteau, of course, had not been idle. He had, indeed, prepared an elaborately pathetic plea and was bitterly frustrated when Judge Cox refused his request to address the jury. The harassed judge explained to Charles that he would ordinarily allow the defendant in a capital case to address the jury; but, Cox admonished, Guiteau's constant improprieties had made this seem unwise. Indignities enough had been inflicted upon the court. But I have only spoken in self-defense, Charles protested. "I have been abused. I had to defend myself. I could not lie down and allow these men to trample on me." The speech itself was crucial. "It reads," Charles implored, "like an oration of Cicero's. It will go thundering down the ages." His speech was vital to the defense—for if even one juror had doubts, it would certainly resolve them in his favor. Despite Cox's repeated refusals, Guiteau never ceased asking permission to deliver his address. 'I have," he coaxed at one point, an encomium upon your Honor in my address to the jury. I hope"—ominously—"that it will not be necessary to withdraw it. If it is necessary your Honor will go down to future ages with a black stain upon your name, and I tell you so to your face." Finally, on Sunday January 15, the day before Scoville began his argument, Charles gave the address he had prepared to reporters; it appeared the next day, covering more than a page of the New York *Herald*.

Unexpectedly, Charles's wish was granted. After Scoville concluded his seemingly endless argument on Friday afternoon, Corkhill rose abruptly and withdrew the government's objection to Guiteau's speaking in his own defense. He wanted no error in the record, he explained, one which might justify a new trial. At this Judge Cox agreed, reversing his previous decision and conceding that a number of his fellow justices had expressed serious doubts as to the propriety of denying the defendant in a capital case the right to address the jury.

Reed and Scoville must have had their qualms—but the other participants were all agreed. Court adjourned early Friday afternoon; on Saturday morning the defendant was to speak in his own behalf. A certain element of novelty was absent, however, since the audience had already enjoyed the opportunity of reading Guiteau's speech in the *Herald* earlier in the week. A number of passages, moreover, were copied from the assassin's "Christmas Address" to the American people; Charles could never resist the temptation of utilizing his more spirited bits of prose as often as and whenever possible. But the overflow audience was not to be disappointed; Charles declaimed his address in a fashion appropriately dramatic. "I am going to sit down," he prefaced his remarks, "because I can talk. I am not afraid of any one shooting me. This shooting business is declining." Charles began with an assortment of heavy-handed compliments. (Even Scoville was granted a few kind words. "Considering his slight experience as an advocate," Guiteau explained, "he showed himself to be a man of marked resources. In other words you cannot tell what there is in a man until he has a chance. Talent lies dormant. A chance develops it. Some men never have a chance, and go down in obscurity. There are plenty of brains in this world. It is only the man who has a chance that develops brains.") Charles soon concluded this informal introduction to his prepared address: "I am not here as a wicked man, or as a lunatic," he explained with dignity, "I am here as a patriot and my speech is as follows. I read from the New York *Herald,* gentlemen. It was sent by telegraph Sunday, and published in all the leading papers in America Monday."

It was a virtuoso performance. After adjusting his glasses, Guiteau began to declaim, holding the paper in one hand, using the other to underline his remarks. At particularly dramatic moments he would close his eyes and glance heavenward, swaying back and forth. At times he lowered his voice, then raised it almost to a treble. Several times he burst into tears or allowed his voice to quaver—his words almost inaudible. On each occasion he abruptly resumed his normal tone. The dramatic highpoint came when Charles, comparing himself to the martyr of abolition, sang—"weirdly chanted" as one reporter described it—a verse from "John Brown's Body."

The speech proper began modestly enough.

If the court please, gentlemen of the jury: I am a patriot. To-day I suffer in bonds as a patriot. Washington was a patriot. Grant was a patriot. Washington led the armies of the Revolution through eight years of bloody war to victory and glory. Grant led the armies of the Union to victory and glory, and today the nation is prosperous and happy. They raised the old war-cry, "Rally round the flag, boys," and thousands of the choicest sons of the Republic went forth to battle, to victory or death. Washington and Grant, by their valor and success in war, won the admiration of mankind. Today I suffer in bonds as a patriot, because I had the inspiration and nerve to unite a great political party, to the end that the nation might be saved another desolating war.

In the grief and mourning that followed President Garfield's death, Guiteau explained, all contention ceased. Charles then began an exposition of his legal position, arguing first that there was no malice, and hence no homicide, and second, that the President had actually died of malpractice. ("The Deity allowed the doctors to finish my work gradually, because he wanted to prepare the people for the change and also confirm my original inspiration.

I am well satisfied with the Deity's conduct of the case thus far, and I have no doubt that He will continue to father it to the end, and that the public will sooner or later see the special providence in the late President's removal.") With each paragraph his argument became increasingly disconnected and repetitive. His feeling for cliché remained consistent.

In the course of his rambling address, however, Charles did manage to picture his inspiration in an unfortunately rational and self-induced fashion; he reaffirmed in his own words the prosecution's contention that he had seen no visions, been visited by no supernatural signs or portents. Charles was too deeply concerned with explaining how he had analyzed the situation, perceptively finding confirmation of his original conception in the worsening political strife. Charles managed as well to amuse his audience by referring repeatedly to the change in opinion that was making Americans so much more favorable to his cause. He read a half-dozen letters and poems sent him by the whimsical; all predicted a glorious future in which Americans would accept the divine origin of his inspiration. "No one," he informed his listeners, "wants to shoot or hang me now save a few cranks, who are so ignorant they can hardly read or write. High-toned people are saying, 'Well, if the Lord did it, let it go.' "

As he began his conclusion, Charles became increasingly solemn, even threatening. He was God's man. "As sure as you are alive, gentlemen," he warned the jurymen, "as sure as you are alive, if a hair of my head is harmed this nation will go down to desolation ... all you can do is put my body in the ground, but this nation will pay for it as sure as you are alive." To hang a man in his mental condition on July 2 would, he continued, be a lasting disgrace to the American people; they did not want the Republican party's savior hung. "The mothers and daughters of the republic are praying that you will vindicate my inspiration, and their prayers I expect will prevail. A woman's instinct is keener than man's, and I pray you listen to the prayers of these ladies." Finally—and to the obvious disappointment of his listeners—the reading ended and court adjourned until Monday morning. It had not been a full day's session but few in the audience could have left feeling that their long wait for seats had been in vain.

Sunday was fortunately a day of rest; Charles was exhausted after Saturday's performance. Yet his optimism was undiminished. Even on the Sabbath he had the pleasure of reading his mail. It came in such quantities, he informed one female "admirer," that his sister had to help in opening letters. Indeed Charles wrote to one prospective mate on Sunday that he planned to visit Paris immediately after his acquittal—but would be happy to stop in Boston en route to discuss their mutual future. "P.S.," he concluded, "what do you think of my speech delivered yesterday with feeling. Send a certified check and I can use it in Washington."

Though Sunday found Charles in an expansive mood, he could not have anticipated Monday with much enthusiasm. Judge Porter, the most experienced and vitriolic of the prosecution counsel, was to close the government's arguments to the jury. And Porter, aroused by the baiting of Scoville and the defendant—the "two Guiteaus" he called them—had prepared himself for an epochal performance. Porter's summation was, indeed, so vituperative that a number of editorialists, all eminently in favor of hanging the assassin, could not help criticizing the New Yorker's courtroom tactics, especially his "steadily blackguarding" the prisoner.

Judge Porter presented a picture of wan bravery as he rose to speak. He had, he said weakly, been working such long hours and with such intense concentration that his health had suffered. For a time indeed, Porter confessed, he had feared that he might not be well enough to speak. "But, gentlemen, the nature of the duty imposed upon me, not by my own seeking or procurement, is such that I feel as if I were almost an accessory after the fact to the prisoner's crime if I omitted to say such words as my strength will permit, to aid you in reaching a just conclusion." Only duty to his country and the memory of the dead President had brought him to Washington but now he could not rest until the crafty and deliberate murderer of the nation's president was safely immured in his death cell. Guiteau and his counsel had already dominated the proceedings to a shocking extent. Reed, Scoville, and Guiteau had presented nine days of argument to the patient jurymen—and in this deluge of accusations and misrepresentations, Porter charged, Guiteau's statements were the least objectionable. "Aside from the impiousness of his allegations, habitual with him through the previous stages of the trial, it was free at least from the deliberate misstatements and perversions of testimony, abounding in the arguments of his two associates." Judge Porter had learned his trade in a rough and tumble school.

As his critics were to point out, a goodly portion of the judge's argument did consist of calling the prisoner names. Even John Wilkes Booth fared well in comparison with Guiteau; at least he was a man of personal valor who sought to perform an act of patriotism. ("This coward, this disappointed office seeker, this malignant, diabolical, crafty, calculating, cold-blooded murderer, carefully providing death for his victim and safety for himself, will you seriously compare him with Wilkes Booth, who, though a misguided, was, at all events, a brave man?") Guiteau was not only a coward, Porter accused, but in all things a calculating egotist, growing more irresponsible and immoral with successive criminal acts.

The evidence shows him to have been cunning, crafty, and remorseless, utterly selfish from his youth up, low and brutal in his instincts, inordinate in his love for notoriety, eaten up by a thirst for money which has gnawed into his soul like a cancer; a beggar, a hypocrite, a canter, a swindler, a lawyer who with many years of practice in two great cities never won

a cause, and you know why; a man who has left in every
State through which he passed a trail of knavery, fraud, and
imposition; a man who has lived at the expense of others, and
when he succeeded in getting possession of their funds
appropriated them to his own private use, in breach of every
honorable obligation and every professional trust; a man
capable of mimicking the manners and aping the bearing of a
gentleman. . . .

Guiteau's religious and patriotic cant was only the more
odious in light of the testimony offered by his own sinful
life. Could one believe that Charles had actually prayed to
the Lord for guidance in deciding upon Garfield's removal?
That a man accustomed to prayer could have ever succumbed to such a temptation? (Guiteau was enraged. "I
pray every night of my life," he shouted; "If you would
pray some you would be a better man. You wouldn't be
here for blood money.") The logical absurdity of the defense case was apparent in its resting, essentially, upon the
honesty of a man dishonest in so many things both small
and large. Porter turned now sympathetically to the jury;
this reprehensible wretch has victimized you too, kept you
here for two and a half months, "imprisoned, isolated from
your families, from your wives, from your children, held
together as if you were criminals."

It was not simply Guiteau's fate that was at stake, the
dignified New Yorker argued. His acquittal would mean a
green light to other such criminal and eccentric types.
Porter sketched in the grim possibilities: honest citizens
might be assaulted, perhaps murdered, their property stolen, houses fired, names forged, wells poisoned, and daughters ravished. The truly insane—those already confined in
institutions—would feel licensed to kill their keepers, "to
open the gates of each asylum and go out, knife and torch
in hand, to spread ruin and conflagration." The majority of
peacable lunatics were, indeed, among those most anxious
to see Guiteau hung; it was they and their keepers who
would be the first victims of their more homicidal fellow

inmates. "Let insane men as a class understand that the law has no hold upon them, and that they can commit with impunity all acts prohibited as crimes, no troops in the command of General Sherman could so guard our asylums as to protect the lives of the inmates from each other, or of the keepers from the inmates."

But again, Porter cautioned, all such arguments were hypothetical—for the prisoner was quite sane on July 2. This was not a case in which the responsibility of a man partially insane had to be assessed. The only ground for assuming Guiteau irrational was the very cold-blooded viciousness of the crime. "I do not deny," Porter conceded, "his title to be regarded as the most cold-blooded and selfish murderer of the last sixty centuries. Certainly there was atrocity enough." But unfortunately Guiteau was not unique in his capacity for atrocious behavior; it was a heritage originating in that distant age when the first-born of the human race slew his brother.

But then, abruptly and with uncharacteristic terseness, Porter concluded the government's case. It was mid-afternoon, Wednesday, January 5. Gentlemen, he urged the jury, you must now do your part in making assassination reprehensible.

Without hesitation, Judge Cox began his charge to the jury. It was, on the whole a thorough and conservative presentation; following it, the jury could not have acquitted the prisoner.

Every accused person, Cox pointed out by way of introduction, was entitled to the protection of the nation's fundamental laws. "With what difficulty and trial of patience this law has been administered in the present case, you have been daily witnesses." Drawn out and unpleasant though the proceedings may have been, all participants could rejoice that none of the prisoner's sacred constitutional guarantees had been infringed in the slightest.

Murder, Cox explained in his precise manner, always

involves three elements—the killing, malice, and a responsible mind in the murderer. Malice, he underlined, need not be proved explicitly, but might be presumed where premeditation existed. Though a defendant was presumed innocent, all men were presumed sane. The initial burden of proof lay, therefore, with the defense; they must provide evidence sufficient to cast at least some doubt upon the presumption of sanity. Only then would the prosecution be obligated to prove a defendant's sanity. If, however, after presentation of such evidence the jury entertained a reasonable doubt as to the prisoner's mental status, he was, of course, entitled to the benefit of the doubt—and to acquittal. As to the facts of the crime, Cox emphasized, there could be no question at all. This issue of malpractice was irrelevant; competent surgeons had testified unanimously that Garfield's wound was necessarily mortal.

The only real issue was the prisoner's sanity. Though the defense of insanity had been subjected to a great deal of unmerited popular abuse, the judge cautioned, it was nevertheless a "perfect defense to an indictment for murder." Guiteau, however, was clearly no raving maniac, but rather one of those marginal persons whose true mental condition represented a diagnostic challenge. But even in a case of partial insanity, Cox explained, the jury must judge whether "the crime charged was the product of the delusion or other morbid condition, and connected with it as effect with cause, and not the result of sane reasoning or natural motives, which the party may be capable of, notwithstanding his circumscribed disorder." Thus, the need to admit the varied types of evidence that had so prolonged the trial; everything "relating to his physical and mental history is relevant, because any conclusion as to his sanity must often rest upon a large number of facts." Similarly, evidence relating to insanity in a defendant's blood relatives was admissible, if not conclusive. Though confronted by a kaleidoscope of evidence, Cox explained to the jurors, they must conform their final judgment to the instructions he had already outlined:

Was his ordinary, permanent, chronic condition of mind such, in consequence of disease, that he was unable to understand the nature of his actions, or to distinguish between right and wrong in his conduct? Was he subject to insane delusions that destroyed his power of so distinguishing? And did this continue down to and embrace the act for which he is tried? If so, he was simply an irresponsible lunatic.
Or, on the other hand, had he the ordinary intelligence of sane people, so that he could distinguish between right and wrong, as to his own actions? If another person had committed the assassination, would he have appreciated the wickedness of it? If he had had no special access of insanity impelling him to it, as he claims was the case, would he have understood the character of such an act and its wrongfulness, if another person had suggested it to him? If you can answer these questions in your own minds, it may aid you toward a conclusion as to the normal or ordinary condition of the prisoner's mind before he thought of this act, and if you are satisfied that his chronic or permanent condition was that of sanity, at least, so far that he knew the character of his own actions and whether they were right or wrong and was not under any permanent insane delusions which destroyed his power of discriminating between right and wrong as to them, then, the only inquiry remaining is, whether there was any special insanity connected with this crime . . .

Was Guiteau's habitual pattern of life a consequence of moral obliquity or long-standing brain disease?

indifference to what is right is not ignorance of it, and depravity is not insanity, and we must be careful not to mistake moral perversion for mental disease. . . . A man who is represented as having always been an affectionate parent and husband, suddenly kills his wife and child. This is something so unnatural for such a man, that a suspicion of his insanity arises at once. On further inquiry, we learn that, instead of being as represented, the man was always passionate,

violent, and brutal in his family. We then see that the act was
the probable result of his bad passions, and not of a
disordered mind.

Another distinction which they must keep firmly in mind,
Cox warned the jury, was that between erroneous, even
bizarre, opinion and insane delusion. "The important thing
is that an insane delusion is never the result of reasoning
and reflection. It is not generated by them, and it cannot
be dispelled by them." Men believed in such things as spirit-
ualism or animal magnetism—and yet there was no necessary irrationality in the mental processes of those holding
these eccentric beliefs; no absurdity in politics, in religion,
in social matters lacked sincere disciples.

Ordinarily, moreover, lunatics convinced of divine inspiration associated this with some supernatural—and presumably hallucinatory—manifestation of divine favor,
voices from above or a blinding light perhaps. By the
defendant's own admission, no such dramatic happenings
heralded *his* vocation. Again and again he boasted of having
"conceived the idea myself"; Guiteau seemed never to have
embarked on his road to Damascus. His conviction that the
President must be removed was reached only after a period
of reflection and analysis. "You are to consider," Cox
explained to the jurymen, "first, whether this evidence
fairly represents the true feelings and ideas which governed
the prisoner at the time of the shooting. If it does," he
added with perhaps an excess of finality, "it represents a
state of things which I have not seen characterized in any
judicial utterance or authoritative work as an insane delusion."

Cox continued with his deliberate exposition of the law
governing criminal responsibility. The law, he explained,
requires an individual possessed of the capacity for reason
to reason correctly, to exercise his cognitive ability by
distinguishing between right and wrong. An individual
might be insanely convinced of divine inspiration in committing some misdeed—and this would absolve him of

responsibility for its consequences. "But, on the other hand, he cannot escape responsibility by baptizing his own spontaneous conceptions and reflections and deliberate resolves with the name of *inspiration*." And there could be no doubt, the Judge added, that the prisoner had been perfectly aware of the law's customary attitude toward his act.

On this final day, court did not adjourn in mid-afternoon; Judge Cox hoped to conclude the proceedings—although counsel and jurors would be dependent on the shifting light of lamps and candles. At 4:35 the judge formally concluded his charge and the jury retired. At 5:40, they returned accompanied by the marshal and bailiffs. All answered quietly as their names were called. "Gentlemen of the jury," the clerk next asked, "have you agreed upon a verdict?" Yes, we have, answered John P. Hamlin, the foreman. "What say you? Is the defendant guilty or not guilty?" "Guilty as indicted, sir," the foreman replied without hesitation.

The last words of his reply were lost in the overwhelming applause that filled the courtroom—applause subsiding only after bailiffs had repeatedly shouted for silence. Scoville, still bitter at the conduct of the proceedings, demanded that the jurors be polled individually. And the prisoner, subdued throughout the afternoon, grew increasingly agitated as the jurors were polled. "My blood be on the head of the jury," he finally shouted, "don't you forget it. That is my answer." Judge Cox explained that motions for a new trial and in arrest of judgment must be filed within four days. Scoville immediately stated that he made exception to the judge's charge and to his refusal to grant the instructions requested by the defense.

It was a Daumier-like scene. Dusk had fallen and the jury had filed in by the light of candles placed on the desks of judge, counsel, and reporters; they shed an uneven flickering light on the cramped and dingy walls, still without the convenience of gaslight. Guiteau's actions seemed more than ordinarily bizarre, as the flickering light magnified his erratic gestures in distorted shadows against the walls. The judge quickly adjourned court.

As Guiteau was led, manacled, through the halls and to the prison van, a crowd of hangers-on—men, teen-aged boys, even children—elbowed their way after the prisoner, shouting mock encouragement—"All America is with you" and the like—and promises of certified checks. Guiteau was strangely and uncharacteristically subdued.

His only consolation lay in what he conceived to be the jury's somewhat disreputable character. As was his usual practice, Charles expressed his disappointment and indignation in a public paper, this one "An Appeal to the American People," which he issued from his cell on the morning of January 26.

> They do not pretend to be Christian men [he wrote of the jury], and therefore did not appreciate the idea of inspiration. They are men of the world, and of moderate intelligence, and therefore are not capable of appreciating the character of my defense. According to one of them, "We had grog at each meal and a cigar afterwards," which showed their style and habits. Men of this kind can not represent the great Christian Nation of America. Had they been high-toned, Christian gentlemen, their verdict would have been "Not Guilty."

Charles had little tolerance for the minor vices.

The defense, as Scoville indicated, was prompt in filing a bill of exceptions and a motion for a new trial. The appeal was argued before the trial judge on Friday, February 3. On Saturday morning, Judge Cox summarily rejected the defense motion.

Guiteau's disappointment seemed oddly disproportionate; he was angrier than he had been at the delivery of the jury's original verdict. Your "jackass theory" convicted me, he shouted at Scoville. His brother-in-law's temper had also grown thin and he shouted back, warning Charles to shut his mouth. This and the bailiff's efforts to control him only increased the prisoner's excitement. He answered almost in rage when the judge asked whether there were any reason why sentence should not be pronounced:

I am not guilty of the charge set forth in the indictment. It was God's act, not mine, and God will take care of it, and don't let the American people forget it. He will take care of it and every officer of the Government, from the Executive down to the Marshal, taking in every man on that jury and every member of this bench will pay for it, and the American nation will roll in blood if my body goes into the ground and I am hung.

Cox did not even break stride. Freed by the jury's verdict from the constraints of impartiality, the judge was eager to lecture the assassin. One cannot doubt, he began, that you understood the nature and consequences of your crime or that you had the moral capacity to recognize its iniquity. Your own wretched sophistry, he continued to snap at the condemned man, not inspiration overcame the promptings of conscience.

Any error of mine, Cox explained, may be appealed to the supreme court of the District sitting in banc. At the moment, however, Cox turned to Guiteau, it is my duty to pronounce "the sentence of the law that you be taken to the common jail of the District, from whence you came, and there to be kept in confinement, and on Friday, the 30th of June, 1882, you will be taken to the place prepared for the execution, within the walls of said jail, and there, between the hours of 12 M. and 2 P.M., you be hanged by the neck until you are dead. And may the Lord have mercy on your soul."

"And may God have mercy on your soul," Guiteau answered. "I had rather stand where I am than where the jury does or where your Honor does." Charles was struggling now and cursing the bailiffs who restrained him. "I am not afraid to die. . . . I know where I stand on this business. I am here as God's man and don't you forget it.

God Almighty will curse every man who has had anything to do with this act." Posterity would certainly applaud his removal of Garfield. In eternity as well, Guiteau continued to shout, his position would be more enviable than that to be occupied by Corkhill and the other devils hounding him to death; the District Attorney was assuredly hellbound.

Six weeks later, on May 22, the court in banc ruled on the defense exceptions; not surprisingly, the judges rejected Scoville's contentions. The assassin's only hope lay now with President Arthur.

Most Americans breathed a sigh of relief. Though perhaps overlong, the trial of President Garfield's assassin was at last completed. Only a handful regretted the jury's decision.

And a predictable handful at that. Most conspicuous among the critics of Guiteau's conviction were the neurological antagonists of the conservative establishment within the asylum superintendent's association. The neurologists, however, faced overwhelming opposition both within and without the profession; it was an opposition stated with the implacability of moral outrage.

The tone and intensity of this hostility tended on the whole to reassure the neurologists in their self-conscious righteousness; the absolutes of science could sanction a pious warmth quite as comforting as any justified by more traditional faiths. Guiteau's conviction merely confirmed their distrust of accepted values in the determination of criminal responsibility and their contempt for the upholders of conservatism in psychiatric ranks. "It is," as the editor of the *Journal of Nervous and Mental Disease* put it, "the old story of Demagogism versus Science. Having indulged in the humiliating spectacle of a prolonged and farcical trial of a lunatic it might perhaps be well to cap the climax and hang him."

In a concrete expression of their concern, members of the neurological circle began to circulate a petition to

President Arthur, asking that he appoint a commission of experts to inquire into Guiteau's mental status. Though originally suggested by Charles Reed, Guiteau's counsel, the petition was soon identified with the names of George M. Beard of New York and W. W. Godding of Washington, the physicians most active in supporting and circulating it among their colleagues. (Both Beard and Godding, it will be recalled, had appeared as witnesses for the defense. The petition itself bore Beard's name and New York address.) There was never, Beard argued, in the history of criminal law, any lunatic brought to trial with a more abundant record of insane behavior than that accumulated by Guiteau. "I have looked up the histories," Beard explained in his characteristically hyperbolic way, "of the most noted criminal lunatics of Europe and America, and I find that Guiteau went into court with a more abundant and more varied record of insanity than any criminal monomaniac that has ever been brought to trial in any country."

Guiteau was clearly a hereditary monomaniac; Beard published this diagnosis in at least four medical journals in the spring of 1882. No American asylum, he stated flatly, would have failed to admit him at any time during the past twenty years; had Guiteau shot some obscure person he would never even have been brought to trial. Medical men friendly to the defense emphasized Guiteau's classically compulsive pattern of letter writing, and especially the striking discontinuity of his thought. "In the immense amount of literature that he has given the world," Beard argued, "it is doubtful whether twelve consecutive, clear, and coherent sentences can be found; certainly not in those that relate even incidentally to his delusions. All the links of the chain are there, but they are not joined, but rather tossed about hither and thither, singly, like quoits."

Most respectable and articulate Americans disagreed, many of them violently. The neurologist's petition was— as the *Independent* explained to its readers—mere "senti-

mental twaddle." Could Americans allow the egocentric
views of a few physicians to be "regarded as better than
that of the jury which convicted the prisoner and of the
court that sentenced him?" A like-thinking editorialist
warned Arthur against possible impulses toward clemency:
"if he wishes to strengthen the hands of social order, he
will let the law take its course." Even if Guiteau were
committable—that is clinically insane—this was unrelated
to his responsibility in law, to his ability to differentiate
between right and wrong. Insanity—and this could not be
emphasized too strongly—did not in itself imply irresponsibility, only certain kinds and degrees of mental illness.

To conscientious editorialists, the most alarming aspect
of the neurologist's position was their deterministic emphasis upon heredity. The acceptance of such theories
would imply a corresponding decrease in the vitality of
traditional emphasis upon individual responsibility. The
Independent's folksy sage, the "sable Reverend Plato John-
son" expressed such fears vividly in a Washington letter;
the times, he warned, had never been so propitious for
thieves and murderers.

Fur w'y? Well, cos de minute you has shot a man de people all
hez sympathy fer yer, an' dey says: "Pore feller, p'raps he
was borned so, an' couldn't help killing folks, so you better let
him go, and jess likes not he won't do so mor'n free or four
times more." Defac' is, dis is w'at the people say: "He
inherited dat pissle-bullet from his gran'mother, an' somebody
else inherited de right to get killed by it, an a'ter a w'le a
good Providence brought de two togedder." When a few weeks
has passed by, we forget dat a murder has bin done, an'
dat someone ought to be hung right off, an', instead ob dat, we
take his picter an' say dat he is a very 'markable man,
only he is a little off his balance.

The courts simply could not accept the fashionable theories
upon which the defense had based its plea. Society, as one
physician put it while discussing the fate of Guiteau, "can-

not and will not make the allowance which an omniscient might and doubtless would. It owes a duty to itself and this it must and will perform, independent of our nice discriminations."

Guiteau's supporters were castigated in proportion to their prominence and to the vigor they displayed in advocating the assassin's cause. The *Nation,* for example, chose George Beard as the particular object for one of its characteristic expressions of moral indignation. It was ridiculous, they editorialized, for Beard in his "obstreperous . . . demands on the patience and good nature of the Government" and the American people, to claim the authority of "Science" in his habitually self-righteous fashion. Psychology was hardly an exact science and could make no absolute claims for the accuracy of the knowledge in its field similar to the claims that could validly be made for the data of astronomy, of chemistry, or of mathematics. "There is no such thing as a science of insanity, any more than a science of health." But such criticism, though doubtless satisfying to its authors, was quite superfluous; the petition asking for the appointment of a lunacy commission had, of course, little chance of success.

On June 22, Dr. Godding, Dr. Beard, and Miss A. A. Chevaillier—the latter a guiding spirit in the reformist association for the protection of the insane—were received by President Arthur; they presented their laboriously circulated petition and Beard spoke earnestly for twenty minutes in its behalf. The President immediately sent a copy of the petition with supporting letters and documents to his Attorney General Benjamin Harris Brewster. The Attorney General provided a prompt and unequivocal answer the next morning. Despite his haste, however, Brewster had taken time to speak with Dr. Godding who, as a Washingtonian, had called in person to explain the petitioners' point of view. The psychiatrist was forced, however, to admit that—aside from the one hundred and sixty signers of the petition—the majority of medical men supported the verdict. But even without Dr. Godding's damaging admission, Brewster wrote to the President, there was clearly no reason to consider a reprieve and the appointment of a lunacy commission. Rarely had a defendant been allowed such latitude in the summoning of witnesses, in the admission of evidence, and in his own courtroom demeanor. Guiteau's case had been reviewed by the whole bench of the District's Supreme Court, which had found no error in fact or law. The evidence had been overwhelming, the judge competent and unbiased. Only four days previously, on the nineteenth, Judge Bradley of the United States Supreme Court had refused the defense a writ of *habeas corpus*. To stay Guiteau's execution, Brewster urged President Arthur, would "establish a dangerous precedent. It will shake the public confidence in the certainty and justice of the courts, by substituting your will for the judgment of the law."

The defense continued its efforts, formal though they knew them to be. As late as June 23, John W. Guiteau completed the assembling of "Letters and Facts not Heretofore Published, Touching the Mental Condition of Charles J. Guiteau since 1865." It was printed immediately and meant to accompany the petition to President Arthur. The pamphlet included letters from Charles's cell dated as late as June 19 in addition to earlier family letters. Most were clearly eccentric in character. On June 27, John Wilson was granted an interview with a sympathetic President Arthur and presented his "Letters and Facts" in person.

With each day, however, the collection of signatures and the gathering of documents by defense partisans assumed an increasingly formalistic character. The writ of execution had been issued and would be carried out.

9

THE CONDEMNED

There seemed little change in the prisoner. He spent most of the day in writing endless letters to judge and counsel, to magazines and newspapers, to President Arthur and to coyly flirtatious lady correspondents. All were confiscated (and a number ultimately found their way into the curio market). Otherwise, Charles wrote to his sister, he had nothing to complain of; his cell was roomy and he dined abundantly on steak, fried potatoes, coffee, and tea.

He worked ceaselessly on the organization of his appeal. With the help of competent counsel, Charles at first felt, he would certainly be released by May. The difficulty lay in raising the funds with which to retain a prominent lawyer to argue his case before the District Supreme Court. Charles's letters appealed tirelessly to Stalwart placeholders for financial assistance; as appointees of President Arthur, he noted sharply, they were direct beneficiaries of his "removal." The defendant sought as well to maintain cordial relations with the considerate Judge Cox. "I desire to appear before you," Charles wrote to him on January 28, "when I plead for a new trial. Scoville," he continued, "is not qualified to represent me in this matter; our main ground will be lack of jurisdiction. Even though I am God's man I intend to use all of my legal rights. . . . P.S.," the assassin concluded casually, "I desire you to defer sentence as long as you can and to see that I am well treated."

Despite his grandiose plans, Charles remained penniless. His only source of income lay in the sale of photographs and autographs. He sent prints of a recent photograph to several national weeklies, suggesting that they use it if they wished—but only if accompanied by an announcement that copies were for sale "only by me or through the trade for a dollar with my autograph. They are sold to the trade with my autograph for nine dollars a dozen." ("This negative," Charles elaborated elsewhere, "will be a great improvement every way on the sitting of July, taken by Bell. My hair is parted and my beard off, and I look ten years younger.") Though Charles took a peculiar delight in disseminating his photographs, they provided, of course, little in the way of income. Guiteau placed his ultimate financial hopes on an autobiography, *The Truth and the Removal,* a strange little book that Charles managed to have printed and copyrighted. The first half reprints his earlier theological contribution, *The Truth;* the second and larger half is a melange of documents and speeches, Charles's comments on the conduct of the trial—and scores of the ironically sympathetic letters he had received.

Such mail continued, of course, to arrive in reassuring quantities. Arch proposals of marriage, elaborately earnest pledges of support, and whimsical bank drafts, diluted the ordinary run of insults and threats. On Valentine's Day, for example, Charles received at least twenty-two valentines, each picturing a noose as his intended.

On May 22, Guiteau's appeal for a new trial was rejected and the clerk of the District Supreme Court issued the formal writ of execution. "You are hereby commanded," began the writ addressed to the warden of the District's prison, "that upon Friday the thirtieth (30th) day of June in the year of our Lord one thousand eight hundred and eighty-two (A.D. 1882), between the hours of twelve (12) o'clock Meridian and two (2) o'clock Post Meridian of the same day . . . that you cause execution to be done upon the said Charles J. Guiteau, in your custody so being, in all things according to said Judgment. And this," the writ concluded with traditional formality, "you are by no means to omit at your peril: and do you return this writ into the Clerk's Office of said Court so endorsed as to show how you have obeyed the same."

The increasing imminence of this event seemed not to have disturbed its principal's customary routine. Charles maintained, for example, his habitual concern with health and physical comfort; the condemned man asked to be vaccinated so as to escape infection from the letters sent him. On June 21, only a week before the scheduled execution, he informed the Washington *Star*—on a page ripped from his Bible, for Warden Crocker had curtailed his supply of writing paper—that

I slept splendidly last night. I had a fine breakfast of Java coffee, broiled steak, omelet, strawberries, and bananas. . . . Last night the papers stated I had a doubt as to my inspiration. *This is untrue.* . . . Only good has come from Garfield's removal and that is the best evidence that the Almighty is backing me. If I am murdered woe unto this Nation and the men who do it! . . . Newspaper men are going to hell as a matter of course. When the Almighty gets after them there will be wailing and gnashing of teeth. They will only get what they deserve for their diabolical spirit towards me. Please publish my poem on heaven and hell.

Guiteau's seeming bravado achieved almost an elegance at times. When told, for example, that $1,000 had been offered for his body, the assassin calmly asked whether a competing dissector might not offer $2,000. He was surprised, Charles wrote President Arthur, to learn that Supreme Court Justice Bradley had denied his appeal for a writ of habeas corpus

as it would be contrary to *LAW*. I am entitled to a full pardon; but I am willing to wait for the public to be educated up to my views and feelings in the matter. In the meantime I suffer in bonds as a patriot. I have concluded to acquiesce in Mr. Reed's suggestion that you respite me until January, so the case can be heard by the Supreme Court in full bench. . . . I am willing to DIE for my inspiration, but it will make a

terrible reckoning for you and this nation. I made you, and saved the American people great trouble. And the least you can do is to let me go; but I appreciate your delicate position, and I am willing to stay here until January, if necessary.
I am God's man in this matter. This is dead sure.

Certainly Charles seemed to possess a self-assurance worthy of God's emissary.

As the date of execution approached, public interest— dimmed somewhat in the weeks since the trial's conclusion —revived markedly. There was, indeed, a good deal of well-meaning anticipation. (One humanitarian did attack hanging as a waste and suggested vivisection instead.) A Chicago engraving firm offered for sale electrotype plates of the execution, prepared from the "official plans" and certainly superior "to the hastily prepared ones printed a week afterwards, when interest has waned." Newspaper vendors stocked comic broadsides, good-humoredly celebrating the assassin's impending dispatch.

Not until the week before his execution was Charles made to accept its inevitability. On June 24, the Reverend W. W. Hicks, a Washington clergyman who had become Guiteau's spiritual advisor, explained to the prisoner that President Arthur had decided not to intervene. It was Guiteau's spiritual duty to prepare himself, to discard the unflagging optimism, even bravado, which has so long sustained him.* When he reported Arthur's refusal, Hicks recalled, Charles became immediately suffused with rage. "Arthur," he shouted, "has sealed his own doom and the doom of this nation. He and his cabinet are possessed of the devil. They oppose God's will and power, but they cannot escape his vengeance. In hell they will understand that God is a little

* Hicks had been chosen for this spiritual task on June 9; from then until Guiteau's execution on the thirtieth, he saw the condemned man each day in his cell. Indeed, Guiteau grew so fond of these lengthy conversations that he made Hicks his executor.

"Tableaux.

"Scene between the Almighty
and my Murderers.

The Almighty,
Why did you murder my
man Guiteau —

(Crocker.) (Crying & wailing)
I was needy, & wanted
my salary.

"No excuse. Go to Hell."

The Almighty (To a thing)
Why did you not
pardon him, Guiteau —

2

"I wanted to; but I was
afraid it would defeat
& My nomination in '84.
"Go excuse, you ingrate!
Go to Hell & Heat up my
Devils!"

the Albany City. (To newspaper
                        men)

Why did you hound my
man to death?

We did not believe he
was your man—
"Go excuse. Go to Hell"

3

The Almighty,
To the American people,

If or your diabolical
spirit towards my man
I will destroy
your nationality as I
did the Jewish Nation.
It took nearly forty years
to get even with the
Jews for killing my man
& I will get even with
you for killing Mr Guiteau
You are doomed!!

U S Jail   Charles Guiteau
June 20, 1882

TABLEAUX.

Scene between the Almighty and my murderers.

The Almighty:
Why did you murder my man Guiteau?

Crocker. (Crying & wailing)
I was warden, & wanted my salary.

"No excuse. Go to Hell."

The Almighty (To Arthur)
Why did you not pardon Mr. Guiteau?

I wanted to; but I was afraid it would defeat my nomination in '84.

"No excuse, you ingrate! Go to Hell. Heat up Mr. Devil!"

The Almighty, (To newspaper men)
Why did you hound my man to death?

We did not believe he was your man.

"No excuse. Go to Hell."

The Almighty, To the American people.
"For your diabolical spirit towards my man I will destroy your nationality as I did the Jewish nation. It took me nearly forty years to get even with the Jews for killing my man & I will get even with you for killing Mr. Guiteau. You are doomed!"

Charles Guiteau

US Jail
June 26, 1882.

Preceding pages and above. A sample of Guiteau's ambitious literary explorations during his last days in the condemned cell. *Rare Book Collection, Harvard Medical Library, Harvard University.*

stronger than the devil, and they will be paid for their cowardice, their treachery and their ingratitude."

And, contrary to the expectations of those who had thought Guiteau a cynical rogue, the condemned man showed no visible signs of distress—nor indeed any alteration in behavior. He continued to eat abundantly and sleep soundly. His literary efforts, however, became gradually more heroic in tone and intent; Charles ventured into poetry as well as prose. On June 17, the Washington *Star* was fortunate enough to publish "God's Ways," Charles's first poem.

> Thou Jehovah!
> All things created
> Save the evil one!
> He being uncreated
> Like Thyself.
> (See my book.)
> . . . .
> The retribution came,
> Quick and sharp,
> In fire and blood,
> In shot and shell,
> In endless pain!
> Like a jumping tooth,
> Lasting for ever and ever!
> (A jumping tooth
> Gives an idea of hell,
> And that is what
> Those Jews got!)

Once he had accepted the inevitability of hanging, Charles joined wholeheartedly in preparations for the spectacle, hoping that it would be staged with appropriate *élan*. He soon decided to mount the scaffold in a white robe and then remove it so as to be hung in his "shirt and drawers alone." At first Scoville and Guiteau's other relatives and sympathizers were unable to persuade him that this underlining of his own Golgotha might not be desirable. It was only the shrewd reasoning of Dr. Hicks that made Charles abandon his planned garb; Washingtonians, the clergyman suggested, would certainly think him insane should he appear in this bizarre and indecent costume. Guiteau, disturbed at the prospect of being considered mad, reluctantly dropped his scheme. He felt only resentment toward the "cranks" who sought to prove him incompetent. But Charles did not, of course, abandon the intention of making his departure from the world a memorable one.

He began the morning of June 30—as Charles had each day of his imprisonment—with exercises in his cell, a bath, and a hearty breakfast. Then, calmly, he sat down with pencil and paper to write a final composition. It was a poem entitled "Simplicity." Charles intended to recite it from the scaffold.

At 11:30 an elaborate dinner arrived; Charles would not miss an opportunity for a lavish meal. (Some minutes before he had sent his shoes to be blackened.) Nineteenth-century Americans were not deliberate eaters and Charles had been through for some minutes when, promptly at noon, the procession to the gallows began. The prisoner was accompanied by the understanding Dr. Hicks; the minister and condemned man had become surprisingly close in the last few weeks.

As the party mounted the scaffold, they became aware of the crowd beneath them in the prison courtyard. Newspapermen, political hangers-on, prison functionaries—a curious and knowing audience, prepared to write and retell the story of the assassin's death. Dr. Hicks began with an invocation, then held a Bible out to the bound man. "I will read a selection," Charles began, "from the tenth chapter of Matthew." Commencing with the words, "And fear not them that kill the body but are not able to kill the soul," Charles continued to read until he had finished some fourteen verses. Finally, he opened another sheet of paper, straightened, then looked forward and down at his motley audience. "Except you become as a little child," he recited earnestly, "ye cannot enter into the kingdom of heaven."

> I am now going to read some verses which are intended to
> indicate my feelings at the moment of leaving this world. If set
> to music they may be rendered very effective. The idea is
> that of a child babbling to his mamma and his papa. I wrote it
> this morning about ten o'clock.

Charles was always precise about such details, small in themselves but of significance to posterity.

Now the practiced player of parts was assuming his final role, that of an innocent child prattling to its parents, a simple child about to meet its Father in Heaven. Charles began in an artificially high-pitched voice to recite the "pathetic" hymn he had just written, quavering shrilly at appropriate moments.

> I am going to the Lordy, I am so glad,
> I am going to the Lordy, I am so glad,
>   I am going to the Lordy,
> Glory hallelujah! Glory Hallelujah!
>   I am going to the Lordy.
> I love the Lordy with all my soul,
>   Glory Hallelujah!
> And that is the reason I am going to the Lord,
> Glory hallelujah! Glory Hallelujah!
>   I am going to the Lord.
> I saved my party and my land,
>   Glory hallelujah!
> But they have murdered me for it,
> And that is the reason I am going to the Lordy,
> Glory hallelujah! Glory hallelujah!
>   I am going to the Lordy!
> I wonder what I will do when I get to the Lordy,
> I guess that I will weep no more
> When I get to the Lordy!
>   Glory hallelujah!
> I wonder what I will see when I get to the Lordy,

> I expect to see most glorious things,
> Beyond all earthly conception,
> When I am with the Lordy!
> Glory hallelujah! Glory hallelujah!
> I am with the Lord.

Fighting back the tears that, precisely scheduled, overcame him during the last stanza, Charles ended his hymn with a vigorous, almost ecstatic shout: "Glory hallelujah! Glory hallelujah! I am with the Lord."

Suddenly the prisoner was silent, pulling back his shoulders and standing militarily erect. Hicks quickly spoke a benediction; the hangman placed the black cap over Guiteau's face. Then, without hesitation, Charles dropped the manuscript which he still held—a prearranged signal for the hangman to proceed—said loudly, "Glory, ready, go" —and the trap was sprung.

"Now," as one evening paper reported the afternoon's work, "the vile assassin has met his just doom at the hands of the hangman, and has gone down to a murderer's grave, execrated and detested by all the civilized world." In Washington at least, there had been extraordinary interest in the hanging. The captain of the guard busied himself in selling individually guaranteed pieces of lining from Guiteau's coffin. Afternoon papers published special editions—one sold out five such extras. The next day detailed accounts of the hanging appeared in newspapers throughout the country.

But for many physicians and lawyers, the case of Guiteau was still open. His true mental condition remained to them a mystery, a dilemma, however, which the assassin's execution and post-mortem might now help to resolve. Would the traces of madness be found in the probings of scalpel and microscope? Though many physicians questioned the inevitability of such signs at autopsy, none doubted their frequent occurrence. The absence of overt pathology could not prove Guiteau sane, but its presence might well indicate his mental abnormality. In any case, however, the necessity for a meticulous post-mortem was obvious. The authors of the official report carefully explained the situation; although most Americans regarded Guiteau as being sane, "a respectable minority continued to agitate the question, and hence the popular demand, as well as the interests of science, religion and law, demanded that all the light possible to be derived from an autopsy of the body be shed upon it."

The neurologists awaited the results with particular anxiety—though with some reservations at the qualifications of the government pathologists overseeing the autopsy. But there were a reassuring number of visitors to report to the medical community, among them W. W. Godding of Washington, Charles Dana of New York, and C. K. Mills of Philadelphia. (A rather sordid tiff did ensue, several of the officials involved in the autopsy objecting—among other things—to the chest cavity having been opened before the brain was investigated.)

The result seemed, in this somatically oriented generation, to bolster the position of those who had considered Guiteau insane.* Many neutrals as well were convinced by

* The official report of the autopsy was reprinted in the *Medical News,* 41 (July 8, 1882): 43–45; (September 9, 1882), 297–99. Guiteau's behavior, as well as his admitted youthful brush with venereal disease, raises the possibility that he may have suffered from syphilitic paresis. To modern eyes, the evidence is inconclusive. Dr. Esmond Long, a distinguished pathologist and historian of pathology, has been kind enough to review the Guiteau autopsy report. "Certain findings," he writes, "are consonant with syphilitic paresis, particularly the perivascular infiltration with lymphocytes, which appears to have been conspicuous and widespread. What are believed to be degenerations of nerve cells are described, but I would be doubtful if the technic of the day was good enough to justify reliance on this apparent finding. Some meningeal adhesions were noted. These occur in paresis, but

signs of what appeared to be a chronic degeneration of gray cells and small blood vessels. The signs were persuasive; brains with fewer and less distinctive pathological changes, as an eminent English alienist summed it up, were not infrequently found in those who had spent years in asylums. "Thus the examination of Guiteau's brain, though it did not positively demonstrate that he had been insane, must be held to add weight to the arguments of those who sustained that opinion."

Indeed, several medical journals, previously hostile to any suggestion that the assassin might have been insane, now reversed their position; reports of the seemingly pathological findings convinced their editors that Guiteau had been genuinely deranged. Spitzka, of course, was confidently jubilant. He emphasized particularly the asymmetry of the convolutions in the late theologian's brain and the primitive development of the right as compared to the left hemisphere—clearly signs of hereditary malformation. And, Spitzka continued smugly, despite the prosecution's statements that Guiteau was in excellent general health, the autopsy proved conclusively his "notoriously . . . wretched physical condition." Guiteau had an abnormal condition of the aorta, tubercules in his lungs, a severe skin eruption, and a suspiciously sallow complexion.

All such evidence had carefully to be weighed; comparatively few minds were changed immediately. Signifi-

---

the microscopic examination suggests that the adhesions in Guiteau's case were of other cause and of no great importance. The appearance of the aorta was not that of syphilis, but patients with cerebral syphilis often escape this particular manifestation of the disease. By and large, I think there is pretty good evidence for chronic malaria, and fairly good evidence for syphilitic involvement of the brain"(Esmond Long to the author, June 20, 1967). Though malaria and syphilis are to some extent antagonistic diseases, Dr. Long warns, it is not at all clear what effect, if any, Guiteau's chronic malaria might have had on syphilis.

cantly, however, those few publicly professing conversion were converted to a belief in Guiteau's insanity. Perhaps more important—and aside from those physicians and lawyers directly involved in the trial—the tone of debate immediately became milder after Guiteau's execution. Once the assassin had been "worked off," there was far less moralistic stridency, far less self-consciously righteous tension in the discussion of Guiteau's mental condition. Except, perhaps, for the neurologists, who were supremely, almost overbearingly, confident in proclaiming that the verdict of history would endorse their position.

10

AFTERMATH

> I tried to play off insane,
>   But found it would not do,
> The people all against me,
>   It proved to make no show.
> The judge he passed the sentence;
>   The clerk he wrote it down.
> On the thirtieth day of June,
>   to die I was condemned.
>
> *from a version of "Charles J. Guiteau," an American folk-song*

And posterity has endorsed the neurologists' opinion. Within a dozen years of Guiteau's execution, few interested physicians doubted that he had been insane, indeed chronically and obviously so. Those harshest in their judgment did not hesitate to call the trial a miscarriage of justice, disgraceful to the legal and medical professions alike.

Guiteau's death helped bring about this change in opinion, discharging as it did emotional energies that made impossible any real debate while the assassin still lived. The manner of Guiteau's death, however, had an equally striking—and to many converting—effect; it seemed impossible that a sane man could have chosen to die as Guiteau had. One St. Louis practitioner expressed a common sentiment when he rose during a medical society discussion and affirmed his belief in the assassin's incompetence, "especially at the last, when he got off that whang-doodle Oh! Lordy song." The position of the neurologists seemed increasingly plausible. In 1885, only three years after Guiteau's hanging, a *Student's Guide to Medical Jurisprudence* could casually explain that if Guiteau's victim had been less prominent, his "obvious imbecility" might "have secured for him an acquittal on the ground of irresponsibility."

Mid-twentieth-century readers will almost certainly sympathize with this shift in opinion. Yet they will find in it an element seemingly paradoxical. For the medical generation of the 1880's and 1890's, so receptive to the broadening of diagnostic categories in mental illness, accepted with equal enthusiasm an increasing and at times overriding emphasis upon heredity in explaining the causation of psychic ills.* The Guiteau case became, indeed, something of a milestone in the popularization of hereditarian explanations of insanity and criminality. By the 1890's, physicians and social thinkers—influenced especially by the criminal anthropology of Lombroso—found it natural to classify Guiteau as a hereditary criminal, a "degenerate of the regicidal class."

Historians of psychiatry have unfortunately concerned themselves to a disproportionate extent with such bravely self-confident etiologies. Twentieth-century historians of psychiatry have, on the whole, tended to project the values of a genetic psychology into the past and in doing so have failed to evaluate with sympathy the ideas of this immediately pre-Freudian generation. Thus, for example, George M. Beard's well-established place in the canon of psychiatric history; for we tend now to see Beard's rather ill-defined idea of neurasthenia as an immediate precursor of the neurosis concept. Hence our respect for his clinical insight. (Among all the participants in the Guiteau trial, Beard's is the only name likely to be familiar to the modern reader of psychiatric literature).

The tendency to make a rigid—and often value-laden —distinction between the somatic and the psychological

* Though a concern with the hereditary component in mental illness is, to an extent, reasserting itself in the mid-twentieth century, it is, of course, stated in a far more moderate and qualified form.

serves largely to obscure an understanding of nineteenth-century psychiatric thought. Unfailing faith in an ultimate somatic pathology need not imply disbelief in a psychologically influenced etiology. The expert testimony during Guiteau's trial demonstrated this clearly; all the witnesses were somaticists, yet all found room in their etiological schemes for an impressively eclectic variety of environmental factors. Spitzka, in one sense the most thoroughgoing somaticist of all, was at the same time quite cautious in his pathological opinions; his European training had made him aware of the difficulties in proving the relationship between specific pathological lesions and behavioral symptoms during life. A number of other neurologists were equally sceptical of the glib pathologies assumed by most physicians to underlie the symptoms of mental illness.

But most physicians could, in any case, ordinarily agree upon a general framework in which to interpret the causation of mental illness—the view, that is, of insanity as normally the consequence of an interaction between the individual, his psychic attributes determined by heredity, and the stress of his environment. Differences arose in regard to emphasis and application, especially in stylized situations such as a criminal process where disagreement would tend to be polarized and exaggerated.

There was, however, one sensitive point upon which disagreement was absolute. This related to the role of heredity in the causation of mental illness and criminality; could it in some cases autonomously produce insanity and antisocial behavior—without the intervention, that is, of environmental factors? This was the position of Spitzka (though he did not, of course, explain *all* mental disease in this deterministic fashion). Or did heredity, as Gray and his supporters argued, at the most weaken and predispose an individual toward mental illness? This debate was inevitably an intense and bitter one, for the social consequences of the new hereditary determinism were obviously alarming.

Yet several new ideas were making hereditarianism

increasingly plausible, and all boasted the authoritative im-
primatur of European acceptance. None of these new
concepts was more important than that of "degeneration."
Pervasive and widely influential throughout the second half
of the nineteenth century, the degeneration concept held
that a basic "neuropathic weakness" might in successive
generations of a particular family manifest itself in such
varied conditions as criminality, alcoholism, insanity, and
mental retardation. Physicians believed, moreover, that
such degenerate families were also prey to a whole spectrum
of constitutional ills, to goiter, to tuberculosis, to cancer.
Such organic ailments underlined the protean nature of the
hereditary weakness that might result in a degenerate misfit
of Guiteau's sort. As one New York neurologist put it

> The wonder is not why Guiteau became insane, but how by
> any possible chance or accident a sound organization could
> come of such a union of mental and physical weakness
> and disease. Guiteau was a crooked limb of a tree that had few
> straight fibres in it, and because he was a little more degenerate
> in organization than his father, the cycle of his existence was
> briefer, and mental disorder came at an earlier period of
> time. . . . that the law of inheritance may help to explain the
> mental characteristics of Guiteau, it is not necessary that insanity
> should have been transmitted to him by a direct and unbroken
> line of descent. Family degeneracy may come from many
> and distant sources, from states of mal-organization in one
> generation that are not easily named, but which when further
> developed in succeeding generations exhibit themselves in
> various states of disease, and in innumerable forms of mental
> and physical deterioration. The offspring of parents who
> are merely of weak organizations may in one instance be
> consumptive; in another, cancerous; in another, epileptic, and
> in another, perhaps, insane; all, however, owing their
> diseased and degenerate organizations to a tendency to family
> deterioration.

In terms of this increasingly fashionable point of view, Guiteau was a hereditary degenerate who might, instead of

being a regicide, have just as well been an idiot, an alcoholic, or perhaps never even survived infancy.

A pervasive concern with evolution helped facilitate acceptance of the degeneration concept. Organic phenomena were seen by late nineteenth century biologists in relation to their place in the evolutionary process; and the development of the nervous system, it was believed, had brought with its increasing complexity the ability to create a complex and moral civilization. Unfortunately, however, this highly evolved nervous system was, by virtue of its very "fineness of organization," vulnerable to the tensions characteristic of the civilization its evolution had made possible. Thus the ease with which stress in business, in religion, in politics might bring about psychic damage. The nervous system was vulnerable as well to congenital damage and hereditary malformation.

Though the neurologists explicitly disowned the faculty psychology it found a place in their thinking, especially in the writings of those preoccupied with problems of legal medicine. The traditionally higher faculties, the aesthetic and moral, were, as a matter of course, identified with those highest in the scale of evolution. (Herbert Spencer called them man's "most altruistic" attributes.) Moral insanity, in the writings of those influenced by these concepts of devolution and degeneration, was simply a failure of the higher and more complex centers—a breakdown which could be caused either by disease or heredity. Such highly integrated mechanisms were naturally more liable to malfunction than simpler ones; civilized man had, to use twentieth century shorthand, too many moving parts. "Stripped" by disease or heredity of his "voluntary" or "altruistic" attributes, man naturally reverted to more primitive patterns of behavior—to rape, to murder, and to theft.

But how was society to deal with such atavistic behavior? This was the problem. "What," as D. H. Tuke, the eminent British psychiatrist, put it in 1885, "is to be done with the man who, from no fault of his own, is born in the nineteenth instead of a long-past century? Are we to punish him for his involuntary anachronism?" And to many American contemporaries, Guiteau presented precisely this dilemma. "It is as illogical to execute Guiteau," one journalist wrote, "as it is to kill a cave fish for not seeing."

In the broadest perspective, however, the Guiteau trial was an incident not only in the intellectual history of psychiatry, but in the larger development of American society, in the shaping of a modern and institutionalized intellectual life. It demonstrated in concrete terms the emotional coherence of a newer generation—that represented by Kiernan and Spitzka. Those ideas and values that shaped and sanctioned the aspirations of these specialists were markedly different in tone and content from those assumed by the so-called Old Guard in the asylum superintendent's association.*

One can, I think, mark the beginning of modern academic medicine and science in the United States from that point in time when American investigators began to care more for the approval and esteem of their disciplinary colleagues than they did for the ordinary standards of success in the society that surrounded them. All students of American intellectual history are aware that the decades between 1850 and 1880 saw Americans in a number of learned fields beginning to accept these values. All students realize, as well, that this process was dependent upon the transfer of European—and, in this generation especially, German— ideas and practices to this country. It was not simply a transfer of scientific data and laboratory techniques, but of values and attitudes as well—convictions that made the life

* Younger and older are, of course, only approximate terms; many younger physicians failed to accept these newer values, while a number of older men did. In the 1880's, an orientation toward the values of world science was still very much an elite—rather than a peculiarly generational— characteristic in American medicine.

of science seem absolutely important and defined the style in which it should be lived. Once he had accepted these values, the American scholar could measure achievement only in terms defined by the world of academic science —ultimately, indeed, only in terms of his colleague's approbation. It would be an oversimplification to see the Guiteau affair as merely an arena for the confrontation of local and cosmopolitan values; yet it would be a useful and in essence meaningful oversimplification.

The course of events during and immediately following the Guiteau trial demonstrated vividly the neurologists' affirmation of the apparently selfless—and in that sense spiritual—absolutes of science. What could be purer or less compromising than a life dedicated to the search for truth? "Very terrible is the religion of truth," as Cesare Lombroso himself put it: "The physiologist is not afraid to reduce love to a play of stamens and pistils, and thought to a molecular movement." Such zealous attitudes could both motivate and sanction an aggressive righteousness. Thus, for example, the neurologist's bumptious and self-confident opposition to lawyers and the law. The attorney, they felt, had to work within a confining network of artificiality—dependent upon the manipulation of "mere verbiage" and obedient to the dicta of "medieval lore" and "hidebound precedent." The scientist, on the other hand, made no such demeaning compromises in his search for knowledge. Those physicians who had sided with the government in the prosecution of Guiteau had not only accepted the artificialities of the law but had submitted themselves with enthusiasm to the intellectually compromising needs of society. These accommodating physicians were the true materialists.

Beard, Spitzka, Kiernan, and Godding all vied in applying their own variety of moral exegesis to the trial. Beard, for example, produced a brief polemic entitled *Salem Witchcraft,* in which he compared Guiteau's trial with that granted Massachusetts' seventeenth-century witches and wizards. The moral was inescapable: "the settled opinion," he declared, "of the future will be that the death of President Garfield was a horrible accident, as though he had been crushed in a railway collision, or suffocated in a burning theatre, or suddenly stabbed while walking the wards of an asylum." There was, Beard wrote, no civilized country in the world—with the exception of his own—in which Guiteau would have been brought to trial, let alone convicted.

Though by no means a completely homogeneous group, the neurologists could also—on the whole—find assurance in their general agreement upon the appropriate diagnosis for Guiteau.* He seemed clearly a case of *"primäre Verrücktheit"* (primary insanity); his inspiration and the President's consequent "removal" were inextricable parts of his systematized delusion. No overt hallucinatory experience need be involved. German sponsorship of this new diagnosis made it only the more plausible. More than a year before the assassination, Spitzka had argued that a fourth of all the mentally ill were victims of this new disease—unwilling though the more conservative might be to concede its existence.

Clearly, the neurologists felt, their Old Guard opponents were pandering to public opinion in arguing as they did that moral insanity had no place in science and that mental disease was infrequently hereditary.** One need not accept

* On many other issues, the neurologists did not agree. Spitzka, for example, with his European training and anatomical sophistication, had only contempt for Beard's "soft" and somewhat opportunistic championing of neurasthenia. W. A. Hammond, another prominent neurologist and sometime Civil War Surgeon-General, agreed that Guiteau was insane —but argued that he should hang, that even the insane could exert some self-control. How else was order maintained in an asylum?

** It should be noted that spokesmen for the asylum superintendents' association also criticized their neurological opponents for pandering to public prejudice—as in their the reality of primary insanity as a specific disease picture; yet one could hardly doubt, the neurologists maintained, these more general and well-attested observations. To question such views, as Beard put it, was "to deny under oath facts of science which were as well-established as the Copernican theory." No really scientific physician denied that heredity was perhaps the most important single factor in the etiology of mental illness; no genuine psychiatrist doubted the existence of "a psychosis of which moral manifestations are the most plain and obvious symptoms." Considerations of social policy could never make that true which is false in fact.

Gradually, of course, impassioned discussions of the Guiteau trial ended. It soon became a memory, an incident in textbooks of psychiatry and legal medicine. Conflict within American psychiatry, however, did not cease; the Guiteau case had served only to help polarize existing antagonisms. In the early 1880's, the short-lived National Association for the Protection of the Insane and the Prevention of Insanity provided—with the continued agitation of the New York Neurological Society—a new focus for attacks by medical and humanitarian reformers upon the conservative and still dominant establishment in the asylum superintendents' association. Not surprisingly, many of the leaders in this crusading Association—most notably George Beard and Miss A. A. Chevaillier—were active in the fight to have President Arthur appoint a lunacy commission to evaluate Guiteau's mental condition. The conflict over psychiatric values and practices culminated symbolically in 1894 in a much-quoted Semi-Centennial Address to the American Medico-Psychological Association. (In 1892, significantly, the Association of Medical Superintendents had changed its name to the American Medico-Psychologi-

---

opposition to asylums and participation in the National Association for the Protection of the Insane and the Prevention of Insanity.

cal Association; the new title clearly implied the beginnings of a new orientattion toward the world of psychiatry.) It was delivered by S. Weir Mitchell, the scientifically eminent yet socially impeccable Philadelphia neurologist. He attacked vigorously—and some must have thought ungraciously—the Association's institutional and administrative failings.

By 1894, of course, the balance of conviction had already begun to shift. The dozen years between Guiteau's execution and the delivery of Mitchell's harsh address had been critical ones in the reshaping of American medicine. New patterns in specialization, the increasing elaboration of knowledge, the growing demand for reform in medical education—all were part of a new world view being accepted by the medical profession's opinion-shaping elite. The establishment within the asylum superintendents' association was—even in the early 1880's—already fighting a rear guard action. The intellectual climate of American psychiatry was clearly changing, paralleling developments reshaping other medical and scientific fields; internal and disciplinary considerations rather than external, social attributes would now ordinarily determine the distribution of status and influence within the psychiatric guild.

In some ways, the psychological medicine of the twentieth century has served merely to reformulate rather than resolve the continuing social dilemma created by the possibly insane criminal. In the immediate aftermath of the Guiteau trial, the problems surrounding the determination of criminal responsibility seemed particularly difficult of solution; the intractable and morally righteous stance of both defense and prosecution experts underlined and exacerbated the difficulties inherent in finding appropriate answers.

The Guiteau affair did, however, make a number of things apparent. One was that the term "moral insanity" no longer served a useful social purpose—though it might express a valid and time-tested clinical insight. Its precise clinical meaning had become quite clouded as well; it was in this sense obsolete, too indeterminate to serve any longer as a specific diagnostic category.

Secondly, the Guiteau case demonstrated anew that the circumstances of a particular case had ordinarily as much to do with its disposition as the precise injunctions of rules of law. (Studies conducted at the University of Chicago within the past decade have demonstrated the continued reality of this commonsensical observation. "Jurors" in mock trials tended to make their decisions in terms of the circumstances of a case, and in light of their own views of mental illness, rather than in strict accordance with differing rules of law presented to them.) Many observers agreed after the trial that if an individual of Guiteau's marked eccentricity had killed an ordinary man—"Patrick Burns who carries a hod," a prominent New York lawyer suggested whimsically—he would almost certainly not have been convicted; very likely he would not even have been brought to trial. Similarly, while Garfield lay on his sickbed, it was commonly assumed that his assailant would be institutionalized if the President should survive. But if not, then not.

Finally, medical men of all ideological and scientific persuasions agreed, in reflecting upon the Guiteau trial that the existing system of expert testimony should somehow be amended. The embarrassing contrasts in medical reasoning, the awkward clash of personalities, the seemingly unavoidable conflict between medical diagnosis and rules of law—all this might have been avoided should some system of court-appointed advisers replace the adversary system. Only Spitzka, oddly enough, expressed reservations. European judges, he warned, though perhaps no more insightful than their American counterparts, were morally obligated to choose as officers of the court men of acknowledged status and authority. With American medical schools still so unfortunate in their selection of faculty, with political and financial considerations still factors in professional success, the commission system in the United States might prove even less successful than the present arrangement. "I grant," he argued, "that if, with the plan as it stands on paper, we could also import the laboratories, the matured educational institutions, and the excellent medico-legal literature of France, Germany, and Italy, there should not be a moment's hesitation about its adoption." But, he concluded, a commission system would be no improvement unless this "exotic can be transplanted with enough of its roots and soil to ensure a healthy domestic growth."

For educated and articulate Americans generally, however, the problem of evaluating criminal responsibility was almost synonymous with the by now familiar yet threatening term, moral insanity; once the word was pronounced all rational discussion ceased. Indeed, one partisan of the defense witnesses in the Guiteau case wrote an elaborate article in which he suggested the use of the term "psychosensory insanity" to describe many of those individuals previously classified under the rubric of moral insanity; this rose might by another name smell far more fragrant.

The tone of fundamentalist irritation in which attacks on moral insanity were phrased only reassured the neurologists in their moral and scientific superiority. But those medical men less assured in their knowledge, more dependent perhaps on their patients' opinion, were always conscious in discussing moral insanity of the public censure its endorsement might bring.* Psychologists, while still anxious to

---

* In January of 1882, for example, John Gray was able to have the following resolution passed unanimously by the Medical Society of the State of New York at their Annual Meeting: *"Resolved,* That the true functions of the medical expert is to expound and interpret the results of pathological conditions, and that in the absence of disease he is not justified in drawing conclusions, as to civil responsibility, from moral manifestations of conduct, that department belonging exclusively to law" (*Transactions,* 1882, p. 59).

have their specialty recognized as a science, must, one spokesman for the establishment warned, guard against the "imputation of having contributed to the demoralization of society." Criminal courts existed to protect the innocent from the depraved—not to act as missionaries or tract distributors to the vicious. Spitzka, not surprisingly, became the particular object of righteous anxiety. J. J. Elwell, for example, a prominent authority on legal medicine, called the New Yorker

a weak echo of a class of modern crazy German pagans, who are trying with what help they can get in America, from such "scientific alienists" as he, to break down all the safeguards of our Christian civilization, by destroying if possible all grounds for human responsibility—putting forth the cold vagaries of agnosticism and nihilistic utilitarianism—accepting nothing beyond the reach of uncertain human experiment and his own fallible reason. . . . Had Dr. Spitzka been present when God said "Let us make man," he would have responded to the "us"; and, while he hardly would have undertaken the main work of creation, he would have made valuable suggestions. . . . With him brain and mind are coexistent and coeval—the death of the material terminates the mental. Depravity and crime are synonymous with disease and circumstance.

The would-be advocate of moral insanity was placed in an extremely awkward position; these hostile attitudes were not only pervasive but were expressed—even by many of the educated and enlightened—with a bitter intensity. The *Nation,* as might have been expected, was particularly cutting: "According to the experts," their editorialist explained sardonically, "the penal justice of society should exist only for the occasional lapses of the class to which it owes nearly everything of value in it—the steady, sober-minded, upright, industrious, and successful."

And even the neurologists had often their difficulties in agreeing upon the diagnosis of a particular case. Many shared the faith of the majority of their fellow Americans in the reality and pervasiveness of sin. Thus, for example,

Charles Folsom, a strong proponent of Guiteau's insanity, and even James G. Kiernan, conceded that the element of depravity might play a part in the total etiology of Guiteau's aberrant personality. And many articulate medical men willing to accept the essential accuracy of the diagnosis made by Spitzka and Kiernan saw no reason to grant such undeniably abnormal individuals immunity from punishment.

Guiteau was dead, his grand destiny fulfilled. Yet the trial's other protagonists—like the intellectual issues it dramatized—remained. Scoville returned to Chicago, Porter to New York and a testimonial dinner—but to a good deal of criticism as well. Corkhill and Davidge too were treated harshly by legal commentators; "Mr. Davidge," as an Albany lawyer put it, "ought to be a little more choice of his epithets. New trials have been granted for an abuse of the public prosecutor's license. . . . As for Corkhill, we give him over." Frances Scoville was adjudged insane in October of 1882—less than a half year after her brother's execution; perhaps the tensions of the trial had been too much for her already tormented mind. (The rumors that pictured Mrs. Scoville as having been insane before the trial may well have had some basis in fact.) Frances did, however, find time to write a "novel," a *roman à clef* entitled *The Stalwarts,* and managed to have it published in 1888. Its hero was one Jules Grieveau, an assassin who had, she hinted darkly, acted as a tool of the Star Route conspirators.

The experts too lived on to practice medicine, to teach, to write, and to appear in court. Not surprisingly, those who had played an active role in the trial did not recant or reconsider. Gray and a number of the other prosecution witnesses wrote elaborate defenses of their position— though in other writings they sometimes assumed more conventionally receptive attitudes toward heredity and moral insanity. Spitzka went on to an eminent and distinguished, if not brilliant, career as an alienist, teacher, and anatomist; and Kiernan to an eventful career as a practitioner and would-be asylum reformer. Hamilton too had a long and successful career in practice and teaching—in the course of which, ironically, he emerged two decades after Guiteau's trial as one of the chief defenders of President McKinley's assasin, Leon Czolgosz. Czolgosz, Hamilton maintained, was clearly and unmistakably insane.* Yet Hamilton never reconsidered his opinion of Guiteau—despite a number of seemingly apparent parallels between his case and that of Czolgosz. In his autobiography, published in 1916, the by-now elderly and honored New Yorker simply reprinted the conclusions he had enunciated at the time of Guiteau's trial; Garfield's assassin was an artful simulator.

And, each spring and fall, dozens of "cranks" still found their way to Washington—seekers after office, supplicants for the payment of fanciful claims. They helped fill boarding houses and hotels, providing amusement as well as annoyance for blasé government clerks. To many Americans, the lasting moral of the Guiteau incident was its proof of the need for somehow sequestering such unhappy souls before they could harm themselves or others.

We are left then with the principal player, with Charles Julius Guiteau. It has frequently been noted that the delusional systems of the mentally ill have a chameleon-like quality, an ability to find themes, tones, specific menaces in the atmosphere and events of their times. The human tragedy of Guiteau is almost blurred indeed by the precise surrealism of his prose, the feeling for the appropriate cliché, the meaningful theme. His prose has the flat, one

---

* This latter pathetic regicide—who considered himself an anarchist somewhat as Guiteau considered himself a "Stalwart of the Stalwarts"—was given the merest caricature of a trial. Intellectual changes within the psychiatric profession had obviously little effect upon social policy in regard to so sensitive a matter.

dimensional quality of a cardboard Victorian novel; one thinks when reading his letters or speeches of one of Horatio Alger's heroes—or perhaps even more of Nathanael West's Lemuel Pitkin. Yet at the same time Guiteau chose unerringly among the most meaningful values and preoccupations of American life—success through morality and self-improvement, evangelical religion, enthusiastic politics, and venturesome business enterprise. He expressed in his ingenuous fashion more covert patterns as well: the mixture of self-conscious gentility and grand inelegance, of an aggressive moralism compensating for the nouveau's insecurity—no word was more important than "high-toned" in Charles's vocabulary. Though perhaps an example of a commonplace illness, he had the ability to portray tragically and unselfconsciously a drama characteristically American as he acted out his sickness.

A NOTE ON SOURCES

The most important single source for this book has been the trial transcript: *Report of the Proceedings in the Case of the United States vs. Charles J. Guiteau, tried in the Supreme Court of the District of Columbia, holding a Criminal Term, and beginning November 14, 1881,* 3 vols. (Washington, 1882). The government, however, published the *Proceedings* in a discreetly small edition and it is something of a rare book. More easily accessible are accounts of the assassination and trial rushed into print by eager publishers at the time; though much abridged from the formal proceedings, they provide in addition something of the courtroom and prison atmosphere surrounding the trial. The best such account is that of H. G. and C. J. Hayes, "Special Stenographic Reporters for the New York Associated Press," in *A Complete History of the Trial of Charles Julius Guiteau, Assassin of President Garfield* ... (Philadelphia, 1882). The summaries of testimony are on the whole quite accurate, and this volume reprints as appendixes the "Autobiography" dictated by Guiteau to Edmund A. Bailey (pp. 405–52), and an account of the "Married Life of Charles Julius Guiteau by his former Wife, Mrs. Annie J. Dunmire" (pp. 455–523).

In addition to these official and quasi-official compilations, contemporary newspapers have provided the most important source in reconstructing the narrative aspects of the trial and events surrounding it. They provide, of course, a running account of the assassination and the atmosphere both during Garfield's illness and the trial itself—and, in addition, interviews with many of the trial's more important protagonists. I have relied most heavily on the Washington *Post,* the New York *Herald,* and the *New York Times.* On the whole, the *Post* provided the most complete and circumstantial account of the trial and events preceding it; the Washington *Sunday Chronicle, Evening Star,* and

Critic, all of which appealed to a "tabloid" audience, yielded comments of a somewhat less dignified cast.

These sources, necessary for describing the trial, have been useful as well in helping reconstruct Guiteau's life before the assassination. The newspapers provided accounts of numerous incidents illuminating Guiteau's years of wandering. And both defense and prosecution introduced scores of documents and letters relating to the defendant's pre-assassination years, the defense, of course, hoping to prove Guiteau chronically insane, the prosecution intent on showing him to have been a petty criminal and schemer. Some of these letters have not survived in other forms.

The sources for Guiteau's life are otherwise scattered and, in many cases, difficult to evaluate—none more so than the numerous accounts that appeared in newspapers and magazines immediately after the assassination. There is a useful and lucid biographical sketch of Guiteau by Stewart Mitchell, "The Man who Murdered Garfield," *Proceedings of the Massachusetts Historical Society,* 68 (1941–44): 452–89. None of the contemporary and sensationalistic pamphlet accounts of the assassin's life are reliable as to fact—though all, of course, are of interest in themselves. Guiteau's brother, John Wilson Guiteau performed a service for the historian in gathering and publishing a number of significant letters while documenting the assassin's appeal for a stay of execution: *Letters and Facts not heretofore Published, Touching the Mental Condition of Charles J. Guiteau since 1865* ... [New York, 1882]. This pamphlet was widely circulated by the neurologist supporters of the defense; the copy in the Library of the College of Physicians of Philadelphia, for example, was presented by George M. Beard. An indispensable source for any prospective psychological study of the assassin are Guiteau's own "theological" writings: *The Truth: A Companion to the Bible. By Charles J. Guiteau, Theologian* (Boston, 1879); *A Reply to Recent Attacks on the Bible, together with some Valuable Ideas on Christ's Second Coming, and on Hades, or the Resting Place of the Dead* (Syracuse, N.Y., 1878).

Several score of Guiteau's letters—the majority written during his imprisonment—have been preserved in manuscript form. The Chicago Historical Society possesses a particularly important group, including several letters from the assassin's youth. A number of other very interesting Guiteau letters and memorabilia were examined through the courtesy of Mr. Justin G. Turner of Los Angeles. Perhaps the most important single source of manuscript materials relating to the actual conduct of the trial is to be found in the National Archives. (Since the Supreme Court of the District of Columbia was a federal court its records have been deposited in the Archives.) The Guiteau trial is Criminal Case #14056, United States Supreme Court for the District of Columbia. This file contains a number of Guiteau's prison letters and, more important, a great number of depositions taken by the district atorney's office in the course of preparing their case. The Archives also contain several invaluable documents printed for the convenience of the prosecution but never formally published. One is a sixteen page statement of John Humphrey Noyes's position in regard to Guiteau's insanity, "Guiteau vs. Oneida Community." Noyes documents Guiteau's tangled relationship with the Community with important contemporary letters—presumably from Noyes's own records. Perhaps even more valuable is a formal printed account of John P. Gray's pretrial interview with the prisoner (*The United States vs. Charles J. Guiteau. Indicted for Murder of James A. Garfield, Twentieth President of the United States. Opinion of John P. Gray, M.D. Superintendent of the Utica Insane Asylum, on the Question of the Sanity of the Prisoner* [Washington, 1882]). This was the interview described at some length in the text. Some of these printed documents—with marginal emphases in ink—are also available at the Library of the Association of the Bar of the City of New York, possibly a gift from John K. Porter.

Other record groups at the National Archives also contain materials concerning the trial and Garfield's illness and funeral. Letters relating to the recruitment of prosecution lawyers are in the records of the Department of Justice and others documenting Garfield's burial and medical expenses are in the Records of the General Accounting Office.

Another valuable body of manuscript materials illuminates in detail Guiteau's last weeks in prison and his execution. This is the collection of the Reverend William W. Hicks, the Washington clergyman who so gained the assassin's confidence during his last weeks of imprisonment. These materials are now in the possession of the Harvard Medical Library in the Francis A. Countway Library of Medicine and I have examined them through the courtesy of Mr. Richard Wolfe, Rare Books Librarian. The most important item in the collection is Hicks's "Personal Note Book and Diary Relating to Charles J. Guiteau." Entries in this diary detail each of the interviews Hicks had with the prisoner from mid-June until Guiteau's execution on the thirtieth as well as accounts of Hicks's role as go-between in attempts to gain the assassin a stay of execution. Hicks also kept the letters he received in connection with the case and a number of Guiteau's literary productions. Also present is Guiteau's own copy of *The Truth and the Removal*, the autobiographical project upon which the assassin spent many of his hours in the condemned cell. It is a paper-covered volume of 237 pages and includes Guiteau's earlier theological contribution, *The Truth* in addition to the prisoner's account of the trial and his reflections upon it. Charles planned to sell the book for two dollars a copy through the mail. Hicks never wrote the book that he originally planned, but did use these materials in a series of articles on "The True Story of Guiteau," which appeared in the New York *Sunday World,* November 12, 19, 26, and December 3, 1893.

I have in addition—and since completing this manuscript—discovered a collection of letters and clippings relating to the trial kept by one of its chief protagonists, Edward Charles Spitzka; these have been consulted through the courtesy of Dr. Robert Ravel, Strafford, Pennsylvania. The Spitzka letters provide a number of revealing insights into the organization of the defense. Several letters, for example, from Miss A. A. Chevaillier of Boston indicate her presence in Washington during the trial and the active role she played in advising the defense. Other letters in this collection illustrate the grossly undignified manner in which histological materials were treated after Guiteau's autopsy; they were—in the words of E. O. Shakespeare, a participant —"inconsiderately handled and hacked to pieces and scattered indiscriminately." Another letter documents District Attorney Corkhill's chilly refusal to allow Spitzka to witness the autopsy. Not least of all, the collection includes a number of examples of that fascinating genre, the abusive and obscene crank letter—of the kind always evoked by such emotion-laden events, but which never, of course, find their way into print.

In reconstructing the assassination and its immediate aftermath, I have relied most heavily on the newspapers already cited and have in a number of instances amplified and corrected these news stories with testimony presented at the trial. The Garfield Papers in the Manuscript Division of the Library of Congress contain a fascinating assortment of letters written to the wounded president, many containing home remedies or offers to exterminate the assassin. The literature on Garfield's wound and its treatment is particularly voluminous and would, indeed, provide the basis for a monograph in itself. Several specific issues were involved. First and most obvious was the question of evaluating the treatment Garfield received; there is a tradition of interest among surgeons in the controverted treatment of famous patients. Moreover, this incident serves as an excellent case study illustrating the confusion surrounding the introduction of antiseptic surgery. For a relatively recent evaluation of Garfield's treatment, see: Stewart A. Fish, "The Death of President Garfield," *Bulletin of the History of Medicine,* 24 (1950): 378–92 and the references cited. Cf: Stewart M. Brooks, *Our Murdered Presidents: The Medical Story* (New York, c. 1966), pp. 55–125; J. Howe Adams, *A History of the Life of D. Hayes Agnew, M.D., Ll.D.* (Philadelphia and London, 1892), pp. 220–49; William A. Hammond, J. Marion Sims, John T. Hodgen, and John Ashurst, Jr., "The Surgical Treatment of President Garfield," *North American Review,* 133 (1881): 578–610. The History of Medicine Division in the National Library of Medicine contains three scrapbooks of clippings from the New York *Herald,* providing a day-by-day account of the President's illness. For a description of attempts to "air-condition" Garfield's sickroom, see: U.S. Navy, *Reports of Officers of the Navy on Ventilating and Cooling the Executive Mansion During the Illness of President Garfield* (Washington, 1882). Even more interesting than the controversy over the president's surgical treatment is the light shed by the incident on contemporary standards of medical ethics and lay attitudes toward the profession. There was not only much invidious discussion of Garfield's treatment but also criticism of the fees submitted by his physicians to the government and of the unseemly competition between Washington physicians for the privilege of treating this eminent patient.

For lay attitudes toward mental illness and criminal responsibility, I have tried to consult a representative assortment of magazines and weekly newspapers. These have, for example, included Methodist, Baptist, Catholic, Episcopal, and free thought weeklies. The *Nation, Harper's Weekly,* and the *Independent* seemed adequately representative of general educated opinion. All of these publications have contributed to the narrative as well, for many published correspondence from Washington visitors, often containing valuable and in some cases extremely vivid descriptions of events during the trial. This was the origin, for example, of the mid-trial analysis of Guiteau's behavior by the reverend editor of the New York *Christian Advocate* cited earlier: J. M. Buckley, "A Study of Guiteau," *Christian Advocate,* 57 (January 12, 1882): 17–18. Cf.: Mary Clemmer, "A Woman's Letter from Washington. The Assassination," *Independent,* 33 (July 21, 1881): 1–3.

The narrative has also benefited from my reading of the formal and eulogistic statements made at the time of Garfield's death. Such materials are overwhelmingly abundant and there seemed little point in conducting an exhaustive search for funeral sermons, orations, and the like; using only the resources of the Library of Congress, the State Historical Society of Wisconsin, and the Columbia University Library, I was able to consult well over two hundred eulogies of the dead President. I had originally planned to use this material—and similar statements drawn from newspapers and periodicals—as the basis for a somewhat extended discussion of American social values, but I soon became dismayed at the logical pitfalls implicit in any attempt to evaluate the themes reiterated in these highly stylized eulogies. (Almost all of which were produced by a comparatively limited if articulate segment of society.) Historians have in recent years been much attracted by the possibilities of using such "mythic" constructs as an index to the configuration of social values at particular moments in time (the assumption being that the values expressed in such essentially collective forms of expression must be those controlling a society's cultural world view). There has, however, been no adequate discussion of the methodological difficulties inherent in the use of such sources. For example, it has never been made clear what the relationship is between such formal values and actual cultural determinants of behavior—or how widely and in what pattern such values are distributed in society. For studies of reactions to the deaths of other nineteenth-century American presidents see: Howard H. Peckham, "Tears for Old Tippecanoe; Religious Interpretations of

President Harrison's Death," *Proceedings of the American Antiquarian Society,* 69 (1959): 17–36; Charles J. Stewart, "Lincoln's Assassination and the Protestant Clergy of the North," *Journal of the Illinois Historical Society,* 54 (1961): 268–93. John William Ward's study of the "symbol" of Andrew Jackson has been particularly influential in this connection (*Andrew Jackson: Symbol for an Age* [New York, 1955]).

There are a number of sources useful in beginning a study of the political life of the period and Garfield's non-mythic career. Two standard biographies of Garfield are available, one by Theodore Smith, which includes many of Garfield's letters and much material relating to the Ohioan's early life, and the other by Robert G. Caldwell, a more narrowly political biography. Both are in some ways in need of revision. (Smith, *The Life and Letters of James Abram Garfield,* 2 vols. [New Haven, 1925]; Caldwell, *James A. Garfield. Party Chieftain* [New York, 1931].) For a more recent and thorough study of the problems surrounding the civil service issue, see: Ari Hoogenboom, *Outlawing the Spoils. A History of the Civil Service Reform Movement 1865–1883* (Urbana, Ill., 1961), especially pp. 179–214. There is also available a study, *The Presidential Election of 1880,* by Herbert J. Clancy, S.J. (Chicago, 1958). One might well also consult Lloyd Lewis and Henry Justin Smith's *Oscar Wilde Discovers America [1882]* (New York, 1936), a rather arbitrary but richly impressionistic picture of American society in the early 1880's.

There have been as well a number of historical accounts of Guiteau and his trial. Probably the best is still that written by near-contemporary William W. Ireland, himself a prominent English alienist (*Through the Ivory Gate: Studies in Psychology and History* [Edinburgh and London, 1889], pp. 160–228). A recent, brief, and readable account is that by Robert J. Donovan, *The Assassins* (New York, 1955), pp. 14–62. Other useful accounts are:

Frederick Fenning, "The Trial of Guiteau," *American Journal of Psychiatry,* 13 (1933): 127–39; E. Hilton Jackson, "The Trial of Guiteau," *Virginia Law Register,* 9 (1904): 1034; John H. Cassity, *The Quality of Murder. A Psychiatric and Legal Evaluation of Motives and Responsibilities in the Plea of Insanity as Revealed in Outstanding Murder Cases of this Century* (New York, 1958), pp. 19–32.

The most difficult interpretive problems in the Guiteau affair relate neither to the assassination, nor to the prisoner's biography, nor even to the actual conduct of the trial, but to understanding the changing and diffuse psychiatric ideas of this generation. Equally confusing is the relation of these medical ideas to the criminal law. There is, unfortunately, no guide or *vade mecum* that allows the common reader convenient access to the issues at stake.

In the area of psychiatric history, moreover, there are a number of persistently confusing dilemmas. One is the polarization already referred to in the conclusion, that between the periods before and after Freud; too many historians of psychiatry have seen pre-twentieth century psychiatric thought almost wholly in terms of its relationship to Freud. This polarization has tended to create a value-laden distinction between the somatic—on the whole to be deplored—and the psychological. As we have seen, however, the psychiatric thought of the late nineteenth century simply does not fit into this either-or, saved or damned, pattern. A second and equally important problem rests in the nature of the traditional canon of psychiatric history. The formal and theoretical aspects of the field have almost completely preempted the historians' interest; correspondingly little attention is paid to the day-to-day care and treatment of the mentally ill. To put the matter crudely, historians of psychiatry have been concerned largely with what has been said, rather than what has been actually done.

Yet in understanding a problem such as the historical

treatment of the possibly insane criminal, descriptive and institutional studies are particularly valuable. We have many discussions of the merits of particular rules for determining criminal responsibility, yet almost no studies of the ways in which insane criminals were actually treated at particular places and particular moments in time. This may perhaps seem—to the non-historian—as a rather antiquarian desire; obviously all legal causes are affected by social values and the circumstances of the individual case. But this is precisely why the events of a trial can be of such value to the social historian, who is concerned directly with the nuances of social attitude inevitably revealed during a criminal process.

Despite these words of caution, however, it is possible to suggest a number of studies useful in pursuing these problems. A brief and unpretentious guide to the history of psychiatry before Freud has been written by Erwin H. Ackerknecht (*A Short History of Psychiatry,* trans. by Sulammith Wolff [New York and London, 1959]). Turning more specifically to the United States, there is a readable and on the whole still reliable social history of psychiatry and the mentally ill by Albert Deutsch (*The Mentally Ill in America. A History of their Care and Treatment from Colonial Times,* 2nd ed. [New York, 1949]). Though superseded in its treatment of a number of issues and thin in its discussion of others, this broadly-conceived study is still the only unified account of the subject. In 1944, the American Psychiatric Association sponsored an ambitious centennial volume, *One Hundred Years of American Psychiatry* (New York, 1944). The contributions that make up the volume are, however, somewhat uneven. Gregory Zilboorg's chapter on the "Legal Aspects of Psychiatry" (pp. 507–84) is insubstantial and fails to give an accurate account of the status of moral insanity in nineteenth-century America. Albert Deutsch's article on "The History of Mental Hygiene" (pp. 325–65) contains some material not included in his general survey and—from our point of view

—much of interest on the history of the National Association for the Protection of the Insane and Prevention of Insanity and the conflict between neurologists and intramural psychiatrists. Several recent studies have replaced or supplemented these standard sources in their treatment of specific issues. The logical place now to begin any study of the status of American psychiatry in the first half of the nineteenth century is Norman Dain's *Concepts of Insanity in the United States, 1789–1865* (New Brunswick, N.J., 1964). The notes to Dain's study provide not only an excellent guide to available primary sources but references to almost all the pertinent historical studies available by 1964. Gerald N. Grob's even more recent history of the Worcester State Hospital (*The State and the Mentally Ill. A History of the Worcester State Hospital in Massachusetts, 1830–1920* [Chapel Hill, N.C., c. 1966]), provides an important companion piece to Dain's *Concepts of Insanity* for its illustration of general intellectual and institutional trends in the well-defined context of a particular hospital. Charles E. Rosenberg's "The Place of George M. Beard in Nineteenth-Century Psychiatry," *Bulletin of the History of Medicine,* 36 (1962): 245–59, provides an analysis of one significant figure in the Guiteau trial. A recent doctoral dissertation provides much added material on the neurologist–asylum superintendent feud: Barbara Sicherman, "The Quest for Mental Health in America, 1880–1917," Ph.D. dissertation, Columbia University, 1967. Two other monographs provide materials useful in gaining an understanding of the popular concepts of personality and responsibility manifested during the Guiteau trial: David Brion Davis, *Homicide in American Fiction, 1789–1860: A Study in Social Values* (Ithaca, N.Y., 1957); John D. Davies, *Phrenology, Fad and Science: A 19th Century American Crusade* (New Haven, 1955).

Moral insanity will certainly prove the most confusing single issue for anyone hoping to gain an understanding of ideas concerning criminal responsibility in the late nineteenth century. Not only was the term used differently at different times and by different writers, but—as we have suggested—it soon came to symbolize a number of socially sensitive legal problems. The term "moral insanity" kept changing, becoming steadily more inclusive throughout the century. A study of the concept—if conceived in terms sufficiently broad and international—would amount to a history of clinical psychiatry in the late eighteenth and nineteenth centuries (with the exception of certain marked conditions, such as severe mental deficiency or deteriorated schizophrenia, which were, of course, never considered under this rubric). There are, however, a number of useful places to begin in a study of this problem: Raymond De Saussure, "The Influence of the Concept of Monomania on French Medico-Legal Psychiatry (From 1825 to 1840)," *Journal of the History of Medicine,* 1 (1946): 365–97; Eric T. Carlson and Norman Dain, "The Meaning of Moral Insanity," *Bulletin of the History of Medicine,* 36 (1962): 130–40; Sidney Maughs, "A Concept of Psychopathy and Psychopathic Personality: Its Evolution and Historical Development," *Journal of Criminal Psychopathology,* 2 (1941): 329–56. (The last-mentioned should be used with caution.) For an understanding of the meaning of moral insanity at any particular moment in time, one must consult contemporary discussions. With reference to the Guiteau trial, an excellent place to begin is a symposium on "The Moral Responsibility of the Insane," published in the *North American Review,* January, 1882, pp. 1–39. Contributors included J. J. Elwell, George M. Beard, E. C. Seguin, J. S. Jewell, and Charles Folsom. For contemporary English opinion see, for example: George H. Savage, "Moral Insanity," *J. Mental Science,* 27 (1881): 147–55; David Nicolson, "The Measure of Individual and Social Responsibility in Criminal Cases," *Ibid.,* 24 (1878): 1–25, 249–73. Nicolson presents forcefully an argument current among English specialists in mental illness—that the M'Naghten rule tended in practice to be ignored and thus ranked as a "mere sophism." For examples of the rejection by physicians of the logical validity of the M'Naghten rule see: William Wood, *Remarks on the Plea of Insanity and on the Management of Criminal Lunatics,* 2nd ed. (London, 1852); John Charles Bucknill, *Unsoundness of Mind in Relation to Criminal Acts. An Essay to which the First Sugden Prize was this Year Awarded by the King and Queen's College of Physicians in Ireland* (London, 1854). D. Hack Tuke and Henry Maudsley, probably England's most prominent psychiatrists of this generation, were both strong advocates of the essential validity of the moral insanity concept. Cf.: Henry Maudsley, *Responsibility in Mental Disease* (New York, 1874); D. Hack Tuke, *Prichard and Symonds. In Especial Relation to Mental Science. With Chapters on Moral Insanity* (London, 1891). In the United States, Isaac Ray was clearly the most prominent and influential exponent of moral insanity and of the essential irresponsibility of those suffering from this ailment. Ray's most influential work was *A Treatise on the Medical Jurisprudence of Insanity,* the first edition of which appeared in Boston in 1837. (A later edition has recently been reprinted by the Harvard University Press with an introduction by Winfred Overholser [Cambridge, 1962].) Ray's *Treatise* was internationally known and was, indeed, quoted at length by the defense in the M'Naghten trial (Bernard L. Diamond, "Isaac Ray and the Trial of Daniel M'Naghten," *American Journal of Psychiatry,* 112 [1955–56]:651–56). Perhaps even more valuable to the historian are Ray's collected essays, most of which relate either to the general problem of criminal responsibility or to particular cases (*Contributions to Mental Pathology* [Boston, 1873]).

The formal legal framework for adjudging cases that involved a possibility of insanity is far easier to determine and evaluate. There was a great deal of legal interest in these problems both immediately before and, of course, during and after the Guiteau trial. I have found the following articles particularly useful. A. G. Sedgwick, "Issues Involving the Fact of Insanity. The Burden of Proof," *American Law Review,* 16 (1882): 118–27; Francis Wharton, "Presumptions in Criminal Cases," *Criminal Law Magazine,* I (1880): 1–46, especially 32–38; William Russell Smith, *Assassination and Insanity: Guiteau's Case Examined and Compared with Analagous Cases from the Earlier to the Present Times* (Washington, 1881); "Insanity as a Defence —Burden of Proof. Alabama Supreme Court. Braswell v. State," *Criminal Law Magazine,* 2 (1881): 32–45; John Ordronaux, "The Plea of Insanity as an Answer to an Indictment," *Criminal Law Magazine,* 1 (1880): 431–51; Ordronaux, "Judicial Problems relating to the Disposal of Insane Criminals," *Criminal Law Magazine,* 2 (1881): 591–618, 729–52; Henry Wade Rogers, "Insanity—Burden of Proof," *Central Law Journal,* 14 (January 6, 1882): 2–7; Francis Wharton, *A Treatise on Mental Unsoundness, Embracing a General View of Psychological Law* (Philadelphia, 1882), pp. 108–201. The New Hampshire doctrine of insanity—which, it will be recalled, Scoville had asked the Court to adopt—represents a fascinating historical problem in itself. Several important recent articles by John Reid provide new insight into its origins: "Understanding the New Hampshire Doctrine of Criminal Insanity," *Yale Law Journal,* 69 (1960): 367–420; "A Speculative Novelty: Judge Doe's Search for Reason in the Law of Evidence," *Boston University Law Review,* 39 (1959): 321–48. A revealing correspondence between Isaac Ray and Charles Doe of the New Hampshire Supreme Court, the architect of the New Hampshire rule, have been conveniently edited and reprinted: Louis E. Reik, "The Doe-Ray Correspondence: A Pioneer Collaboration in the Jurisprudence of Mental Disease," *Yale Law Journal,* 63 (1953): 183–96. For a few contemporary evaluations of the continuing problems involving the possibly mentally ill offender see, for example: John Biggs, *The Guilty Mind; Psychiatry and the Law of Homicide* (New York, 1955); Philip Q. Roche, *The Criminal Mind; A Study in Com-*

munication between the Criminal Law and Psychiatry (New York, 1958); American Bar Foundation, *The Mentally Disabled and the Law; the Report on the Rights of the Mentally Ill,* ed. Frank T. Lindman and Donald M. McIntyre (Chicago, 1961); American Law Institute, *Model Penal Code. Tentative Drafts Nos. 1, 2, 3 and 4* (Philadelphia, 1956), especially Appendix C, "Excerpts from Correspondence Between Dr. Manfred Guttmacher and Herbert Wechsler Relating to the Problem of Defining the Criteria of Irresponsibility in the Model Penal Code," pp. 182–92; Rita M. James, "Juror's Assessment of Criminal Responsibility," *Social Problems,* 7 (1959): 58–69; Abe Krash, "The Durham Rule and Judicial Administration of the Insanity Defense in the District of Columbia," *Yale Law Journal,* 70 (1961): 905–52. For an illuminating recent reevaluation of the common-law origins of the M'Naghten test see: Anthony Platt and Bernard L. Diamond, "The Origins of the 'Right and Wrong' Test of Criminal Responsibility and its Subsequent Development in the United States: An Historical Survey," *California Law Review,* 54 (1966): 1227–260. I have also found the discussions of the M'Naghten test in the report of the Royal Commission on Capital Punishment extremely valuable (United Kingdom, Royal Commission on Capital Punishment, 1949–1953, *Report Presented to Parliament by Command of Her Majesty September, 1953.* [London, 1953], especially pp. 73–144, 391–428).

In the research for this book, I sought to arrive at some feeling for consensus in the legal community by consulting a cross-section of legal periodicals. The following seemed to me of particular relevance: New York *Daily Register,* July, 1881–June 30, 1882; *The Criminal Law Magazine* (Jersey City), 1–3, 1880–82; *Albany Law Journal,* 14–15, 1881–82 (weekly); *Washington Law Reporter,* 9–10, 1881–82 (weekly); *Central Law Journal* (St. Louis), 13–14, July, 1881–July, 1882 (weekly); *American Law Review* (Boston, 15–16, 1881–82 (monthly).

As a class, the most illuminating materials relating to the psychiatric aspects of the Guiteau trial were journal articles written by physicians who participated in it. An understanding of the trial's psychiatric testimony and of the extra-courtroom hostilities demands, as has been noted, some familiarity with the personal and intellectual disagreements that had simmered—and sometimes boiled—for a half-dozen years before the assassination. I refer most immediately to the bitter conflict between the neurologists and their superintendent opponents. Much of the material documenting this feud appeared in the three American medical journals specifically dedicated to the field of psychiatry; these were the *American Journal of Insanity,* organ of the "establishment," and the *Journal of Nervous and Mental Disease* and *Alienist and Neurologist*—the latter two were more impartial, but sympathetic on the whole to the neurologists. The *Chicago Medical Review* and the *St. Louis Clinical Record* also printed editorials and articles critical of Gray and the asylum superintendents. The *American Journal of Neurology and Psychiatry,* founded in 1882, served as an additional sounding board for the neurologists —but this was hardly surprising since Spitzka, T. A. McBride, and L. C. Gray, three activist members of the New York Neurological Society, were its editors. The medical press provided in general mixed reports both on the Guiteau trial and the neurologist-superintendent controversy. It would be fair to say, however, that a clear majority of medical editorialists and correspondents assumed a conservative stance in regard to the question of criminal responsibility. This is typified, for example, by the editorialists of the influential Philadelphia weekly *Medical News,* who conceded after the Guiteau autopsy that the neurologists' diagnosis of the assassin was probably right but that far greater danger to society lurked in the exculpation of such dangerous criminals than in the occasional execution of a morally insane offender ("Guiteau—Finis," *Medical News,* 41 [July 1, 1882]: 12).

There is, unfortunately, no detailed account of the extended and complex feud between the neurologists and asylum superintendents, and many of its details are still obscure. The studies by Deutsch and Sicherman previously cited do contain valuable material, however, especially as relating to the National Association for the Protection of the Insane and the Prevention of Insanity. The basic sources for the controversy are still to be found in the publications of this organization and in the pamphlets and articles that constituted the ammunition for both sides. For the NAPIPI see, for example: *Papers and Proceedings, at the Stated Meeting Held in New York City, January 20, 1882* (New York, 1882); *National Association for the Protection of the Insane and the Prevention of Insanity* (Boston, 1880). This later pamphlet contains papers by E. C. Seguin and George M. Beard as well as letters of endorsement and programmatic statements relating to the founding of the Association. Before its premature demise, the NAPIPI also published a journal in 1883–84 and 1884–85, the *American Psychological Journal*. The struggle in New York State, especially relevant to the Guiteau case because of the central roles played by Spitzka and Gray, can be sampled in the following pamphlets: *Report of the Proceedings for Establishing a Board of Commissioners in Lunacy, for the State of New York* (New York, 1880); State of New York, *Report of the Committee on Public Health Relative to Lunatic Asylums. In Senate. May 22, 1879. No. 64* (Albany, 1879); New York Neurological Society, *The Answer of the New York Neurological Society to the Document known as the Report of the Committee on Public Health Relative to Lunatic Asylums. Nr. 64 . . .* (New York, 1880); New York Medico-Legal Society, *Report of the Permanent Commission of the Medico-Legal Society, In Answer to the Senate Resolutions of January 4, 1882, in Reply to the Letter of the Attorney-General and State Commissioner in Lunacy of the State of New York* (n.d.). Of course, one must also consult the writings of spokesmen for the asylum superintendent's association; they returned in good measure the neurologists' abuse. Eugene Grissom of North Carolina was particularly virulent in his language and often chose to answer attacks on the Association and its leadership: "Mechanical Protection for the Violent Insane," *American Journal of Insanity,* 34 (1877–78): 27–58; "True and False Experts," *Ibid.,* 35 (1878–79): 1–36. Similarly vitriolic is a lengthy article by Orpheus Everts in the *AJI* for October, 1881, "The American System of Public Provision for the Insane, and Despotism in Lunatic Asylums." Everts—a prosecution witness at the Guiteau trial—called his opponents "born agitators" and "professional reformers" who themselves moved about the axes of insanity. As a coda to this controversy, one might well consult S. Weir Mitchell's "Address before the American Medico-Psychological Association," reprinted from the *Journal of Nervous and Mental Disease,* July, 1894. This address includes a substantial appendix (pp. 31–61) reprinting the responses of prominent American physicians to a circular letter asking their opinion of asylum conditions and asylum administration. A characteristically outspoken letter from Spitzka (pp. 55–57) indicates that his position had changed but little since the conclusion of the Guiteau case a dozen years before.

The historian of the Guiteau trial is remarkably fortunate in the number of accounts of the affair written by immediate participants. On the prosecution side, John Gray was clearly the most influential and articulate figure, and as editor of the *American Journal of Insanity* he was never modest in committing his words to print. He wrote a lengthy account of the trial and defense of his theoretical position in the *AJI* for January of 1882 (vol. 38, pp. 303–448). Gray's position on the issue of moral insanity and the limits of criminal responsibility was remarkably consistent both before and during the Guiteau trial. Cf.: "Responsibility of the Insane—Homicide in Insanity," *Ibid.,* 32 (1875–76): 1–51, 153–83; "Lord Chief Justice Cockburn on the

Responsibility of the Insane," *Ibid.,* 38 (1881–82): 60–72. For other accounts by prosecution witnesses, see: Henry P. Stearns, "A Contribution in re Guiteau," *Archives of Medicine,* 7 (1882): 286–307; Samuel Worcester, "A Review of the Guiteau Case," *New England Medical Gazette,* 17 (1882): 114–22, 148–58. The most complex in orientation among the prosecution witnesses was Allan McLane Hamilton. Hamilton represented a younger generation than Gray and was flexible enough to accept the diagnostic category of *primäre Verrücktheit* as clinically valid, but refused, on the other hand, to grant such individuals immunity from responsibility (Hamilton, *A Manual of Medical Jurisprudence, with Special Reference to Diseases and Injuries of the Nervous System* [New York and London, 1883], pp. 62–68). Hamilton never altered his opinion of Guiteau, though he reversed his position completely in the somewhat analogous case of Leon Czolgosz, assassin of President McKinley (cf.: Hamilton, "The Case of Guiteau," *Boston Medical & Surgical Journal,* 106 [March 9, 1882]: 235–38; Hamilton, *Recollections of an Alienist. Personal and Professional* [New York, 1916], pp. 350–60). For an account of the Czolgosz affair see: L. Vernon Briggs, *The Manner of Man that Kills* (Boston, 1921), pp. 233–344. Dr. Hamilton was, in any case, in bad odor among neurologists in the early 1880's for other reasons; his appearance for the prosecution in the Guiteau case only confirmed their suspicions. See, for example, the bitter and hostile review of Hamilton's text on *Nervous Diseases* in the *Journal of Nervous and Mental Disease,* 9 (1882): 184–95.

Guiteau's defenders produced an even larger volume of narrative and justification. And just as John Gray was the leading spirit in the prosecution's war of words, so Spitzka played the leading role in defending the position of the defense experts. In addition to the New Yorker's extensive testimony during the trial, he recorded his explicit judgments on both Guiteau and the conduct of the trial in a number of places: "The Case of Guiteau," *Boston Medical and Surgical Journal,* 106 (March 23, 1882): 285–86; "A Contribution to the Mental Status of Guiteau and the History of his Trial," *Alienist and Neurologist,* 4 (1883): 201–20; "A Reply to J. J. Elwell, M.D. *in re* Guiteau," *Ibid.:* 417–38; [E.C.S.], "Editorial Notes and Comments. The Guiteau Autopsy," *American Journal of Neurology and Psychiatry,* 1 (1882): 381–92. One may obtain convenient access to Spitzka's ideas generally and a number of additional references to the Guiteau case in his influential textbook, *Insanity. Its Classification, Diagnosis and Treatment. A Manual for Students and Practitioners of Medicine* (New York, 1883). For good examples of Spitzka's argumentative, even abusive style in his continuing feud with the asylum superintendent's establishment see: "Merits and Motives of the Movement for Asylum Reform," *Journal of Nervous and Mental Disease,* 5 (1878): 694–714; "Reform in the Scientific Study of Psychiatry," *Ibid.:* 201–29. There is no biography of Spitzka—whose career never flourished as it might, possibly because of the very acidity of his personality—but there is much material relating to him in Victor Robinson's biography of S. V. Clevenger, a close friend of Spitzka, *The Don Quixote of Psychiatry* (New York, 1919). A bibliography of Spitzka's works and a brief sketch of his life may be found in the *Journal of Nervous and Mental Disease,* 41 (1914): 209–19. In understanding Spitzka's certainty in his diagnosis of Guiteau, it is important to recall the intensity of his devotion to the opinions of his German teachers—and at the same time the prominence of monomania or *primäre Verrücktheit* in the changing clinical pictures of European academic psychiatry in this period. Even before Garfield's assassination, it will be recalled, Spitzka had argued that fully one fourth of the insane fell into this category ("On the Scientific Necessity for a Clinical Demarcation of the Various Forms of Insanity," *Medical Gazette,* 8 [May 15, 1880]: 310–311). Compare Spitzka's articles on "Monomania, or Primaere Verruecktheit," *St. Louis Clinical Record,* 7 (1880): 256–71 and "A Practical Definition of Insanity," *Chicago Medical Review,* 6 (July 15, 1882): 322–23. It is also important— and in a sense crucial—to understand the differences between the somaticism of Spitzka and that professed by Gray. The older man's belief in an ultimate somatic pathology for all mental illness was an article of faith, an intellectual absolute that he could not modify. Spitzka was far more cautious in his somaticism, except for the issue of heredity, to which Gray felt unable to concede even the slightest kind of autonomy in the production of mental illness. Behavioral manifestations of mental disease were still primary in Spitzka's nosological schemes, although he was, like many of his European contemporaries, fascinated by the seductive certitudes of correlating physical lesions or congenital malformations with clinical symptoms. Spitzka remained, however, consistently sceptical of extreme and uncritical advocates of a deterministic hereditarianism, especially as it manifested itself in the guise of Lombroso's criminal anthropology ("Remarks on the Czolgosz Case and Allied Questions, as Presented by Dr. Talbot," *Medical Critic,* 1 (1902): 17–28; "Regenticides not Abnormal as a Class—A Protest against the Chimera of 'Degeneracy,'" *Philadelphia Medical Journal,* 9 [February 8, 1902]: 261–68).

W. W. Godding, superintendent of the government asylum in the District of Columbia was, with Spitzka, a stalwart defender of Guiteau, although his personal style was far less pyrotechnic. The Washington psychiatrist was also responsible for the best written and most thorough account of the Guiteau affair left us by any of its immediate participants: W. W. Godding, *Two Hard Cases. Sketches from a Physician's Portfolio* (Boston, 1882, pp. 34–257; Godding, "The Last Chapter in the Life of Guiteau," *Alienist and Neurologist,* 3 (1882): 550–57. Other defense witnesses writing accounts of the trial were T. W. Fisher, Charles Folsom, Walter Channing, and J. G. Kiernan;

T. W. Fisher, "Was Guiteau Sane and Responsible for the Assassination of President Garfield," *Boston Medical & Surgical Journal,* 106 (June 22, 1882): 601–5; Channing, "The Mental Status of Guiteau, the Assassin of President Garfield," *Ibid.,* 106 (March 30, 1882): 290–96; Folsom "The Case of Guiteau, Assassin of the President of the United States," *Ibid.,* 106 (February 16, 1882): 145–53, reprinted without change in: *Studies in Criminal Responsibility and Limited Responsibility* (privately printed, 1909); Folsom, "The Responsibility of Guiteau," *American Law Review,* 16 (1882): 85–100; Kiernan, "The Case of Guiteau," *Chicago Medical Review,* 4 (1881): 544–45.

George M. Beard, although his testimony was never officially admitted, was extremely—others in the NAPIPI felt agressively and arrogantly—active in the petition fight. Beard was something of a compulsive writer, and he could hardly have failed to take advantage of the rich opportunity offered by the Guiteau case. Cf.: *The Psychology of the Salem Witchcraft Excitement of 1692 and its Practical Application to Our Own Time* (New York, 1882) and "The Case of Guiteau—A Psychological Study," *Journal of Nervous and Mental Disease,* 9 (1882): 90–125. Spitzka, it should be noted, considered Beard something of charlatan, a kind of Barnum of American medicine (Rosenberg, "The Place of George M. Beard," *Bulletin of the History of Medicine,* 36 [1962]: 258).

As we have already suggested, many physicians accepted neither the position of the defense nor that of the prosecution. The most influential compromise view was presented by William A. Hammond, sometime Surgeon-General and articulate writer on psychiatric subjects. To Hammond it was clear that Guiteau was a "reasoning maniac"—roughly the equivalent of "morally insane" in earlier terminologies —but equally clear that such persons must be held responsible before the law; society had indeed more to fear from such disturbed souls than it did from ordinary criminals. Though Guiteau was a maniac, Hammond explained, he should be executed as an example to those similarly constituted; even in an asylum fear and retribution were understood and used to maintain order ("Reasoning Mania: Its Medical and Medico-Legal Relations; with Special Reference to the Case of Charles J. Guiteau," *Journal of Nervous and Mental Disease,* 9 [1882]: 1–26; "The Punishability of the Insane," *International Review,* 11 [1881]: 440–50). Hammond never reconsidered this point of view. In 1888, for example, he argued that Jack the Ripper was almost certainly such a reasoning and responsible maniac ("Madness and Murder," *North American Review,* 148 [1888]: 626–37).

In the years immediately following the trial, partisans of both sides continued to review its arguments and events, creating an essentially repetitious but occasionally valuable literature. Possibly the most valuable of such "briefs" was written by Dr. M. J. Madigan of Brooklyn, a defense partisan. "Was Guiteau Insane? A Reply to Dr. Elwell's Rejoinder," *Alienist and Neurologist,* 5 (1884): 227–59, 386–430. Even more influential were the writings of C. H. Hughes, a St. Louis physician and editor. Hughes was not only a decided advocate of Guiteau's insanity, but a leading proponent of the essential validity of the moral insanity concept—even if, as he argued, the term itself was too clouded by controversy to be of any further practical use (Hughes, "A Psychical Analysis of a Legally Sane Character: The Mental Status of Guiteau as Gleaned from his Speech and Conduct," *Alienist and Neurologist,* 3 [1882]: 588–617; "The Essential Factors of an Unsound Mind and the Mental Status of Guiteau,'" *St. Louis Medical & Surgical Journal,* 44 [1883]: 35–54; "Moral (Affective) Insanity—Psycho-Sensory Insanity," *Alienist and Neurologist,* 5 [1884]: 297–314, 431–68). Aside from Gray himself, the strongest and most vitriolic defender of the government position was J. J. Elwell, a well-known writer on medicolegal subjects. His moral outrage against Spitzka and what he conceived to be the forces of social disorder was in its very intensity revelatory of the values that—to a lesser degree or less overtly—shaped the hostility of many other educated Americans toward Guiteau and his defenders. Cf.: "Guiteau.—A Case of Alleged Moral Insanity," *Alienist and Neurologist,* 4 (1883): 193–201; "Guiteau.—A Case of Alleged Moral Insanity. A Rejoinder, by J. J. Elwell, to Reply of E. C. Spitzka, M.D., N. Y.," *Ibid.,* 4 (1883): 621–45. The controversy between Spitzka and Elwell illustrates, perhaps better than any other writings produced by the Guiteau affair, the tone and bitterness of the incident. A fascinating index to grassroots opinion within the medical profession are the informal debates provoked at local medical societies by papers on Guiteau's mental status. For an example of such a spirited discussion, see: *St. Louis Medical & Surgical Journal,* 44 (1883): 65–74. There was almost as extensive a post-mortem on the Guiteau case in legal as in medical circles. This debate included discussions both of the M'Naghten rule, and of the general conduct of the trial—particularly the courtroom decisions of Judge Cox and the rhetoric of the prosecution lawyers. For representative reviews of the trial's legal aspects, see: Charles E. Grinnell, "Review of the Month: Concerning Some Criticisms upon the Trial of Guiteau," *American Law Review,* 16 (1882), 50–55; George F. Edmunds, "The Conduct of the Guiteau Trial," *North American Review,* 134 (1882): 221–31. The question of Guiteau's true mental condition was, of course, widely discussed by European authorities; an unmistakable majority concluded that the assassin was insane and irresponsible. This is true irrespective of the nationality of the psychiatrists expressing themselves on this controversial issue.

A particularly immediate context into which the Guiteau case should be placed was the growing influence of hereditarian explanations not only of insanity, but of antisocial behavior generally. The idea of degeneration, which helped justify and express these deterministic doctrines, was based, it will be recalled, upon the existence of some "neuropathic weakness" that might manifest itself in insanity, mental retardation, pauperism or criminality. Lombroso's criminal anthropology was related to and derivative from these ideas; and in Lombroso's system, as we have seen, Guiteau was an atavism, a throwback to an earlier stage of human development. The basic study of the degeneration idea is still that by G.-P.-H. Genil-Perrin, *Histoire des origines et de l'évolution de l'idée de degenerescence en medecine mentale,* Paris, Faculté de Médicine, Doctoral Thesis, 1913. A useful short summary in English is that by Erwin H. Ackerknecht, *A Short History of Psychiatry,* trans. Sulammith Wolfe (New York and London, 1959), pp. 47–51. For a survey of such ideas in America, see the relevant chapters and references in: Arthur E. Fink, *Causes of Crime. Biological Theories in the United States. 1880–1915.* (Philadelphia, 1938). Cf.: Mark H. Haller, *Eugenics. Hereditarian Attitudes in American Thought, 1870–1930* (New Brunswick, N.J., 1963); Charles Rosenberg, "Charles Benedict Davenport and the Beginning of Human Genetics," *Bulletin of the History of Medicine,* 35 (1961): 266–76. Charles H. Hughes, cited previously as an articulate defender of Guiteau's irresponsibility, was as well a pioneer popularizer of these ideas—urging as early as 1883, for example, the eugenic doctine that the insane should not be allowed to reproduce ("The Rights of the Insane," *Alienist and Neurologist,* 4 (1883): 183–89; "History of the O. Z. Family; an Illustration of Rapid Neuropathic Degeneracy," *Ibid.,* 3 (1882): 535–38. For Lombroso's own diagnosis of Guiteau see: *Genio e Follia. In Rapporto alla medicina legale, alla critica ed alla storia,* 4th ed. (Turin, 1882), pp. 331–39.

Index